# The Functional Analysis
# of English

# The Functional Analysis of English

## A Hallidayan Approach

**Thomas Bloor**
**and**
**Meriel Bloor**

A member of the Hodder Headline Group
LONDON • NEW YORK • SYDNEY • AUCKLAND

First published in Great Britain in 1995 by
Arnold, a member of the Hodder Headline Group
338 Euston Road, London NW1 3BH
175 Fifth Avenue, New York, NY 10010

Distributed exclusively in the USA by
St Martin's Press Inc.,
175 Fifth Avenue
New York, NY 10010

*British Library Cataloguing in Publication Data*
A catalogue entry for this book is available from the British Library

*Library of Congress Cataloging-in-Publication Data*
Bloor, Thomas, 1935–
    The functional analysis of English : a Hallidayan approach/
Thomas Bloor and Meriel Bloor.
        p.    cm.
    Includes bibliographical references and index.
    ISBN 0–340–60012–8
    1. English language—Grammar.   2. Functionalism (Linguistics)
3. Halliday, M. A. K. (Michael Alexander Kirkwood), 1925–
I. Bloor, Meriel, 1934–    . II. Title.
PE1106.B56    1995
425—dc20                                                              95–11092
                                                                          CIP

ISBN 0 340 60012 8

1 2 3 4 5    95 96 97 98 99

Typeset by Phoenix Photosetting, Lordswood, Chatham, Kent
Printed and bound in Great Britain by JW Arrowsmith Ltd, Bristol

# Contents

# Preface

This book presents a short account of Systemic Functional Grammar. It aims to introduce this particular model of grammar, to provide the reader with the tools for analysing real samples of English and to offer a partial description of the language. Within the constraints imposed by space and level of complexity, we have tried to minimize deviation from the version of this grammar presented by Halliday in his *Introduction to Functional Grammar*, but we have consciously omitted a good deal.

The first two chapters are introductory. Chapter 2, in particular, deals with basic concepts which may be familiar to some readers, who might therefore wish to move rapidly to Chapter 3. Chapter 5 specifically addresses the issue of text, and Chapter 11 discusses applications of the grammar. Chapter 12 is to some extent independent, providing a brief overview of some past and present approaches in an attempt to set Halliday's work in a historical perspective. It could just as well be read first as last.

The rest of the book is primarily concerned with the grammar of the clause. All chapters except 12 are best read in sequence, since chapters to a certain extent presuppose knowledge of previous ones. In the interests of clarity, though, we have occasionally repeated information. We have assumed no prior knowledge of linguistics and have tried to explain even fairly basic terms. Even so, we appreciate that the large number of technical terms does present difficulties, and the glossary is intended as an *aide-mémoire* for the reader. It consists largely of brief explanatory descriptions rather than precise definitions, and the glosses are not intended to be accessible independently of the rest of the book.

Each chapter ends with a brief summary of the ground covered and, in most, we have added a short section headed 'Further study', which raises more abstruse points and/or suggests further reading. Chapters 1 to 10 also feature short exercises.

# Acknowledgements

We would like to express our gratitude to the many colleagues who have helped directly or indirectly: to Michael Halliday for early encouragement, for submitting with courtesy and kindness to prolonged interrogation and for providing the grammar; to Lesley Riddle of Arnold for inviting us to write the book, and her successor, Naomi Meredith, for her care, support and infinite patience; to colleagues at Aston and Warwick who, in spite of enormous workloads, ungrudgingly gave us time; to our graduate students who, knowingly or not, served as guinea-pigs for our material and, with their valuable comments and questions, helped us form our ideas; to colleagues in other universities, particularly Birmingham, Lancaster, Liverpool, and Nottingham; to Roger Woods, Mary Bodfish and Anne Beale for practical help; and, especially, for comments and advice, to Malcolm Coulthard, Helen Drury, Gill Francis, Chris Gledhill, Dick Hudson, Susan Hunston, Lorraine Lawrence, Hilary Nesi, Shelagh Rixon, Jane Willis and Dave Willis. None of the above is in any way responsible for any errors or shortcomings in this book.

# 1

# Preliminaries

## 1.1 *Introduction*

This book provides an introduction to the analysis of English. The aim is to provide the reader with the grammatical tools needed to take samples of English apart and find out how the language works. It is by the process of analysis that linguists build up descriptions of the language and gradually discover more about how people use language in social communication.

The analytical approach taken in this book is, in the main, drawn from the work of the major modern linguist Michael Halliday, in particular the model of grammar that he sets out in *Introduction to Functional Grammar*. The work of other linguists working in a similar tradition is also a significant influence on some sections of this book. Since some readers may not be familiar with this approach to the analysis of English, there is some simplification of Halliday's more complex and comprehensive work and only the briefest of introductions to the work of others. For this reason, most chapters include a section called 'Further study' that suggests additional readings and presents controversial or more complex issues.

Halliday's work is based on certain theoretical and practical principles that influence the type of analysis that he undertakes. In this chapter, therefore, it is important, as a first step, to outline the nature of these principles. In Chapter 12, we explain how these principles can be seen as part of a historical tradition in linguistics and indicate something of how they differ from other theoretical approaches.

## 1.2 *Grammar and meaning*

For Halliday, language is a 'system of meanings'. That is to say that, when people use language, their language acts are the expression of meaning. From this point of view the grammar becomes a study of how meanings are built up through the use of words and other linguistic forms such as tone and emphasis. This may seem fairly obvious to most people since it accords with a commonsense view of language, but not all linguists have been concerned with meaning in such a direct way as Halliday.

Linguists have approached the study of English from different points of view; some, for example, have tried to account for formal aspects of the grammar of language largely divorced from meanings. Others have started out by looking at words and sentences (language forms) and then asking how the forms of the language represent meanings. For Halliday, the only approach to the construction of grammars that is likely to be successful will be one that recognizes meaning and use as central features of language and tackles the grammar from this point of view. It follows from this that Halliday's grammar is *semantic* (concerned with meaning) and *functional* (concerned with how the language is used).

## 1.3   *Linguistic choice*

Halliday's explanation of how language works (his *theory of language*) involves the idea that a language consists of a set of systems, each of which offers the speaker (or writer) a choice of ways of expressing meanings. Thus, if I want to know the time, I might choose either of the following expressions (or any one of many more ways that the language offers us):

(1)   What's the time?
(2)   Tell me the time, please.
(3)   I'd like to know the time.

The first expression uses the *interrogative form*, the second uses the *imperative form* and the third uses the *declarative form*. (These forms are discussed further in Chapters 2 and 3.)

Linguistic choice is not only available to speakers with regard to interrogatives, imperatives and declaratives; it operates at every point of production in speech. We may, for example, refer to a grocer's as 'the supermarket' or 'the store'; we may address our father as 'Dad', 'Daddy', 'Pa' or by the use of his personal name. Linguistic choice also permits us to change the order of groups of words. For example, in exceptional circumstances, we might use an interrogative but change the word order to:

(4)   The time, what is it?

Most of the linguistic choices we make are unconscious. We do not stop and think about whether to use a past tense or a present tense verb, for example. The choice between the active and passive voice verbs in Examples (5) and (6) (in a book for parents[1] on the subject of teaching children to fish) depends on the circumstances of use.

(5)   Last summer, my boys finally *caught* their first fish.

(6) It is said that many more fish *are caught* in May or June than in any other months.

In (5) the past tense, active verb ('caught') is used because the language makes this form available for completed actions that took place in the past. In (6) the present tense, passive verb ('are caught') is used; this form is available for events that happen regularly or often. In (6) the passive form is necessary because the writer has chosen to make 'the fish' the Subject of the verb 'are caught' rather than name the people who catch the fish.

It is not that the author has made a *conscious* choice among the available language forms. He has chosen the forms that best express the meanings that he is trying to convey and that do not express superfluous meanings.

## 1.4  *Language in use*

When people use language to express meanings, they do so in specific situations, and the form of the language that they use is influenced by the complex elements of those situations.

Thus, to offer some obvious examples, we greet people in different ways depending on the time of day, where we are and who we are talking to. Teachers speak differently when they are addressing naughty children from when they are talking to the headteacher or a shop assistant. Teachers who fail to adapt their speech to different situations and talk to everyone as though they were naughty children will become, at best, objects of humour, and, at worst, targets of serious resentment.

Situation also affects the expression of meaning in written English. A business letter requesting payment of a debt (known as a 'letter of collection' in business) is likely to be very different in format and style from a letter on a similar topic written to an old friend who owes the correspondent some money. The situation not only affects the choice of words but also the grammar that is used.

The situation can have such a constraining effect on language that society often develops clear conventions of use (like those associated with business letters or formal greetings) which have to be learned before newcomers to the circumstances can behave appropriately.

The number of situations to which most very young children are exposed is relatively limited – usually the situations found in the home environment in the company of family and friends – but, as children grow and move into the wider society of the school and community, the range of situations in which they can use language expands. Most of this language use is acquired without conscious attention, but some situations require such complex language production that training is necessary. Our education system accounts for some of this training; children are helped in school to write narratives or to prepare reports of scientific experiments, for example, and later they may practise debating or public speaking, where they need to communicate with a larger audience than is found in face-to-face interaction.

One result of this is that, faced with a fragment of written text or a sound recording of speech, adult English-speakers do not usually find it difficult to recognize the situations in which particular instances of language were used. A recording of a speaker (for example, a sermon by a bishop in a cathedral, a speech in the house of commons, or a senior medical officer talking to his junior staff in a teaching hospital) can be easily recognized and described by the person in the street. (You can try your hand at recognizing the situations in which some written texts were created in the exercises at the end of this chapter.)

Since a speaker's or writer's choice of words is constrained by the situation of utterance, and since words and groups of words take on special significance in particular contexts, the grammar must be able to account for the way in which the language is used in social situations.

## 1.5    *The study of texts*

An important feature of Halliday's approach to linguistic study is its insistence on studying actual instances of language that have been used (or are being used) by speakers or writers. That is not to say that we may never take an interest in sentences that we, as speakers of the language, have thought of 'in our heads', but that, on the whole, we are more likely to arrive at interesting useful descriptions of English if we investigate *authentic texts*.

A *text* in Halliday's terminology is a chunk of language that is actually spoken or written for the purposes of communication by real people in actual circumstances. Both spoken and written texts are equally valid as objects for analysis. When linguists study or analyse a spoken text, they usually write down the text or, more often nowadays, record it electronically and then transcribe it (that is to say write it down as accurately as possible, using some system that can represent pronunciation and intonation). The fact that linguists study fixed written forms of texts could suggest that language itself is somehow fixed or static. This, of course, is not true. A spoken conversation, for example, moves forward in time, and the basis on which speakers and listeners express and interpret meaning is constantly changing. Communication is an interactive process through which meaning is negotiated. Even a written text has something interactive about it. When we read a successful detective story, for example, our knowledge of the background to the case is introduced in stages by the author so that our perceptions change and we eventually see the logic of the final secret of the plot.

In order to explain how human language works, contemporary linguists are often interested in this aspect of language (sometimes called *discourse*) and functional linguists have been in the forefront of this type of work. The text is the data that is used as the object of study, but we have to remember that it was originally produced as language within a communicative event.

It is via the analysis of texts that we are able to increase our understanding of the linguistic system and of how it enables speakers and writers to produce and process coherent meaning.

In Halliday's view, a grammar that was only satisfactory for the analysis of individual sentences would be incomplete. We need a grammar that can also account for conversations or other types of spoken or written English longer than a sentence. For one thing, the choice of words and the word order of one sentence often depends on the sentence that it follows. For another, the language has special words, such as pronouns, that can refer to the same entities as previously used words. For example, in Text 1A, the second and third sentences, and two further clauses in the third sentence, answer the question 'Where do turtles live?' They begin with words that direct the reader to turtles, a topic that is introduced in the question that begins the passage. The words that refer to turtles (or groups of turtles) are in bold type in the text.

---

*Where do turtles live?*
**They** live throughout the warmer sections of the world. **Some** are aquatic, **others** are amphibious; and **a third group**, the tortoises, don't go near the water except to drink.

---

**Text 1A**   (Schwartz, *How to fly a kite, catch a fish, grow a flower*[1]).

These words are *They, Some, others,* and *a third group.*

The linguistic analysis of texts has many practical applications above and beyond knowledge about language for its own sake. It can help us to find out why some texts are more effective than other texts at communicating information or persuading people to do or buy something. It can help us to understand the nature of propaganda, the success or failure of some types of political speeches, or how breakdowns in communication can occur. It can also sometimes help in the identification of a criminal by revealing the likely author of a text or of a speaker on a recorded telephone conversation. That is to say, text analysis can be used as a tool for the *evaluation* of texts. In addition, text analysis is currently being used to give us a better understanding of the nature of language use in English in specific fields such as business or science, and such work can be applied to the design of teaching syllabuses for language learners. (Some applications of text analysis are discussed in more detail in Chapter 11.)

## 1.6   *The notion of rank*

Although the analysis of longer stretches of language is of the greatest importance in linguistics, there is a sense in which the meaning of a text is constructed out of its component parts: its sentences, its clauses, its words, and so on. Certainly, in order for us to understand the grammatical systems of English, we have to look at smaller stretches of language.

| Sentence | Recent research is shedding new light on how acupuncture might work though we still have no definite answers. |
|---|---|
| Clause | Recent research is shedding new light on how acupuncture might work<br><br>(though) we still have no definite answers |
| Group | Recent research<br>is shedding<br>new light<br>no definite answers |
| Word | answers<br>still |
| Morpheme | answer            shed[d]<br>-s                   -ing |

**Fig. 1.1**   Examples of rank

Hallidayan linguistics employs the notion of *rank*. In brief, this simply states that a **sentence** consists of one or more clauses; a **clause** consists of one or more groups; a **group** consists of one or more words; and a **word** consists of one or more **morphemes**. Each of these ranks refers to a unit of meaning. The examples in Fig. 1.1 provide illustrations of each rank from Example (7).

(7) Recent research is shedding new light on how acupuncture might work though we still have no definite answers.

Fig. 1.1 does not give a full analysis of the ranks that make up the sentence, but only examples of each. This sentence is made up of two clauses, the first of which alone has eleven words. The word *answers* has two morphemes: *answer* (the lexical item) and *-s* (the plural morpheme). The nature of morphemes, words, and so on will be discussed in more detail in Chapter 2, and much of this book is about the structure of clauses and groups and about how their structure reflects meaning.

### 1.6.1   The clause and its constituents

In functional grammar, the basic unit is often said to be the *clause*. What this means is that in the language itself the clause has a special place in expressing meaning because it is at this rank that we can begin to talk about how things exist, how things happen and how people feel in the world around us. It is also at the rank of clause that we usually use language to interact with others. In other words, instead of simply uttering sounds or single words like *father, fish, river*, the available systems of the clause allow us to express ideas like *Father is fishing in the river* or ask a question *Is father fishing in the river?*

As we said above, a sentence may consist of one or more clauses. As an illustration, the following sentence from Text 1A consists of four clauses:

*Clause 1:*   Some are aquatic
*Clause 2:*   others are amphibious
*Clause 3:*   a third group, the tortoises, don't go near the water
*Clause 4:*   except to drink

This can be represented diagrammatically as in Fig. 1.2. This type of diagram is known as either a tree diagram, because it looks like an upside-down tree with a trunk and branches, or a constituency diagram, because it shows the constituents of the higher rank.

Constituency is concerned with the structural organization of the sentence or how the sentence is built up out of its various parts. As we can see from the tree diagram in Fig. 1.2, the clause is a constituent unit of the sentence. Similarly, a group is a constituent unit of a clause, and a word is a constituent unit of a group (*see* Fig. 1.3). In a functional grammar, constituency is closely related to the principle of the rank scale.

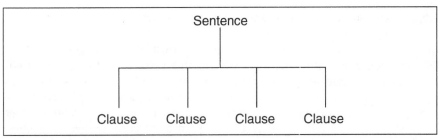

**Fig. 1.2**   Sentence constituency

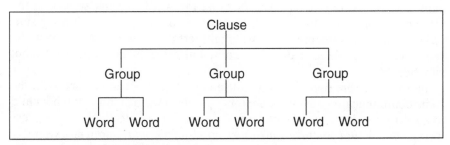

**Fig. 1.3**   Constituency of a clause

## 1.7    *Functions and metafunctions*

In Section 1.2 above we said that the grammar described in this book is *functional* and we explained this as being concerned with *language in use*. In fact, the notion of function in grammar is more complex than this. In this section, we discuss two different uses of the word function in linguistics and applied linguistics and then we consider Halliday's approach to meta-function.

### 1.7.1    Grammatical functions

In a lexicogrammar, each element (each word or group or clause, for example) has to be seen as part of the systems of the language. This means (in part) that it is seen in relation to the elements that are next to it in the text. Each element is said, therefore, to have some *function* in relation to the linguistic system. One type of language analysis depends on assigning grammatical functions to linguistic elements. Hence we might say that in the clause *Some are aquatic* (from Text 1A), *some* functions as Subject. Much of this book is about how grammatical function works in English and many examples illustrate the idea.

### 1.7.2    The communicative function of utterances

In language teaching and applied linguistics nowadays, many people equate the term *function* with situational use. In this sense we can say that each individual utterance in a given context has a particular *use*. For example, a speaker might say the words, 'Good afternoon' as a means of greeting a friend at an appropriate time of day. We can say that the *communicative function* of 'Good afternoon' is *greeting*. In a different context the same words can have a different function. For example, if a student is late for morning school and misses part of the first lesson, the teacher might sarcastically say, 'Good afternoon'. The fact that the words are not spoken in the afternoon indicates to the listeners that in this case the function is not a simple *greeting*, but something that we might term *reprimand*. In this way, the same words can have a different communicative function in a different situation.

In a similar (but opposite) way, different utterances can be used with the same communicative function. So, for example, a woman might tell her child to take off his shoes in a direct way (*Take your shoes off, Robin*) or in a less direct way (*Would you take your shoes off please, Robin?*) or in an extremely indirect way (*You haven't taken your shoes off, Robin*). In each case the function of directing the child to take his shoes off is similar even though the wording and the tone are different.

Halliday (1994: p. 95) makes the point that the relationship between the forms of utterances and the types of meaning they can express is a complex one which is based on the principle that what speakers say makes sense in the context in which they are saying it. He claims in addition, however, that all adult language is organized around a small number of 'functional components' which correspond to metafunctions (or the purposes which underlie all language use) and that these *metafunctions* have a systematic relationship with the lexicogrammar of the language. We now turn to a discussion of metafunctions.

### 1.7.3   Metafunctions

*[handwritten: metafunctions = the purposes which underlie all language use.]*

The ways in which human beings use language are classified by Halliday into three broad categories.

1. Language is used to organize, understand and express our perceptions of the world and of our own consciousness. This function is known as the *ideational function*. The ideational function can be classified into two subfunctions: the *experiential* and the *logical*. The experiential function is largely concerned with content or ideas. The logical function is concerned with the relationship between ideas.
2. Language is used to enable us to participate in communicative acts with other people, to take on roles and to express and understand feelings, attitude and judgements. This function is known as the *interpersonal function*.
3. Language is used to relate what is said (or written) to the real world and to other linguistic events. This involves the use of language to organize the text itself. This is known as the *textual function*.

Since the grammar of any language has developed through the ages to serve people's language needs, Halliday argues that 'these functions have moulded the shape of language and fixed the course of its evolution'. This very strong claim is the basis of the theory of functional grammar.

Newcomers to functional grammar are sometimes confused by metafunctions because they expect them to operate independently and discretely. This is a mistaken expectation. In almost any instance of language use, all three metafunctions operate simultaneously in the expression of meaning. This is because certain aspects of the grammar realize the ideational function, other aspects realize the interpersonal function, and yet others realize the textual function. We can see examples of the metafunctions in Text 1B, but we will not analyse it in detail at this stage since much of this book is concerned with explaining (and expanding on) the ideas in this section.

> There are four things a young child ought to learn about fishing his first time out. *First*, hooks are sharp. Demonstrate this by lightly pressing the point against the fleshy part of his thumb. *Second*, a pole is held in a certain way (usually at the end in two hands, one above the other). *Third*, noise frightens the fish away. *Fourth*, the fisherman must be patient. Perhaps the best way to teach patience is to be patient yourself, since his attitude will depend to a considerable extent on how you behave.

**Text 1B**   (Schwartz, *How to fly a kite, catch a fish, grow a flower*[1]).

This passage is mainly concerned with giving information about the state of the world. Hence, much of the language expresses the ideational function (for example, *hooks are sharp*, *noise frightens the fish away*). Another aspect of the ideational function is realised in *since* in the last sentence. *Since* establishes the logical relationship (in this case of *reason*) between the two main ideas in the sentence.

However, the writer also reveals his attitude and shows that he is expressing an opinion through the use of modality (for example, *ought to*, *perhaps*). This reflects the interpersonal function. The writer is giving advice to the reader.

Incidentally, he also shows, by the use of *he* and *fisherman*, that he expects the child who is learning to fish to be a boy rather than a girl, a view that we might wish to question. This use of language also reveals certain attitudes of the writer, but in this case he is presenting the ideas as being representative of the world as he sees it and so his attitude could be said to be 'hidden' within the ideational framework.

The textual function is realized through the word order of the sentences, through which the writer orders the message for the reader, and also through the numerals, *first*, *second*, *third* and *fourth*, which the writer uses to signal the salient points of his message.

It is the meshing of these functions in the lexicogrammar of the clause that realizes the meaning of the text as an act of communication between the writer and his readers.

## Summary

In this chapter we have looked at various points of grammatical theory. We began in 1.2 by explaining the importance of *meaning* in a functional grammar. Then, in 1.3, we discussed the question of *linguistic choice* as an inherent part of the potential of language. Section 1.4 introduced the importance of *situation* in the creation of *language in use* and the principle that the grammar of the language is constrained by the situation. This was followed, in 1.5, by an explanation of what is meant by *text* and a discussion of why we need a grammar that will allow for the analysis of texts. Section 1.6 briefly introduced the notion of *rank*, and finally, in 1.7, we looked at two different uses of the term *function*, grammatical and communicative function, ending the chapter with an explanation of the three metafunctions: ideational, interpersonal and textual.

## Exercises

Many of these exercises can be done very effectively in discussion with a partner or in a small group.

### Exercise 1.1

Imagine you are in room with someone you know well. You would like the other person to turn on a heater (or, if you live in a hot country, an air-conditioner). Think of three ways of asking them to turn the heater on, using an interrogative form, a declarative form and an imperative form.

### Exercise 1.2

How many ways can you think of asking someone to stop smoking? Would the way you speak differ depending on whether you are talking to: (a) your boss (or professor); (b) a boy of twelve; (c) a person whom you find very attractive but don't know very well; (d) your mother?

### Exercise 1.3

Each of the following short texts is taken from a different published source. They were all, originally, written to be read. Read them carefully and decide on the possible origin of each text.

a) Are you disqualified by a court from holding or obtaining a driving licence?
b) Mix all the ingredients together and drop spoonfuls of the mixture onto a greased baking sheet. Cook them in a hot oven for about twelve minutes. While they are still hot, curl them round the handle of a wooden spoon and leave them to dry.
c) Granulated flourspar being fed into a steel making furnace.
d) Feet should be clean and dry. Moisten adhesive surface of pad with water and apply to foot with aperture directly over painful or sensitive area. Press pad down firmly to ensure complete adhesion.
e) There are A kg of apples in one bag, and B kg of apples in another bag. What is the total weight of apples in the two bags?

## Answers

*Exercise 1.1*

There are, of course, many possible ways of wording this request. Here are three attempts:

|  |  |
|---|---|
| Interrogative: | Would you turn on the heater, please? |
| Imperative: | Turn on the heater, please. |
| Declarative: | I'd like the heater on. |

*Exercise 1.2*

Once more, there is a wide variety of possible answers. Here are some of them:

I don't think you ought to smoke in here.
Why on earth are you smoking?
Stop smoking for goodness sake!
Put that filthy cigarette out.
Be an angel will you and stop smoking?
I'd be very grateful if you'd put your cigarette out.

*Exercise 1.3*

a) A question on the form of application for a driving licence, UK 1991.
b) From the method section of a recipe for brandy snaps from *Robin McDouall's Cookery Book for the Greedy*, Penguin, 1955.
c) The caption under an illustration in an undergraduate engineering text-book.
d) From the directions on a packet of Scholl (UK) Felt Callous Pads for the treatment of sore feet.
e) A mathematics exercise from a school textbook, *A First Course in Modern Mathematics, Volume 1*, by Marie Anderson, Heinemann Educational Books (Metric Edition), 1973.

## Note

1.   Schwartz, Alvin 1967: *How to fly a kite, catch a fish, grow a flower.* New York: Macmillan Pocket Books.

# 2

## Labels

### 2.1 *Music, mathematics, medicine and motor-vehicle maintenance*

All disciplines use technical terms. The field of music uses the labels *chord*, *note*, *semitone*, *octave*, *tonic*, *dominant*, *subdominant* and many, many more. In mathematics books, we find terms such as *angle*, *decimal*, *fraction*, *factor*, *hypotenuse* and *ratio*. Doctors talk about *hypothermia*, *gastritis*, *lesions* and *oedema*. Motor-vehicle mechanics make use of terms such as *crankshaft*, *gear*, *big-end*, *ignition coil*, *manifold* and *carburettor*. The study of language also has its specialized vocabulary of technical terms.

### 2.2 *A political allegory*

Suppose some mad dictator, believing that people who worked in garages were using specialist language in order to bewilder and cheat their customers, decided to ban the use of technical terms for motor-vehicle maintenance. Under this lunatic regime, mechanics would be permitted to talk about the parts of an engine in 'ordinary' language, but would not be allowed to use the specialist terms which they use today. For example, mechanics might refer to the *brake* as the *thing that puts pressure on the wheels to stop them turning* but they could not refer to it as a *brake*. (This assumes that *wheel* is not a technical term, which is a questionable assumption.) It does not require a great leap of the imagination to see that insuperable difficulties would arise, particularly when they came to talking about items which are known in the repair shops of more reasonable societies as the *primary throttle return spring adjusting screw* or the *reverse gear selector pivot pin*. Almost certainly, this mad enterprise is entirely impossible. Even if it were possible, mechanics would fairly soon be using shorthand terms for these descriptions: the *thing that puts pressure on the wheels to stop them turning* might be called the *wheelstopper* or the *squeezer*. Would the dictator's thought police feel that this was a breach of the law? How long would it be before names like *brake*, *primary throttle return spring adjusting screw* or *reverse gear selector pivot pin* re-emerged?

Clearly, the whole scenario is ridiculous. Yet our hypothetical dictator's position is not a million miles from the attitude taken by some people to the use of technical terms in the study of language. Some people seem to perceive grammatical terminology as part of a conspiracy to baffle the general public. Some think that we can make the discussion of language easier by using descriptive statements rather than labels, or, if labels are used, they prefer labels which sound less technical: for example, the label *naming word* instead of *noun*; *doing word* instead of *verb*. There are a number of problems here which parallel those in our hypothetical dictatorship. Such terms have very limited potential for application, and we would soon run out of them. If an *adjective* (such as *quick*) is called a 'describing word', what are we to call an *adverb* (such as *quickly*)? And how accurate is it to call a verb a 'doing word'? *Are* is a verb in the sentence *Whales are mammals*, but it cannot with any precision of meaning be called a 'doing word'.

Some people argue that it is not necessary to use technical terms for language because we can use language efficiently enough without describing it in this way. It is true that people may have an excellent command of their mother tongue and know little about the analysis and labelling of the language that they speak; it is even possible to learn a foreign language without conscious recourse to such considerations. The fact remains, however, that if you wish to talk about language you must have a vocabulary for doing so. After all, it is not inconceivable (though it is not very likely, either) that people might repair motor-car engines, play musical instruments or even perform an appendectomy without acquiring related technical terminology, but, in order to systematically discuss these matters, they would have to acquire or invent the appropriate language for such discussion. No one questions this obvious truth in mathematics, medicine, music or motor-vehicle maintenance; it is only in the field of language and, with rare exceptions, only in the Anglophone world, that this happens.

Language for talking about language is *metalanguage*, and it has come into existence because there is a need for it. Linguists are not unique in using metalanguage. All people talk about language with varying degrees of metalinguistic detail. When a child says that a book has a lot of long words in it, that is a metalinguistic comment. The term *word* itself is a technical term used in discussing language; it just happens to be one that most people are very familiar with. The word *greeting* is a metalinguistic term of a different kind, in this case identifying a speech act, as are *question, answer, denial*. Such terms are accepted by the anti-terminology lobby because they are familiar and obviously serve a useful purpose. However, linguists need a very large technical vocabulary for language just as mechanics need a large technical vocabulary for car engines. How familiar we need to be with linguistic descriptions will vary in accordance with our professional concerns and our personal interests and motivation.

One difference between labelling parts of an internal combustion engine and labelling language items is that the former are concrete physical phenomena and the latter are not – or at least only partially so. Language form is essentially an abstraction although it is realized concretely as sounds or written symbols. Moreover, by and large, motor-car parts each have one function so that we need only one label for any individual unit. A language is vastly more complex than an automobile engine, and linguistic items, being multifunctional, can be looked at from more than one point of view, and hence given more than one label on different occasions even within the same analytical framework.

## 2.3   Word classes

One of the great contributions that the grammarians of ancient Greece and Rome made to our understanding of language was the development of a set of categories for classifying words. These categories came to be known in English as *parts of speech*, and traditionally eight (or sometimes nine) of these are presented as a full and true account of the possible classes into which words fall. These are usually given as *noun, verb, adjective, adverb, pronoun, preposition, conjunction, article* and/or *interjection*.

Nowadays, among linguists the term *parts of speech* is not often used, and categories of this kind are called *word classes*. Modern linguists have raised a number of objections to the traditional classification and particularly to the criteria for assigning these labels to items, yet most of them still use all or most of these labels to indicate the word classes of lexical items. Although they serve a purpose, there is nothing sacrosanct about these labels; nor are they self-evident. Indeed, it took the ancient Greeks several centuries to work their way from two identified word classes to the eight that they ended up with, and the categories were not always the same as the ones listed above. Some of the eight are also subdivided into various subcategories.

Like traditional grammar, Hallidayan grammar also features eight word classes, but they are not quite the same as the traditional ones. They are *noun, adjective, numeral, determiner, verb, preposition, adverb* and *conjunction*. One way of analysing a sentence is to label each word in it according to word class. The analysis of Example (1) given in Fig. 2.1 (overleaf) reveals samples of all eight of Halliday's word classes.

(1)   Soon a massive system was developed, consisting largely of numerous flood barriers, two dams and several branch canals.

### 2.3.1   Nouns

Some of these items can be subclassified, for example, *noun* subdivides into *common noun, proper noun* and *pronoun*. These have qualities in common, hence their overall classification as *noun*, but they are also grammatically

| noun | system, flood, barriers, dams, branch, canals |
|------|-----------------------------------------------|
| adjective | massive |
| numeral | numerous, two, several |
| determiner | a |
| verb | was, developed, consisting |
| preposition | of |
| adverb | soon, largely |
| conjunction | and |

**Fig. 2.1**

distinct from each other in some respects, and so there are distinguishing labels available, too. All the nouns in Example (1) are common nouns, but we can find other subclasses in further examples.

(2)  Wedgwood experimented ceaselessly.

In Example (2), *Wedgwood* belongs to a subclass of nouns known as *proper nouns*, which are traditionally described as the individual names of persons (such as *Abdullah, Picasso, Shakespeare, Michael Halliday*), places (such as *Sydney, Japan, Alberta, South Island*), ships, trains and aeroplanes (such as *the Orient Express, Concorde*), institutions and organizations (such as *Toyota, United Nations*), and similar categories. In English they are normally written with a capital letter. Nouns (other than pronouns) which do not fall into this class are labelled *common nouns* (for example, *ant, cheese, concept, donkey, evidence, faith, grass*). These words too have often been described as 'naming words'.

Some linguists prefer to identify word classes not in such conceptual terms but rather in terms of (i) their potential for interaction with other parts of the linguistic system and (ii) their morphology, that is, the 'shapes' they can take, their 'endings', etc. Thus a noun might be described as: (i) a linguistic item which can function as (among other things) Head of a Nominal Group (*see* Section 2.5), the Nominal Group being a unit which can (among other things) realize the function of Subject or Complement in a clause (*see* Section 2.4 and Chapter 3); or (ii) an item which can take a possessive inflection (as in *Shakespeare's, donkey's*). A *common noun* might be described as an item that may be preceded by *the*; a *countable noun* might be described as a noun which may be modified by *a/an* or a numeral, and which may have plural inflection (an added -*s*), and so on.

It is not entirely frivolous to suggest that one defining characteristic of a noun is that it is not one of the other categories in the set: not a verb, adjective, adverb, preposition, and so on, for it is only by contrast with (and by interaction with) the other items in the same subset of linguistic items that a word class has significance.

## 2.3.2   Pronouns

Why are pronouns included within the broad category of nouns in Halliday's grammar? Consider the following example, written by the medieval Italian traveller, Marco Polo.

> (3) Let me add only that the Great Khan has no authority over them and they render no tribute or other acknowledgement.

Pronouns in this example are *me*, *them* and *they*. They are classed as a type of noun because they realize the same grammatical functions as common and proper nouns. In the example given, the pronoun *me* refers to the writer. If someone else told the story, *me* might be replaced by *he* or by *Marco*. *Them* and *they* refer to some third party, an already identified group of people. Grammatically, it makes little difference whether we write 'the Great Khan has no authority over *them*' or 'the Great Khan has no authority over *these people*'; '*they* render no tribute' or '*these people* render no tribute'. Contrariwise, instead of using the expression *the Great Khan*, the author could have written *he*. These choices differ in the amount of information that is made explicit, and there may be good textual reasons for preferring one or the other, but they perform similar grammatical functions. To some extent, then, pronouns are like other items that are classed as nouns, and there is a case for treating them as members of the same class.

There are also, however, characteristics which set them apart from the other two types of noun, which is why we want to subclassify them, giving them the distinguishing label of *pronoun*. Common and proper nouns are *open sets*; that is to say that the community that uses the language can go on adding new members to the set with little difficulty. If, for instance, a new gadget is invented, it may be given a new name, thereby extending the set of nouns in English (as occurred with the *computer*). In the seventeenth and eighteenth centuries, English vocabulary expanded enormously to accommodate new scientific concepts, adding words like *biology*, *botany*, *hydrogen* and *oxygen*. More recently we have acquired *cybernetics*, *ecology*, *hyperspace*, *microchip* and *software*. English readily takes in nouns from other languages; a large portion of English vocabulary was acquired by such borrowing. Obvious modern examples are sports terms such as *judo* and *karate* from Japanese, and *ski* from Norwegian; or food terms such as *biryani*, *pizza* and *sushi*, from various sources.

Pronouns, in contrast, are a closed set of items which cannot easily be added to or diminished, as witness the seeming impossibility of introducing a gender-neutral pronoun for human beings (*he/she*), for which there has recently been some demand. Also, unlike common nouns, but like most (not all) proper nouns, pronouns cannot normally be preceded by words like *the* or *a/an* (determiners).

There are various kinds of pronouns, including the personal pronouns in Fig. 2.2. The personal pronouns in the right-hand column can be distinguished from those to their left by the fact that they occur as modifiers of other nouns (for example, *my book, her prize*) whereas the ones on the left can 'stand alone' (*mine* referring to *my book*, *hers* to *her prize*, and so on, but without the common noun *book* or *prize* being mentioned).

Another class of pronouns is the so-called wh-pronouns (*who, whom, whose, which, what*) and *that* when it means *who /whom* or *which* (for example, *the book that you gave me*). This account does not exhaust the class of pronouns, but it covers most of them.

| Singular | | |
|---|---|---|
| First person | I, me, mine | my |
| Second person | you, yours | your |
| Third person | he, him, his | his |
| | she, her, hers | her |
| | it, its | its |
| Plural | | |
| First person | we, us, ours | our |
| Second person | you, yours | your |
| Third person | they, them, theirs | their |

**Fig. 2.2**   Personal pronouns

### 2.3.3   Verbs

Traditionally defined as words which express an action or state (a rather feeble definition), verbs show the greatest degree of variation in form (morphology) of any of the word classes. Verbs can be subdivided in many different ways. Halliday lists three basic subclasses – lexical, auxiliary and finite – but there are many possible approaches.

Somewhat confusingly, the term *verb* has long been used to refer to such items as *write, writes, wrote, writing, written,* and to *is, was, were, has,* and also to *was writing, were writing, has written,* and so on. That is to say that conventionally *verb* may refer to Verbal Groups as well as to the components of those groups.

The structures *writes, wrote, am writing, are writing, is writing, was writing, were writing, has written, have written, has been writing, have been writing*, *had been writing*, *will write*, *may write* (one could continue) can be described as different forms of the verb *write*. Thus *write* is the form by which we may refer collectively to all or any of the forms in the list just given; it is the *citation form*. If we look for the word in a dictionary we do not look under the heading *wrote*, or *was writing* or any of the other forms but under this citation form *write*. (Some people tend to give the *to*-form for citation purposes: *to write*.)

The various forms of *write* in the incomplete list above are in some instances supported by other verbal elements (*am*, *are*, *is*, *was*, *were*, *has*, *had*, and so on). We can distinguish *write* as the *stem* and *is*, *are*, *was*, *were*, *has*, and so on, as *finites*. Since *write* is a dictionary item in a way that none of the finites is, we can also refer to it as a *lexical verb*. Most grammars do not make the division between finites and auxiliaries as such, but speak of *finite auxiliary* and *nonfinite auxiliary*. In *might have been reading*, *might* is the *finite* (modal auxiliary) and *have* and *been* are (non-finite) *auxiliaries*.

The finites and auxiliaries are closed sets; lexical verbs are an open set: *write*, *chase*, *conceal*, *dig*, *diversify*, *sweat*, *overcompensate*; there is virtually no limit. As with nouns, though perhaps not quite so productively, new concepts can inspire new verbs to express them linguistically; computer activity has given us such newly coined verbs as *hack*, *boot up*, *download* and *interface*, just as physics once gave us verbs like *electrify* and *electrocute*. It is hard to imagine how we could add to the set of auxiliary verbs. This is not to say that auxiliaries are inevitably and eternally impervious to change, but they are strikingly different from lexical verbs in their resistance to innovation.

A significant subset of finites is the set of *modal auxiliaries* (or *modals*): *can*, *could*, *may*, *might*, *must*, *shall*, *should*, *will*, *would*. One distinctive characteristic of these verbs is that they do not add -*s* for third person singular: *she can* but not **she cans*. (An asterisk before an item indicates an ungrammatical form.)

Another way of looking at verbs, setting aside the issue of auxiliaries, is to consider the forms which each lexical root can take. Thus, if we count the *to*-form as a separate entity, we can say that *dig* is a five-form verb showing up as *dig*, *to dig*, *digs*, *dug*, *digging*, whereas *write* is a six-form verb: *write*, *to write*, *writes*, *wrote*, *writing*, *written*. More limited are verbs like *cut*, which is a four-form verb: *cut*, *to cut*, *cuts*, *cutting*. The reason for the variation in the number of forms is largely historical accident: *cut* serves for present simple tense (excluding third person singular, which adds -*s*), past simple tense, and *past participle*, whereas *dig* has *dug* as simple past and past participle only; and *write* distinguishes simple past and past participle in the forms *wrote* and *written*. The -*en* morpheme is the most distinctive past participle marker since it serves no other purpose in verb morphology; the most common past participle morpheme is -(*e*)*d*, but that is also the most common past simple tense morpheme. All present participles have the ending -*ing*.

In all lexical verbs, the base form (*dig*, *write*, *cut*) doubles as (i) all persons of the simple present tense except third person singular (*I write, you write, we write* and *they write*); and (ii) what is sometimes called the *bare infinitive* (the form we referred to earlier as the citation form), which combines with modal auxiliaries to give, for example, *may write, must write, can write*. The form with *to* is known as the *to-infinitive*.

The richest variety in English verb forms is found in the verb *be*, which has nine forms: *be, to be, am, is, are, was, were, been, being*. Most English verbs distinguish third person singular from the other persons in the present tense, but *be* is the only verb in English that does so for the past simple tense: *was/were*. Compared with most European languages and many others, the variation in morphology of English verbs is extremely limited, but it is still greater than for any other word class in English.

In addition to *person* (first, second, third), *number* (singular/plural) and *tense* (present/past), an important system affecting verbs is that of *voice*: *active* or *passive*. When passive voice is selected, some form of the auxiliary *be* (or less frequently *get*) is always present, and the lexical verb is in the form of a past participle, as in Example (4) (italics added).

(4)   Current from one input *is channelled* to two or more different gates.

We return to these and other characteristics of verbs in Section 2.4 and Chapter 3.

### 2.3.4   Adjectives

*Adjectives* have two main functions: (i) as modifiers of nouns (a *large* deficit); (ii) as Head of a group that is Complement of a copular verb such as *be, seem, become*; for example – The deficit is *large*. (Groups are discussed later in this chapter and also in Chapter 7. Complement and related functions are discussed in Chapter 3.) The typical morphological potential of an adjective is inflection for comparative and superlative forms: *-(e)r* and *-(e)st*; for example: *larger, largest*. Comparative and superlative may also be indicated by *more* or *most* placed before the adjective. Also most adjectives can be modified by items like *very, fairly, rather, quite, somewhat*; hence *very large, quite large*, and so on.

However, not all adjectives have this potential for comparative, superlative or other grading; exceptions are known as *nongradable adjectives*, and include such items as *male, female, left, right, single, married, total* and *unique*. Only when playing with words, as a sort of joke, do we speak of someone being *very female* or *slightly married*, since one either is or is not female, married and so on, or so the language suggests. The fact that many people describe things as *rather unique* or *very unique* probably says something about their perception of the meaning of the word as a near-synonym of *rare* rather than as meaning, in the words of the *Shorter Oxford Dictionary*, 'of which there is only one; single, sole, solitary'.

## 2.3.5 Determiners

The term *determiner* is a more comprehensive category than *article*. The articles in English are *the* (*definite article*) and *a/an* (*indefinite article*); but these two make up only a subclass of words that have a similar grammatical role, or, to put it differently, that show up in the same positions. Others include the words *this*, *that*, *these*, *those*; for example, the italicized words in (5) and (6). Like pronouns, determiners are a closed set.

(5) *This* microprocessor directs *the* car's engine-control system.
(6) *These* two groups of figures are binary and decimal equivalents.

The words *some* and *any* are also determiners when in the modifying function as in Example (7).

(7) He melted down *some* silver coins.

In traditional grammar, determiners other than articles (and sometimes articles, too) were classed as *adjectives* on the grounds that they modify nouns, but there are very good reasons for treating them as separate from adjectives. Although it is true that they modify nouns, they do not do so in the same way as adjectives, and they have a different *distribution*, which is to say that they do not show up in quite the same positions and they differ on the question of grammatical obligatoriness. Where both occur together, determiners precede adjectives as in Example (8) but not vice versa as in (8a).

(8) The greater danger is that of flooding.
(8a) *Greater the danger is that of flooding.

Sometimes a determiner before a noun is a grammatically obligatory requirement whereas an adjective never is: we can say (9) or (9a) but not (9b).

(9) *A* microprocessor works by responding to electrical impulses.
(9a) *This* microprocessor works by responding to electrical impulses.
(9b) *Microprocessor works by responding to electrical impulses.

Putting an adjective before the noun does not solve the problem, as we see from Example (9c):

(9c) *New* microprocessor works by responding to electrical impulses.

## 2.3.6 Numerals

Numerals were also frequently classed as adjectives in traditional grammars, but again their grammatical role is sufficiently dissimilar to justify classing them separately. In fact, in some instances – certainly not all – numerals are more like determiners than like adjectives. On some occasions (for example, in abstract mathematical calculations such as *five times ten equals fifty*), they seem rather to resemble nouns. In fact, numerals are a rather anomalous set and are perhaps best treated as a class of their own.

Unfortunately, questions of classification rarely have an obvious or conclusive answer, and so analysts may disagree on how to classify items without anyone necessarily being wrong or, for that matter, entirely right. Hence you will find considerable variation in different publications on this as on many of the issues discussed here.

### 2.3.7   Adverbs

The most unsatisfactory word class is that of *adverb*, which is often described by commentators as a ragbag or dustbin category; in other words, it is the category into which an amorphous collection of linguistic items goes when they cannot be fitted in anywhere else. Traditionally, the adverb category was even more comprehensive than it is now, but it has to be admitted that in modern linguistics it still embraces a range of markedly dissimilar items. Since adverbs vary so greatly, it is difficult – perhaps even impossible – to come up with any feature which they all share.

One of the primary functions of adverbs is as the Head word of a group functioning as Adjunct at the rank of clause (see Chapter 3 for a fuller explanation of this statement). One type of adverb is characterized by the morphological feature *-ly*: *quickly*, *cleverly*, *silently*, *bravely*, and so on. Obviously these items have a regular correspondence to certain adjectives and are said to *derive from* the corresponding adjectival forms: *quick*, *clever*, *silent*, *brave*. Sometimes, the *-ly* suffix is missing and we have what appears to be the same word for both adjective and adverb; for example, *fast* in Example (10) is adjective in the first instance and adverb in the second.

(10)   He is a fast runner but he can't swim very fast.

Another set of adverbs (depending on what criteria we use to group them, traditionally usually semantic criteria) includes *now, then, later, earlier*, and yet another *here, there, everywhere, nowhere, anywhere*. Thus we can speak of adverbs of manner (*quickly*), time (*now*) and place (*here*). Items like *seldom, never, often, frequently, always, invariably* are sometimes described as adverbs of frequency. *Upwards, downwards, sideways, left, right, forwards, backwards* and so on are often called directional adverbs. Another set includes such items as *however, moreover, nevertheless, thus, consequently, finally*, and, closely related to this group, *frankly, honestly, clearly, apparently*; both these types often occur at the beginning of a clause and they are sometimes called sentence adverbs. (See the discussion of Adjuncts in Section 3.4.)

All these subgroups have a strong family resemblance at least, and one can see why they end up with the same label. More questionable are items like *very*, *fairly*, *rather*, *quite*, *somewhat*, whose function, as mentioned above, includes the modification of gradable adjectives. It also includes the modification of gradable adverbs (*very quickly*, *very quietly*). There is something very messy about putting these items in the same large class as adverbs of time, manner and place, and some grammarians set them apart as *intensifiers*; there is a lot to be said for this approach, but it is common to treat intensifiers as a subclass of adverbs.

The rules regarding the sequential position of adverbs in relation to other items in the clause are very complicated and vary according to the subclasses of adverb. We will not pursue this further here, but the invented Example (11) gives some indication of a range of adverb types and their distribution in the clause.

(11) *Honestly*, they are *usually still* working *very energetically now*, but *tonight* they are *probably* waiting *outside* or going *home late once again*.


### 2.3.8 Prepositions

One area of potential confusion is with words like *up*, *on*, *in*, *over*, *under*, *near*, *by*, *inside*, *outside*. These often occur in a role which suggests that they are adverbs. Perhaps even more frequently they seem to be prepositions. Consider Example (12) from an introductory book on computers.

(12) For example, they can process sounds coming in through a microphone and reproduce them through speakers or onto special disks. They can monitor temperatures in laboratories or manipulate images on television.

The first occurrence of *in* (*sounds coming in*) is an adverb; the second occurrence of *in* (*in laboratories*) is a preposition. Other prepositions in this example are *through* (*through a microphone*), *onto* (*onto special disks*) and *on* (*on television*). *Through* can also be an adverb as in Example (13):

(13) I can't get through.

Perhaps the easiest way to deal with this problem is to say that they are homonymous pairs (looking and sounding alike but different in meaning): that just as there is an adjective *fast* and an adverb *fast* (not to mention a semantically unrelated verb *fast* – abstain from eating – and noun *fast*), there is also an adverb *in* and a preposition *in*, two different words belonging to different word classes but which happen to be pronounced and written in the same way. The same applies to *through*, or any of the others. Not all linguists would accept this position, however.

By definition, prepositions occur in prepositional phrases with a Nominal Group as Complement (*see* Section 2.5). A preposition does not vary in its form.

### 2.3.9   Conjunctions

Conjunctions are of two types: *linking conjunctions* or *linkers* (also known as co-ordinating conjunctions or co-ordinators) and *binding conjunctions* or *binders* (also known as subordinating conjunctions or subordinators). The linkers are a small set: *and*, *but*, *or*, and possibly *for*, *so* and *then*. Of course, in some cases, what appear to be the same 'words' may be items of a different word class that happen to look and sound alike. For example, in (14) the item *for* is a conjunction; in (15) *for* is a preposition.

> (14) Such a picture neatly explains A. V. Hill's observations, for clearly the number of molecules of APT consumed will depend on the length of rope hauled in.
> (15) The Air Force surrounded him with medical orderlies specially cleared for security.

The binding conjunctions are a larger group and they include: *because, since, when, whenever, until, before, after, while, if, unless, whether, although, even though, in case, given that, so that,* and many more. A clause which begins with a linking conjunction must follow the clause to which it is linked, but a clause which begins with a binding conjunction may generally follow it or precede it. Note that once again duplication occurs: there are items here which are identical in pronunciation and spelling to items classed as prepositions or adverbs.

It is undeniable that the proliferation of terminology presents problems for the student of grammar. In part the profusion of terms is arbitrary; simply due to the fact that there is no systematic attempt by the profession to agree on one set of labels. A more significant cause is that different linguists have different perceptions and so break language down differently. This is exacerbated by the fact that most categories in language are not discrete, neatly separable classes but *clines*, or gradations with clear central examples and more peripheral ones shading into other classes. For example, *and* and *or* are the most central – or most typical – examples of conjunction.

However, one point that we want to make is that there are good reasons why one linguistic realization (word, group of words, and so on) may carry more than one label even within the same model of grammar. Therefore, we will suspend discussion of word classes and look further at nouns and the groups in which nouns and other word classes play a key role.

## 2.4   *Subjects*

A traditional term (not a word class) still widely used is *Subject*. In Example (2), repeated here, *Wedgwood* is the Subject. It is also a noun.

> (2) Wedgwood experimented ceaselessly.

To say out of context that *Wedgwood* is a noun is quite viable. The quality of being a noun is a feature of the word *Wedgwood* in virtually all circumstances. We cannot say out of context that *Wedgwood* is a Subject, however, since being a Subject is not an intrinsic feature of the word *Wedgwood* but only a function which it sometimes realizes. Now consider Example (16).

(16)  Money is the root of all evil.

Exactly the same is true of *money* that we have said of *Wedgwood*. It is always a noun and in this example it is a Subject. It is not always a Subject, however. For instance, in (17) and (18), *money* is a noun but it iṣ not a Subject.

(17)  They offered money.
(18)  He is obsessed with money.

It is only in some specific instance of a sentence (or, more precisely, of a clause) that an item can be labelled Subject. In Systemic Functional Grammar, *money* in (17) is said to be the *Complement* (*see* Chapter 3), and the pronoun *they* is the Subject. In Example (18) *he* is the Subject and *money* is part of a prepositional phrase (*with money*).

Not all the personal pronouns in Fig. 2.2 can function alone as Subject in Standard English clauses. *I, you, he, she, it, we, they*, from the left-hand column, and *mine, yours, his, hers, its, ours, theirs* may do so. For example, in Standard English, we can say *They offered money* but not *\*Them offered money*. In fact, *I, she, he, we, they* nearly always realize the function of Subject (one exception is intensive structures like *It is I*, which most native speakers avoid as pedantic). *Me, her, us* and *them* never realize Subject in Standard English (though they do in some dialects).

How do we decide then whether some word or group of words is the Subject? With pronouns, as we have just seen, the form of the word itself (its morphology) often reflects its function. *I, he, she, we* and *they* are all forms which realize the Subject function, and *me, him, her, us* and *them* realize Complements. However, pronouns are untypical in this respect. In some languages, most words consistently vary according to their function, but in English most words do not. So what formal clues are there to help in identifying the Subject? One is that it often determines the form of the verb. Thus we say *He is obsessed with money* but *They are obsessed with money* or *I am obsessed with money*. As we have already seen, the verb *be* has more forms than other English verbs and so this *agreement* (or *concord*) with the Subject is noticeable more frequently than with other verbs, where evidence tends to more restricted. Most verbs require an *-s* in the third person singular form, so that a singular third person Subject such as *The computer chip* co-occurs with the verb form *uses* as in (19), but with a plural Subject as in (19a) there is no *-s* inflection on the verb. (It is a strange quirk of English morphology that *-s* is the suffix denoting singularity in verbs and plurality in nouns. No one, presumably, would wish to suggest that the *-s* on verbs is grammatically the same morpheme as the -*s* on nouns even though they look and sound the same.)

> (19)   The computer chip uses this battery of information [...]
> (19a) Computer chips use this battery of information [...]

However, once again English does not always display even these limited distinctions, and, as already mentioned, verbs like *can*, *may* and *should* (the modal auxiliaries) and most past tense main verbs do not vary according to Subject – or for any other reason.

Halliday proposes one diagnostic test for Subject which works fairly well. He says that it is the item in the clause which is picked up in the pronoun in a *question tag*. A tag question is a question which is made up of a clause with a short form interrogative tagged on at the end; for example (19b) or (19c). The tag is the bit at the end.

> (19b) The computer chip uses this battery of information, doesn't it?
> (19c) Computer chips use this battery of information, don't they?

*It* in the first example is the pronoun equivalent of *the computer chip* and *they* in the second example picks up from *computer chips*. Hearing a sentence like Example (20) we can deduce not only the Subject but also the gender of the person the Subject refers to.

> (20)   The doctor prescribed these pills, didn't she?

The choice of *she* is not intrinsically identified with the word *doctor*, but determined by an aspect of the situation, in this case the sex of the doctor in question. If the doctor were a man the pronoun would reflect the fact. Further evidence that grammar is intimately bound up with context of situation and not just relationships within the clause!

Even given a declarative clause without a tag, the analyst can easily imagine a tag and thereby identify the Subject. We look at this issue again in Chapter 3.

## 2.5   *Groups*

Not all nouns can stand alone in the way that proper nouns and many personal pronouns usually do or as some common nouns may, for example, *money* in Example (16). The nouns *computer* and *microchip*, for example, when they occur in the singular form, are always modified in some way by a word such as *the* or *a* (a determiner) or the numeral *one*. (Such nouns are labelled *count* or *countable nouns*. Nouns like *money* are *non-count* or *uncountable*.)

Nouns can also, of course, occur with more extensive modification. We can speak of *a sophisticated computer* or *a computer with an external drive*, or, if we are being more expansive, *a sophisticated computer with an exter-*

*nal drive that meets all the requirements.* In a modern analysis we would say that, in Example (21), the Subject is *a computer with an external drive,* and not just the noun *computer.*

(21)  A computer with an external drive works in the same way.

It is not quite right therefore to say that a *noun* can realize the Subject. It is rather a *Nominal Group* that has this potential. Thus, in Example (21), *a computer with an external drive* is a Nominal Group functioning as Subject of the clause. In fact, in all the examples the Subject is realized by a Nominal Group, regardless of the number of words involved. *The Great Khan, current from one input, this microprocessor, these two groups of figures, the greater danger, a microprocessor, such a picture, the number of molecules consumed, the Air Force, the doctor, a computer with an external drive* are all Nominal Groups, but so are *Wedgwood, money,* and *he.*

It may seem surprising that we should label a simple unmodified noun (*Wedgwood, money* or *he*) as a Nominal Group, but this is in keeping with the hierarchical, paradigmatic structure of the grammar. According to the rank scale (introduced in Chapter 1), a group is made up of *one or more* words and a clause is made up of *one or more* groups.

The key grammatical item in the group is called the Head. The remaining elements are Modifiers. Some of the Nominal Groups functioning as Subject that we have already considered are (with the Head in italics): *current* from one input, this *microprocessor,* these two *groups* of figures, the greater *danger,* a *microprocessor,* such a *picture,* the *number* of molecules consumed, the *Air Force,* the *doctor,* a *computer* with an external drive; *Wedgwood, money,* and *he.*

Thus, a Nominal Group is typically a group with a noun (or pronoun) as its Head, and that noun may be modified, but it does not have to be modified in order to constitute a group in this technical sense. To make an analogy with a nonlinguistic situation: a boat has a crew, and one person is the captain of that boat, but a boat may have a crew of one, and that one is by definition the captain. We have also seen that one of the functions which a Nominal Group can realize is that of Subject. We can now deal very briefly with other groups.

Just as a Nominal Group may consist of a simple noun, a *Verbal Group* may consist of a simple verb; for example *directs* in Example (5), *is* in (8), *works* in (9). A Verbal Group may also be more complex, as with *was developed* in (1); *is obsessed* in (18); *must be based* in (22) or *had been developing* in (23).

(22)  Price movements must be based on the beliefs of the investing public.
(23)  They had been developing a similar process before this.

Finiteness is a quality which is not exclusive to the subclass of *finites.* Where the Verbal Group is a single word (e.g., *directs, uses, prescribed, works* in the previous examples), it may be referred to as a *simple finite verb.* That word is the Head of its group. Where the verb is more complex, the Head is the finite element: *must* in *must be based* in (22), *had* in *had been developing* (23). The Verbal Group *may have been being written* has five elements. The breakdown here is as follows:

*may*: finite (modal)
*have*: auxiliary (bare infinitive)
*been*: auxiliary (past participle)
*being*: auxiliary (present participle)
*written*: lexical verb (past participle)

In fact, a more abstract analysis would cut across most of the words to give:

*have* plus the past participle morpheme (*-en*), which together indicate perfect aspect (completion)
*be* plus present participle morpheme (*-ing*), which together indicate progressive (i.e., continuous) aspect
*be* plus past participle morpheme (*-ed*), which together indicate passive voice

So, on this analysis, this Verbal Group is modal perfect progressive passive. In (22) *must be based* is modal passive, and in (23) *had been developing* is past perfect progressive. There is further discussion of the Verbal Group in Chapter 3.

*Adverbial Groups* tend to have simpler structure than Nominal or Verbal Groups. The Adverbial Group normally has an adverb as its Head. In Example (24), *somewhat earlier* is the Adverbial Group; *earlier* is the Head, and *somewhat* the Modifier.

(24) Somewhat earlier the first application of glaze to pottery was made.

A *Conjunction Group* usually consists of just the conjunction as Head, and is rarely analysed as such. Conjunctions can have modifiers, however: in the clause *just until you go*, the conjunction *until* is modified by *just*; in *even if he answers*, *if* is the Head and *even* the Modifier. Linking conjunctions are not modified.

A *Preposition Group* has a preposition as Head and this is not often modified. Some Preposition Groups do contain Modifiers, however; for instance: *just inside* has *inside* as Head and *just* as Modifier. Other examples are *right on* (as in *right on target*), *slightly over* (as in *slightly over the edge*), *far beyond* in *far beyond our expectations*.

Except in elliptical structures, a Preposition Group (with or without modification) always occurs with a Nominal Group to make up a *prepositional phrase*; for example *in the office* is a prepositional phrase made up of a preposition (strictly speaking an unmodified Preposition Group) *in* and a Nominal Group *the office*; *slightly off the point* is a prepositional phrase made up of a Preposition Group *slightly off* and a Nominal Group *the point*.

Groups of the same type can be linked together to make up a group complex. *Jack and Jill* is a Nominal Group complex, and so is *the truth, the whole truth and nothing but the truth* in *Do you swear to tell the truth, the whole truth and nothing but the truth?* A Verbal Group complex can be formed similarly: She *speaks and thinks* like a lawyer. Also classed as Verbal Group complexes are the italicized items in: She *wants to understand*; Things are *beginning to develop*; They *seem to thrive* here.

## 2.6 *Three ways of looking at a clause*

We have said that any item of language may have more than one function. Any sample of language would serve to illustrate this. Take the following sentence, for instance:

(25)  Boole had already written an important paper on this subject.

We can examine this from various points of view. We can analyse the structural relations of the clause, commenting on its *mood*, which concerns the fact that it is a statement (in grammatical terms, a *declarative*) and not a question (an *interrogative*), and therefore the Subject *Boole* comes before *had*. If the sentence were a question, the interrogative form would require *had* to be placed before *Boole* to give (25a).

(25a) Had Boole already written an important paper on this subject?

This has something to do with the nature of the exchange between the speaker (or writer) and the listener (or reader). The fact that the writer is asking rather than telling leads to her choice of a particular ordering in the wording, a choice made from a number of possible options in the structure of clauses in English. In order to examine this aspect more fully, we would need to consider such matters as which items take on the functions of Subject, Complement, and so on. In this case, *Boole* is the Subject. The remaining functions will be discussed in Chapter 3.

On the other hand, we might be more interested in considering what some people might think of as the 'meaning' of the clause, but what for Systemic Functional linguists is just one of several kinds of meaning. What kind of event or state of affairs is being represented here? Or, in the words of the limerick: Who does what, which way up, and to whom? Here, the analyst's attention is directed to the question of whether the process is one involving action, or thought/feeling, or speech, or whether it specifies some relationship such as identity or similarity. In this case, we might label *Boole* as *Actor* on the grounds that this is an action and that Boole is the one who performs it. So we see that we have now labelled *Boole* twice: once as Subject and once as Actor. Each label says something different about the function of the item *Boole* in this clause.

There is yet another way in which we can look at it. We can concentrate attention on the choice the writer has made about which item to place first in the clause. Once a declarative has been opted for, *Boole* is the obvious choice for starting point, because in most declarative clauses in English the Subject comes first. The grammar of English would also permit other choices, for example one of the following:

(25b)  Already, Boole had written an important paper on this subject.
(25c)  On this subject, Boole had already written an important paper.
(25d)  An important paper Boole had already written on this subject.

It is true that some of the choices seem less likely than others, but all are possible. In all these alternatives, the function of Subject is realized by the Nominal Group *Boole*, and in all of them *Boole* has the role of Actor; but in (25b), (25c) and (25d) the author has chosen to start off with something other than the Subject/Actor. The item with which we start a clause can usually be labelled the *Theme*. In the original, authentic example, (25), *Boole* is Subject, Actor and Theme. In the others *Boole* is Subject and Actor, but not Theme. The Themes in the other Examples are as follows: *Already*, *On this subject*, and *An important paper*. Chapters 4 and 5 return to the question of Theme and related issues. If (25d) seems a little odd out of context, compare Example (26) from the same page of the same text.

(26)  He also began to have some ideas of his own. These he wrote up [. . .]

In the second sentence here, we have the same sort of structure as (25d). The author might have chosen to place the Subject/Actor *he* first in the clause, as in (26a), but for textual reasons opted for *These*, thereby pushing the Subject into second place.

(26a)  He also began to have ideas of his own. He wrote these up [. . .]

So, we have suggested three different ways of looking at the clause. The first, involving such functions as Subject, is described in Halliday's grammar as the Clause as Exchange and relates primarily to the interpersonal metafunction. The second, involving such role labels as Actor, is the Clause as Representation and relates primarily to the ideational metafunction. The third, which concerns the choice of starting point and the optional ordering of elements and which involves the function Theme, is the Clause as Message and relates primarily to the textual metafunction. Each of these will be discussed further in subsequent chapters.

## Summary

In this chapter we have argued that grammatical terminology, rather than being a device intended to exclude the public from the deliberations of specialists, is valuable, even necessary, for talking about the way in which a language works. Starting with the familiar notion of word classes (or parts of speech), we see that the criteria for classification may produce different groupings of items, and we list Halliday's eight word classes, paying particular attention to nouns and their subclass, pronouns. Verbs can be described in a number of different ways and various subclassifications emerge. The functions Subject, Actor and Theme serve as an illustration of the fact that the same bits of language can be usefully labelled in more than one way, reflecting co-existing dimensions. Functions such as Subject are realized not so much by nouns as by Nominal Groups. Nominal Groups consist of a Head (usually a noun) and possibly Modifiers.

## *Further study*

There is a good discussion of the parts of speech in the chapter so named in Huddleston (1984). Among other things, he shows the shortcomings of traditional criteria, easier than coming up with satisfying alternatives. In fact, Huddleston acknowledges strengths as well as weaknesses in the traditional classification. He also addresses the issue of groups (which, as most non-systemic linguists do, he calls *phrases*).

Many linguists working within a systemic-functional framework posit the existence of *Adjectival Group* with an adjective as Head (for example, Fawcett, 1974; Downing and Locke, 1992). This appears to be consistent and predictable in terms of the analysis of other groups. (Note that adjectives which occur as Modifier in a Nominal Group are not themselves groups.) Halliday himself, however, dispenses with Adjectival Groups, classifying these structures as Nominal Groups with adjective as Head on the grounds that, like Nominal Groups with noun as Head, they frequently function as Complement (*see* Chapter 3) and in other roles typical of groups with noun as Head. In comparing Fawcett and Halliday on this point, Butler (1985, p. 101) seems to favour Fawcett.

There are also variations in the use of the term *Preposition Group* by different Systemic-Functional linguists. In most of the Systemic literature, the Preposition Group applies to combinations of a preposition and a Nominal Group: for example: *on your bike, over the rainbow*. Halliday, at least in later writings, calls this structure a prepositional phrase, and treats it, somewhat ambivalently, as outside the rank scale of clause, group, word, morpheme. As explained in Section 2.5, he applies the term Preposition Group to the preposition itself (as Head) plus Modifiers, if any (Halliday, 1994: sections 6.4.3 and 6.5).

Halliday (1994: section 6.3) discusses the Verbal Group in somewhat different terms from those used here. His treatment of tense and aspect in particular is strikingly different from that of most other linguists. More conventional treatments of verbs can be found in Palmer (1974; 1979; 1986).

*Exercises*

*Exercise 2.1*

Read Text 2A and carry out the tasks below.

[1] Water makes up over three-quarters of most living things and is constantly used up in cell processes. [2] Small plants are kept upright by being distended with water [3] just as a motor car tyre is firm when filled with air. [5] A tyre, [4] when it is flat, [5 *continued*] cannot support the car, and [6] a plant short of water on a hot day wilts. [7] Most of the water taken up by a plant is lost by evaporation from the leaves, a process called transpiration. [8] A maize plant loses about two litres a day because, [9] when the stomata are open to exchange gases during photosynthesis, [10] water vapour is lost very rapidly.[11] Transpiration actually helps to draw water up the plant in a way similar to sucking liquid up a straw.

**Text 2A**   (Martin *et al.* (eds.), *The Penguin book of the natural world ,*[1] p. 42, numbers added).

1. (a) Identify the Nominal Groups which function as the Subjects of the numbered clauses in the text. (Clauses without an explicit subject are not numbered.)
   (b) Identify the Head noun in each Group.
2. Identify each word in the last sentence according to its word class. (Treat *to draw* as a single unit.)
3. Label the following groups as Nominal, Verbal, Adverbial or Conjunction. Clause numbers are given in parentheses.

   constantly (1)           evaporation from the leaves (7)
   cell processes (1)       about two litres a day (8)
   just as (3)              is lost (10)
   wilts (6)                very rapidly (10)

*Exercise 2.2*

(a) Identify the Verbal Groups in the following examples and label them as active or passive.
(b) Label the elements of the Verbal Groups as lexical, non-finite auxiliary, finite, modal finite; **plus** (simple present), (simple past), (infinitive), (present participle), (past participle).
(c) Identify the nouns and label them as: common noun, proper noun or pronoun.
(d) Identify prepositional phrases and label the preposition and Nominal Group.
1. Robins had quoted a passage from Stevenson.

2. The government was willing to use that strategy.
3. Johnson must have smiled.
4. Eventually seventeen people were wiretapped by the FBI.
5. One more ingredient must be mentioned [...]
6. He worked with Bronstein, who had been brought into the firm by Kaplan.
7. [...] we did not know it at that time [...]
8. Her future in corporate public relations must have looked rather dim at that moment.

*Exercise 2.3*

One of the eight parts of speech in the most widespread version of traditional grammar is *interjection*. This is exemplified by such expressions as *Ouch! Oh! Ah! Help!* Try to think of reasons why many grammars exclude this category.

*Exercise 2.4*

From texts of your own choice, find examples of *numerals* functioning as (a) Modifier of a Head noun (b) as Head.

*Exercise 2.5*

Think about the alternating pronouns in the following examples or discuss them with a friend or colleague. You might consider questions of 'correctness', common usage versus grammatical regularity, and so on.

1. (a) Unlike She Who Must Be Obeyed, he was kind enough to laugh.
   (b) Unlike Her Who Must Be Obeyed, he was kind enough to laugh.
2. (a) I don't mind giving money to they who need it.
   (b) I don't mind giving money to them who need it.
3. (a) He first met my wife and I during our honeymoon.
   (b) He first met my wife and me during our honeymoon.
4. (a) Me and Bill go back a long way.
   (b) Bill and I go back a long way.
5. (a) Speaker 1: Who did this? Speaker 2: It was I.
   (b) Speaker 1: Who did this? Speaker 2: It was me.

## Answers

*Exercise 2.1*

1. (a) and (b). (Head nouns in italics.)
   [1] *Water.* [2] Small *plants.* [3] a motor car *tyre.* [4] *it.* [5] a *tyre.* [6] a

*plant* short of water on a hot day. [7] Most of the *water* taken up by a plant. [8] A maize *plant*. [9] the *stomata*. [10] water *vapour*. [11] *Transpiration*.

2. *Transpiration*: noun; *actually*: adverb; *helps*: verb; *to draw*: verb; *water*: noun; *up*: preposition; *the*: determiner (or definite article); *plant*: noun; *in*: preposition; *a*: determiner (or indefinite article); *way*: noun; *similar*: adjective; *to*: preposition; *sucking*: verb (or, arguably, noun); *liquid*: noun; *up*: preposition; *a*: determiner (or indefinite article); *straw*: noun.

3. *constantly*: Adverbial; *cell processes*: Nominal; *just as*: Conjunction; *wilts*: Verbal; *evaporation from the leaves*: Nominal; *about two litres a day*: Nominal; *is lost*: Verbal; *very rapidly*: Adverbial.


*Exercise 2.2*

1. (a) *had quoted*: active. (b) *had*: finite; *quoted*: lexical (past participle). (c) *Robins, Stevenson*: proper nouns; *passage*: common noun.

2. (a) *was willing to use*: active. (b) *was*: finite; *willing*: lexical (present participle); *to use*: lexical (infinitive). (c) *government*: common noun; *strategy*: common noun.

3. (a) *must have smiled*: active. (b) *must*: modal finite; *have*: non-finite auxiliary; *smiled*: lexical (past participle). (c) *Johnson*: proper noun.

4. (a) *were wiretapped*: passive. (b) *were*: finite; *wiretapped*: lexical (past participle). (c) *people*: common noun; *the FBI*: proper noun. (d) *by the FBI*: *by* preposition; *the FBI*: Nominal Group.

5. (a) *must be mentioned*: passive. (b) *must*: modal finite; *be*: nonfinite auxiliary; *mentioned*: lexical (past participle). (c) *ingredient*: common noun.

6. (a) *worked*: active. (b) *worked*: lexical (simple past); (a) *had been brought*: passive. (b) *had*: finite; *been*: non-finite auxiliary (past participle); *brought*: lexical (past participle). (c) *He, who*: pronouns; *Bronstein, Kaplan*: proper nouns. (d) *with Bronstein*: *with*: preposition; *Kaplan*: Nominal Group. *into the group*: *into*: preposition; *the group*: Nominal Group. *by Kaplan*: *by*: preposition; *Kaplan*: Nominal Group.

7. (a) *did ... know*: active. (b) *did*: finite; *know*: lexical (infinitive). (c) *we, it*: pronouns; *time*: common noun. (d) *at that time*: *at*: preposition; *that time*: Nominal Group.

8. (a) *must have looked*: active. (b) *must*: modal finite; *have*: non-finite auxiliary (infinitive); *looked*: lexical (past participle). (c) *her*: pronoun. *future, relations, moment*: common nouns. (d) *in corporate public relations*; *in*: preposition; *corporate public relations*: Nominal Group. *at that moment*: *at*: preposition; *that moment*: Nominal Group.


*Exercise 2.3*

This is an open question, but plausible answers might include the following considerations. Such expressions do not play an integral part in the structure of clauses; they do not interact with other word classes. Some might argue that most examples are not strictly speaking items of vocabulary or grammatical items at all but rather represent emotive noises. Items like *Help!* seem to be included on dubious grounds since *help* occurs in other contexts as a verb and a noun, and there seems to be some confusion here between grammatical word classes and utterance classifications such as exclamations. *Rubbish* is a noun. The fact that it is regularly uttered as an exclamation does not make it something other than a noun. The same might be said of *Help!* though it is a moot point whether it is a noun or a verb in exclamations. However, some categorial term seems to be needed for items like *Ouch!*, and *interjection* is as good as any other, but perhaps this is not a category on a par with nouns, verbs, or even conjunctions and prepositions.

## Exercise 2.4

Open question. Examples follow:

**as modifier:** the supply of food would increase *six* times; Most experts agree that a daily intake of about *3,000* calories is adequate; each person needing *70* grams per day.

**as head:** less than *2* per square kilometre; it is hoped to increase Australia's present population of *11.5 million* to *20 million*; *thousands* have to be recruited.

## Exercise 2.5

This is an open question about personal pronouns, raising points about prescriptivism and individual/dialectal, conscious and unconscious variation in usage.

Many speakers of English sometimes use 'subject pronouns' in non-Subject functions while others sometimes use 'object pronouns' in Subject functions. The (a) versions in Examples 2 and 3 show the 'subject-pronoun' preference, and the (b) examples offer the 'corrected' version. Some people condemn this usage, exemplified in the (a) version, but it is widespread. It seems to occur when the pronoun in question is modified as in (1) and (2) or when it is linked with another noun or pronoun as in Example 3. 'Subject-pronoun' preference may be partly due to over-correction. (Only in a few regional dialects do we find it with simple pronouns: *I don't mind giving money to they* or *He met I*.)

Example 1(a) is exceptional. In John Mortimer's *The Trials Of Rumpole*, *She Who Must be Obeyed* is a comic nickname Rumpole gives to his wife; thus, the phrase is treated as though it were a single noun and therefore invariable. In (2) the structure is somewhat stilted and (2a) could be a result of over-correction. It may be influenced by *who* being Subject in its own clause (see Chapter 8). Doubtful speakers might choose to say *those who*, thereby avoiding the problem.

In (4a) an 'object-pronoun' is used in a Subject function. 3(a) seems to some people to suggest insecure carefulness whereas 4(a) is more dialectal and unselfconscious; or, possibly, aiming at an informal, colloquial effect. Some speakers substitute the reflexive pronoun *myself* in combinations of this kind, possibly reflecting the widespread insecurity about the appropriate form. 5(a), though it can be rationally defended, is contrary to common and educated usage, which is typified by 5(b).

**Note**

1.   Martin, E., Larkin, S. and Bernbaum, L. (eds) 1976: *The Penguin book of the natural world.* Harmondsworth: Penguin.

# 3

# Subject and related functions

The night before Easter Sunday, 1920, Otto Loewi, an Austrian physiologist, awoke in the night with an idea which he jotted down on a tiny slip of paper and then went back to sleep. When he awoke again about six, he remembered that he had written down something of the greatest importance, but he could not decipher his own scrawl. The next night, at three a.m., the idea returned. It was a way of determining whether there is any chemical substance involved in nerve transmission.

The nerve impulse was known to be electrical in nature, but it was a mystery why some nerves stimulate an organ and others depress it. For instance, the vagus nerves slow down the rate of heartbeat, while the accelerator nerves increase it. Seventeen years before, it had struck Loewi that there might be a connection between this fact and the way in which some drugs stimulate while others depress.

**Text 3A**  (Taylor, *The science of life*,[1] p. 298).

## 3.1  *Subject revisited*

In Chapter 2, we pointed out that the Subject (S) is a function which is realized by a Nominal Group. At its simplest, this can be a personal pronoun such as *he* in a clause like Example (1).

(1)  [. . .] he could not decipher his own scrawl [. . .]

Or it may be an 'empty' pronoun such as *there*, as in the clause in Example (2).

(2)  [. . .] (whether) there is any chemical substance involved in nerve transmission.

It can also consist of a straightforward Nominal Group with a common noun as Head such as *the idea* in (3).

(3)  The next night, at three a.m., the idea returned.

### 3.1.1    Apposition

The subject of the first clause in Text 3A, Example (4), is *Otto Loewi, an Austrian physiologist*, which is complicated slightly by the Nominal Group *an Austrian physiologist*, placed alongside the personal name. Such a group is said to be *in apposition*; in this instance, *an Austrian physiologist* is in apposition to the nominal group *Otto Loewi*.

> (4)  The night before Easter Sunday, 1920, Otto Loewi, an Austrian physiologist, awoke in the night with an idea which he jotted down on a tiny slip of paper...

With some sacrifice of informational detail, the author could have chosen to place either *Otto Loewi* or *an Austrian physiologist* alone as Subject to give (4a) or (4b):

> (4a)  Otto Loewi awoke in the night [...]
> (4b)  an Austrian physiologist awoke in the night [...]

Both expressions refer to the same individual. In (4a), the Subject function is realized by a proper name, and in (4b) it is realized by a more complicated Nominal Group with a common noun *physiologist* as its Head. In the event, the author combined the two by using the device of apposition. We can describe this in either of two ways: (i) that the subject is *Otto Loewi* and that the apposition element *an Austrian physiologist* is not part of the structure of the clause but an interpolation, or (ii) that the whole thing *Otto Loewi, an Austrian physiologist* is the Subject. We shall choose the second, regarding *Otto Loewi, an Austrian physiologist* as a *group complex*.

### 3.1.2    Subject-Finite agreement test

We mentioned in Chapter 2 that, although agreement with the finite element of the verb is one key to the identification of the Subject, this is often – perhaps usually – not a reliable guide, because English verbs rarely vary in form except in the third person singular present tense, where they often add -*s*. In such instances, it is easy to see that a change of number or person in the Subject may coincide with a change of number in the verb (where by 'number' we mean the choice of singular or plural and by 'person' we mean: first – *I* and *we*; second – *you*; and third – anyone else).

In Text 3A, the prevailing tense is past simple and so the agreement feature is not manifest. The verb *awake*, for example, is invariably *awoke* in the past, regardless of how many people are involved or whether the person doing the awaking is the speaker or the addressee or some third person.

Texts written predominantly in the present tense, therefore, obviously offer more examples of explicit subject-verb agreement. A geography textbook, describing existing conditions or general truths, is a case in point, offering such examples as (5), (6), (7) and (8), all with verbs in the present.

(5) Erosion depletes the grasslands [...]
(6) The failure of the rain brings disaster.
(7) All savanna lands experience a period of drought [...]
(8) Rich pastures support more animals [...]

In Examples (5) and (6) the verbs end with -*s* and so we know they are singular; in (7) and (8), they do not, and so they are plural (or, at least, obviously not third person singular). In (5) there are two Nominal Groups: *erosion* and *grasslands*. The Nominal Group *erosion* is singular; the Nominal Group *the grasslands* is plural. Therefore the Subject is *erosion*.

In (7) we also have two Nominal Groups: *all savanna lands* and *a period of drought*. The verb is plural; *all savanna lands* is plural whereas *a period of drought* is singular. Therefore the Subject is *all savanna lands*.

In these two cases the relation between the Subject and the verb is very clear. In examples (6) and (8) the test does not work quite so well. In (6) both the Nominal Groups are singular and in (8) they are both plural. The test can still work if we ask ourselves what effect it would have to change the *number* of the Nominal Groups (from singular to plural or vice versa). In (6) if we change *disaster* to *disasters*, it has no effect on the verb. But if we change *the failure of the rain* to *the failures* (or some other plural group) we have to change the verb from *brings* to *bring*. Therefore, *the failure of the rain* is Subject, and not *disaster*. The same sort of thing happens in reverse for (8).

This test works for the past tense with the verb *be* only. The text gives us Example (9), where *It* is a third person singular pronoun referring to *the idea*, mentioned in the previous sentence:

(9) It was a way of determining whether there is any chemical substance [...]

If there had been more than one idea the pronoun would have been *they* and the verb would have been *were* as in (9a):

(9a) They were ways/a way of determining whether there is any chemical substance.

### 3.1.3 Question-tag test

We mentioned in Chapter 2 a more reliable test for Subject, since it works in more instances. This is based on the fact that in a tag question, the Subject of the main clause is reflected in the tag. Thus, we can test for the subject of a declarative clause by adding a question tag to it. Adapting our original Example (4) from the source text, this gives, for example, (4c):

(4c) Otto Loewi awoke in the night with an idea, didn't he?

The pronoun in the tag reflects *Otto Loewi* and so takes the form *he* rather than *it*, which it would have to do if it reflected *the night* or *the idea*. In

Example (3), where the subject actually is *the idea*, the tag would be *it*, as in (3a):

> (3a)  The next night, at three a.m., the idea returned, didn't it?

The application of the tag test on Examples (5), (6), (7) and (8) works as a diagnostic for Subject in a similar way to the Subject-Agreement test, that is, more straightforwardly for (5) and (7) than for (6) and (8) (*see* (5a) to (8a) below):

> (5a)  Erosion depletes the grasslands, doesn't it?
> (6a)  The failure of the rain brings disaster, doesn't it?
> (7a)  All savanna lands experience a period of drought, don't they?
> (8a)  Rich pastures support more animals, don't they?

### 3.1.4   Passive clauses

In the first sentence of the second paragraph of the text about Loewi, we have the clause given below as (10):

> (10)  The nerve impulse was known to be electrical in nature [. . .]

This is a passive clause, a clause in which the Verbal Group includes some form of the auxiliary verb *be* and a past participle, in this instance, *known*. The tests suggest that *the nerve impulse* is Subject.

Passive clauses are, in a sense, the inverted form of corresponding active clauses. To take an example not included in the above extract:

> (11)  Loewi was obsessed by the idea.

This has a hypothetical corresponding active clause (11a):

> (11a)  The idea obsessed Loewi.

In the first one, the passive clause, the hypothetical tag is *wasn't he?* and in the second, the active, the tag is *didn't it?* Thus we can ascertain that the Subject of the first example is *Loewi* but that of the second is *the idea*.

In passive clauses, there is sometimes a phrase made up of *by* plus a Nominal Group, as in Example (11). The by-phrase in the passive matches the Subject of the corresponding active clause; that is, the Nominal Group following *by* in the passive clause is the same as the Nominal Group realizing the Subject in the corresponding active clause. (*See* Fig. 3.1.)

| Voice | Subject | | |
|---|---|---|---|
| ACTIVE | The idea | obsessed | Loewi |
| PASSIVE | Loewi | was obsessed | by the idea |

Fig. 3.1

Much more frequently, however, we find passives without a by-phrase. This brings us back to the first clause in the second paragraph of the source text, our Example (10) above (*The nerve impulse was known to be electrical in nature*), which is an instance of exactly this phenomenon. Presumably, there is some hypothetical 'knower' assumed, but there is no mention of this person and we cannot safely deduce who it might be; in fact, there is an implication that the precise identity of the knower is not significant.

### 3.1.5 'Empty' Subjects

We mentioned above the 'Empty' Subject *there* which occurs in the first paragraph of the source text. Such Subjects are also known as 'dummy' Subjects. In the second paragraph, we find another of these. This time the pronoun is the first *it* in Example (12):

(12) [...] it was a mystery why some nerves stimulate an organ and others depress it.

What is the function of the first *it* in this clause? Superficially, it resembles the *it* in the previous sentence of the text, our Example (9), but there is a significant difference. In Example (9) (*It was a way of determining* [...]), the pronoun *it* refers to the same concept as the Nominal Group *the idea* in the sentence before that, but in Example (12) the Subject *it* is simply a sort of stand-in, holding the Subject position until the meat of the Subject comes along, namely: *why some nerves stimulate an organ and others depress it*.

The second *it* in the same sentence, Example (12), is a fully referring pronoun (not a 'dummy') and is co-referential with *an organ*.

Where empty *it* temporarily stands in for more substantial matter (that is, as a dummy), we say that the 'postponed' structure is an embedded clause (*see* Chapter 8). We analyse the dummy *it* and the embedded clause together as making up the Subject. Thus, the subject of Example (9) is: *it* [...] *why some nerves stimulate an organ and others depress it*. (We return to this kind of structure in detail in Chapter 8.)

### 3.2 Finites and Predicators

Verbal Groups realize the functions of *Finite* (F) and *Predicator* (P), and the two are often combined in a single word. If we take all the simple Verbal Groups from the source text, we have: *awoke, jotted (down), went, remembered, returned, stimulate, depress, slow (down),* and *increase,* some occurring more than once. Each of these is analysed as a simple Verbal Group realizing the functions of Finite and Predicator at the same time. In each instance, the Finite and Predicator are said to be *fused*. Where the Verbal

Group consists of one word, the fused Finite/Predicator function is represented as F/P.

It can perhaps be more easily understood what this means if we look at the instances of unfused Finites and Predicators. These can be found among the remaining Verbal Groups: *had written, could not decipher, was known* and *had struck*. Each of these falls into two parts, the first part being Finite and the second part Predicator. The Finite is that part of the Verbal Group which carries the agreement (person and number), in so far as it shows up at all in English; the Predicator is the remainder of the Verbal Group.

In this text, as it happens, we have no examples with more than two verbal elements, but noncomplex Verbal Groups can contain up to five words, not counting the negative polarity element *not* or the particles (for example, *down* in *had written down* or *slow down*). An example of a five-part Verbal Group is *might have been being written* as in *It might have been being written during that period*. Admittedly, such instances are not very common, but four-word Verbal Groups (*might have been written*) are, and so are groups of three words or two. In all such instances the first element (in our example, *might*) realizes the Finite function whilst the rest of the Verbal Group (in our examples, *have been being written* or *have been writing*) realizes the Predicator function (*see* Fig. 3.2).

In other words, the Predicator is realized by the lexical verb, that part of the verb which you might look up in a dictionary (*awake, jot, go, remember,* and so on), but it also incorporates all auxiliary elements other than the finite, which carries the agreement function (though agreement is not always made manifest in the substance of the language). So, in *might have been writing*, only *might* realizes the Finite function, whereas *have been writing* realizes the Predicator. In *has been writing*, *has* is Finite and *been writing* is Predicator. Fig. 3.2 offers a random selection of various Verbal Groups with *write* as the lexical verb, analysed into the functions Finite and Predicator.

In any Verbal Group made up of more than one word in English, only the Finite carries the burden of agreement, and there is only one Finite to a group. When they stand alone, finite forms of *be* (*am, is, are, was, were*) and finite

| Finite | Predicator |
|--------|------------|
| was | writing |
| had | written |
| was | written |
| has | been writing |
| might | have been writing |
| might | have been being written |

**Fig. 3.2**

forms of *have* (*has, have, had*) are usually analysed as Finite and not as fused forms. Clauses featuring Finites of this kind have no Predicator, for example the first clause partially analysed in Fig. 3.3(i). Compare this with the other two clauses: (ii) a fused Finite and Predicator and (iii) a separate Finite and Predicator.

| (i) | it | was | a way of determining . . . | |
|-----|-----|-----|-----|-----|
|     | **S** | **F** | | |

| (ii) | he | awoke | again about six | |
|------|-----|-----|-----|-----|
|      | **S** | **F/P** | | |

| (iii) | he | has | written | the letter |
|-------|-----|-----|-----|-----|
|       | **S** | **F** | **P** | |

**Fig. 3.3**

### 3.2.1  Negatives and interrogatives

In English, the grammar of interrogatives and negatives (and certain related structures) is much more complicated than in many other languages, such as most other European languages.

Where the positive declarative contains a separate Finite and Predicator, as in *had written* in our source text, the negative counterpart is identical except that *not* (or *n't*) is present immediately after the Finite. Let us consider modified data to avoid some confusing problems irrelevant to our present concerns. Thus, illustrating the positive-negative options, we have the pairing (13) and (13a).

(13)   He has written the letter.
(13a)  He has not written the letter.

Interrogatives likewise have a fairly straightforward systematic correspondence with declaratives in that the Finite and the Subject are inverted; thus we have (13b).

(13b)  Has he written the letter?

So far, so good. Look at it from the point of view of the non-English speaker (say, a German teenager) trying to master English usage. This corresponds very nicely with what happens in her own language. In German, for example, she might say (14) when forming a positive declarative, (14a) when forming a negative and (14b) when forming an interrogative:

(14)   Er hat den Brief geschrieben.
       (lit: *He has the letter written.*)

(14a)  Er hat den Brief nicht geschrieben.
      (lit: *He has the letter not written.*)
(14b)  Hat er den Brief geschrieben?
      (lit. *Has he the letter written?*)

The order of the words is not quite the same, but the relationship between the two is otherwise consistent with the English pattern.

So long as we stick to samples where the Verbal Group in the positive declarative realizes distinct Finite and Predicator, all is well, but the unsuspecting young German will get into linguistic trouble if she tries to do the same thing with all verbs since, working on the same principles, she could come up with the paradigm (15):

(15)  He awoke in the night.
      *He awoke not in the night.
      *Awoke he in the night?

That sort of thing might have been all very well for Shakespeare, but it will not do for English today. In modern English, we have the paradigm (15a), analysed for S, F and P in Fig. 3.4:

(15a)  He awoke in the night.
      He did not awake in the night.
      Did he awake in the night?

This particular complication in English grammar, which has no parallel in German (or French, Spanish, Italian or most other) grammar, requires that the negative or interrogative counterparts of positive declaratives with a simple verb must feature a form of the verb *do* as Finite. Put another way, the rules in English are as follows.

1.  To convert a positive declarative into a negative, add *not* after the Finite. If there is no separate Finite make *do* the Finite and add *not*.
2.  To convert a declarative into an interrogative, invert the order of Finite and Subject. If there is no separate Finite, make *do* the Finite and place it before the Subject.

| He | awoke | in the night. |
|---|---|---|
| S | F/P | |

| He | did not | awake | in the night. |
|---|---|---|---|
| S | F | P | |

| Did | he | awake | in the night? |
|---|---|---|---|
| F | S | P | |

**Fig. 3.4**

The native English student learning German needs only the first part of each rule, since the second part is unique to English.

Incidentally, *do* and other finite auxiliary verbs often occur in isolation in elliptical structures such as short form answers to yes/no questions (*Yes, I did; No, they can't*); short form emphatic agreement (*So they did! So they should!*); and many others, including question tags. These are clear instances of Finite without a Predicator.

Of course, we are not obliged to look at the relationship between regularly corresponding clause types as involving some kind of conversion process from one to another. This is just one of the many metaphorical devices we may employ in talking about language. Another might present the whole of the vocabulary and grammar of the language as a vast network of inter-related systems, through which the users thread their way each time they use the language, committing themselves to a series of options, some of which determine later choices to varying extents. This last metaphor is closer to the Hallidayan perception.

### 3.2.2  Mood

In Section 3.2.1, we looked at some of the grammatical characteristics of declaratives and interrogatives. This leads us to a brief consideration of Halliday's treatment of Mood.

Halliday divides the clause into two parts: the Mood and the Residue. The Mood is made up of the Subject and Finite; the Residue is the rest of the functions in the clause (Predicator, Complements and Adjuncts).

Recall that we have mentioned the representation of the grammar as an intricate set of sets of choices. Each of these sets is called a system and the systems link up with each other as networks. The realization of the Mood function in any clause involves making choices from the Mood system (*see* Fig. 3.5).

Not all clauses have Mood. Examples of moodless clauses are (16), (17), or the italicized section of (18) (*see* Chapter 8).

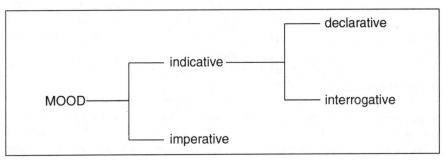

**Fig 3.5**

(16)  Closed for lunch.
(17)  Happy New Year!
(18)  *Subsequently released*, he escaped to England.

In clauses which do have mood, an obligatory choice is made between indicative and imperative. (We could call indicative 'non-imperative'.) If indicative is chosen, an obligatory choice is made between declarative and interrogative. Each choice precludes the others; that is to say, you cannot have a clause which is simultaneously declarative and interrogative, or imperative and declarative, and so on. In the network, this Mood system links up with the system of Polarity shown in Fig. 3.6. In addition to selecting one of the three options from the Mood system, we are required to choose between positive and negative.

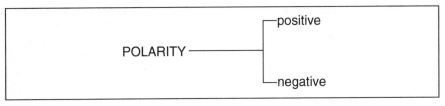

**Fig. 3.6**

In the second sentence in Text 3A, presented here as Example (19), there are four clauses. All of them realize the choice *declarative* from the Mood system; the first three realize the choice of Positive and the last one realizes the choice of negative from the Polarity system.

(19)  When he awoke again about six: *positive declarative*
      he remembered: *positive declarative*
      that he had written down something of the greatest importance: *positive declarative*
      but he could not decipher his own scrawl: *negative declarative*

Subject and Finite are the key exponents of the Mood choices in that (i) the sequencing of Subject and Finite is affected by the choice between declarative and interrogative (already discussed above) and (ii) the choice of imperative permits us to leave out the Subject. Polarity has a bearing on Mood because, as we have pointed out, with verbs in the simple present tense and simple past tense, Finite and Predicator are fused in a single word in the positive option, but in the negative option the separate auxiliary finite *do* must realize the function of Finite.

To label the rest of the clause 'Residue' is not to suggest that it is of little importance. It is simply the Residue (what remains) after the Mood is taken out. Incidentally, it is possible to analyse a clause in terms of the functions SFPCA without mentioning Mood and Residue, but they are part of the same package.

### 3.3 *Complements*

If you are familiar with traditional grammar, you may have already learned to identify the term *complement* with a particular concept. (In other grammars the term is used with a number of meanings.) The use of the term in Hallidayan linguistics is more comprehensive than in traditional grammar. In her seminal *Introduction to Systemic Linguistics*, Margaret Berry (1975: p. 64) identifies it as follows: 'A complement is the part of a sentence which answers the question "Who or what?" (or, if one wishes to be pedantic, "Whom or what?") *after* the verb.'

Berry refers to definitions of this type as 'helpful but unscientific' (Berry, 1975: p. 84), and that is a fair comment. If we were to apply it to Text 3A, we would find it helpful in some cases, less helpful in others. Since our aim here is to elucidate rather than confuse, we will take the liberty of being selective in our application.

If on reading the first sentence, shortened here as (20), we ask 'Loewi awoke who or what?', there is no obvious candidate to fill the *Who or what?* slot.

(20) Loewi awoke in the night.

Loewi awoke *in the night*, but *in the night* does not answer the question *Who or what?* The sentence goes on to say that he awoke in the night *with an idea*, but this too fails to meet the *Who or what?* criterion. Ergo, there is no Complement.

This is a correct deduction. In fact, many clauses have no Complements. It happens that, even though it doesn't have a Complement in this instance, the verb *awoke* could have one, though this is not true for all verbs. For example, Loewi might have decided to tell his bright idea to his wife, assuming that he had one and that she was present. In this case, we might wish to say (21).

(21) He awoke his wife.

Now, if we were to ask the Berry question, we get the answer *his wife*. Thus the Complement is *his wife*. In Example (22), however, there is no possibility of a Complement.

(22) Night fell.

Dipping into Text 3A at a later point, we get (23):

(23) [. . .] he had written down something of the greatest importance [. . .]

This time when we apply Berry's question as *He had written down who or what?*, we get the answer: *something of the greatest importance*. We have identified a Complement. This time, the presence of the Complement is obligatory since *written down* must take a Complement (*see* Fig. 3.7).

A further dip into the text brings out Example (3) again, repeated here:

(3) The next night, at three a.m., the idea returned.

| he | had | written down | something of the greatest importance |
|----|-----|--------------|--------------------------------------|
| F | S | P | C |

**Fig. 3.7**

*The idea returned who or what?* we ask. No answer. So again, no Complement.

Try again with (9), also repeated:

(9)   It was a way of determining whether there is any chemical substance in nerve transmission.

Berry question: *It was who or what?* Answer: *a way of determining whether there is any chemical substance in nerve transmission.* We have identified another Complement, a long and complicated one this time, but there is nothing in the grammar that says that Complements cannot be long and complicated.

One last dip. This time we take a dependent clause (*see* Chapter 8), Example (24):

(24)   [...] while the accelerator nerves decrease it [...]

Berry question: *While the accelerator nerves decrease who or what?* Answer: *it*. Therefore, the Complement is *it*. A complement does not have to be long and complicated, then, or even very explicit out of context.

Alas, this test is no more rigorous or reliable than the tests for Subject. The best that can be said for it is that it usually works. If you try the rest of the clauses in the extract, you may well get into difficulties at times. This is the price of using authentic data rather than invented 'The cat chased the mouse' type of sentences that are designed to suit the needs of the moment. Some of the problems will be resolved in later chapters. Part of the source text is analysed and labelled for SFPCA in Section 3.5.

### 3.3.1   More delicate complement analysis

Like flowers, Complements come in various kinds. On one occasion, it may be enough to describe an object as a *flower*; on another occasion, we may wish to be more specific and refer to it as a *rose* or *jasmine* or *magnolia*. Some people might want to specify what kind of rose they are talking about and so they classify it as a *tea-rose* or *a rambling rose*. Rose growers may go into even greater refinements of categorization. In the same way, with many grammatical categories, we can classify items with varying degrees of delicacy. Though they are less variegated than flowers, Complements are no exception to this tendency. For some purposes, we may be happy with the label Complement; sometimes we may wish to go further and say what kind of Complement we are dealing with.

The Complements (italicized) in the clauses 'he awoke *his wife*'; 'he had written down *something of the greatest importance*'; 'he could not decipher *his own scrawl*'; 'others depress *it*' are all classed, with greater delicacy, as *Object Complements*. Or, at somewhere around the 'rambling rose' stage of delicacy, they can be classed as *Direct Object Complements* (C$^{do}$).

The long, complicated Complement in Example (9) (*a way of determining whether there is any chemical substance involved in nerve transmission*) is an *Intensive Complement* (C$^{int}$). This categorization is not related to its length or complexity, but rather to the fact that it follows a form of the verb *be* (a copular verb). The item following the Predicator would still be an Intensive Complement even if the clause said: 'It was *cabbage*.'

Direct Object Complements (C$^{do}$) normally follow those verbs listed in dictionaries as transitive: *decipher, depress, stimulate*, from our extract; or *identify, liberate, control, secrete, block, destroy, cram* from a later paragraph in the same book. Verbs marked in the dictionary as intransitive tend to occur without an Object Complement. One problem for someone trying to give a neat account of all this is that most verbs in English (not all) seem to be able to function both 'transitively' and 'intransitively'; that is, with or without a Complement. For example, in the extract we find both (25) and, a little later, (26) (with Object Complement in italics):

(25) [...] some nerves stimulate *an organ* and others depress *it*.
(26) [...] some drugs stimulate while others depress.

A Complement which follows a copular verb (such as *be, seem, appear, become*) is called an *Intensive Complement* (C$^{int}$). Examples: Brasilia is *the capital city*; she seems *a brilliant woman*; he appears *stupid*; the terrain eventually became *a desert*. The text provides a more complicated example of this in (9), repeated here with added italics.

(9) It was *a way of determining* (*whether there is any chemical substance* [...])

Some verbs allow two Object Complements: a Direct Object Complement and an *Indirect Object Complement* (C$^{io}$) (*see* Fig. 3.8). Example (27) is taken from another chapter of the source text.[1]

(27) Mendel promptly sent him 140 packets.

Here the Direct Object Complement is *140 packets* and the Indirect Object Complement is the pronoun *him*. The verbs that permit Indirect Object Complements, called *ditransitive* verbs, are a limited set; typical ones are *give, send, offer*. In a simple independent declarative clause the Indirect

| Mendel | promptly | sent | him | 140 packets. |
|--------|----------|------|-----|--------------|
| S | | F/P | C$^{io}$ | C$^{do}$ |

**Fig. 3.8**

Object Complement normally comes immediately after the verb and the Direct Object Complement follows it (as in the example above). Such clauses systematically correspond to clauses where the Direct Object Complement immediately follows the Predicator and the other Complement is expressed as a prepositional phrase with *to*. Thus the author might have written (27a):

(27a)  Mendel promptly sent 140 packets to him.

Most linguists reserve the term Indirect Object for the structure without the preposition. One label that has been applied to the *to*-phrase in such structures is *Oblique Complement* ($C^{ob}$). Some class it as an Adjunct. However, some analysts prefer to apply the term Indirect Object Complement to both structures, regardless of the form and sequence.

| Mendel | promptly | sent | 140 packets | to him |
|--------|----------|------|-------------|--------|
| S | | F/P | $C^{do}$ | $C^{io}$ or $C^{ob}$ |

**Fig. 3.9**

Sometimes Indirect Object Complements correspond not with a *to*-phrase but with a *for*-phrase, but it is analysed similarly. For example, in the case of the invented clause (27b), the corresponding clause is (27c):

(27b)  Mendel bought him 140 packets.
(27c)  Mendel bought 140 packets for him.

A different kind of structure with two Complements is to be found in the next example, (28):

(28)  Loewi called the substance released by the vagus nerve 'vagus-stuff'.

There are two Complements here: (i) *the substance released by the vagus nerve*, and (ii) *vagus-stuff*. The first is the Direct Object Complement, but the second is another kind of Intensive Complement (*see* Fig. 3.10). (Two is the maximum number of Complements that a (simple) clause can contain.)

A standard textbook example of this type of structure is (29):

(29)  They elected him President.

Here *him* is Direct Object Complement and *President* is Intensive Complement. Comparable structures in common use are the so-called performative expressions, such as (30), (31) and (32):

| Loewi | called | the substance ... | 'vagus-stuff'. |
|-------|--------|-------------------|----------------|
| S | F/P | $C^{do}$ | $C^{int}$ |

**Fig. 3.10**

(30) I now pronounce you man and wife.
(31) I find you not guilty.
(32) I declare this supermarket open.

A literary example of Direct and Direct Object Complement and Intensive Complement is the well-known first sentence of the great American novel *Moby Dick*: 'Call me Ishmael' (which because it is imperative lacks a Subject). An old joke plays on the potential ambiguity of such structures:

> Hotel guest: Call me a taxi!
> Hotel porter: All right, you're a taxi.

Normally in our analysis we label Complement as C without indicating the more delicate subcategory. Only when the distinction is important for the purposes of the discussion do we go into the more delicate analysis.

## 3.4  *Adjuncts*

*Adjuncts*, as their name suggests (etymologically: something 'joined to'), are slightly peripheral in the clause. That is not to say that they are necessarily of less importance informationally than S, F, P or C items, but they are for the most part grammatically optional in a way that the others are not.

The first sentence in Text 3A begins with an Adjunct: *The night before Easter Sunday, 1920*. Other Adjuncts in the same sentence are: *in the night, with an idea, on a tiny slip of paper* and *then*. (Some analysts might want to add *down*, but we have decided to place it with the verb as part of the Predicator.) In the following sentences in the same paragraph, we find: *again, about six, the next night, at three a.m.*, and *in nerve transmission*.

Adjuncts fall into three subtypes: Circumstantial, Conjunctive and Modal, corresponding more or less to the three macrofunctions: Ideational, Textual and Interpersonal. As in the case of Complement, whether or not we need to go into such details depends on the immediate purpose of our analysis. It may be enough to classify an item as Adjunct or we may wish to subclassify it.

### 3.4.1  Circumstantial Adjuncts

Most of the Adjuncts in the first paragraph concern information about time or place; in other words, they deal with the *circumstances* of the events or states described in the text. For this reason, such Adjuncts are called *Circumstantial Adjuncts* ($A^{cir}$).

The realizations of the Circumstantial Adjuncts cited here are as follows:

*the night before Easter Sunday, 1920*: Nominal Group
*in the night*: prepositional phrase
*with an idea which he jotted down on a tiny slip of paper*: prepositional phrase

*on a tiny slip of paper*: prepositional phrase
*about six*: prepositional phrase
*the next night*: Nominal Group
*at three a.m.*: prepositional phrase
*in nerve transmission*: prepositional phrase.

As you can see, Adjuncts have considerable flexibility with regard to the items which realize them. Most typically, though, they are realized by prepositional phrases or adverbs. Nominal Groups which express points of time and to that extent resemble adverbs are also not rare. In this extract prepositional phrases dominate.

Circumstantial Adjuncts express information about the circumstances of a process: they convey information about such matters as place, time, manner, the associated participants (with whom? with what?); they are, therefore, part of the ideational meaning of the clause.

The by-phrase in passive clauses is also a Circumstantial Adjunct because it expresses the meaning: by what? Example (11) is analysed as in Fig. 3.11.

| Loewi | was | obsessed | by the idea. |
|-------|-----|----------|--------------|
| S | F | P | $A^{cir}$ |

**Fig. 3.11**

You may note that we omitted from the list of realizations above the adverbs *then* and *again*, although we originally identified them as Adjuncts. This is because *then* and *again* have subtly different functions from the items in the list, and are therefore discussed in the next section.

### 3.4.2   Conjunctive Adjuncts

Before we continue with the adverb *then*, let us consider the second paragraph of the extract, where we find an Adjunct that is clearly of a different kind from the Circumstantial Adjuncts listed.

> (33) For instance, the vagus nerves slow down the rate of heartbeat, while the accelerator nerve increases it.

In Example (33) the prepositional phrase *for instance* functions to show the link between the clause it introduces and the previous text. In the sentence that precedes Example (33) in the text, we have a general statement: *some nerves stimulate an organ and others depress it*. The information that (33) offers is a specific example of the type of thing initially described in these general terms. It is an instance of the discourse pattern: Generalization: Example (Hoey, 1983). What the expression *For instance* does is to signal the nature of that relationship. It does not actually add to the propositional content of the second sentence, but it does make clear for the reader how it fits into the text. It helps to show the link between this clause and what precedes it. For this reason, Adjuncts of this type are called *Conjunctive Adjuncts* (A$^{con}$).

To return to *then* (in the clause *and then went back to sleep*), although it resembles most of our examples of Circumstantial Adjuncts in that it is concerned with time, its primary function seems to be to relate this event to the events previously recounted in the text. This seems to suggest that it is a Conjunctive Adjunct. The adverb *again* in *When he awoke again* is similar. By the same reasoning, *Seventeen years before* might also be classed as a Conjunctive Adjunct (though this is perhaps more debatable).

Here we have an example of the way that labelling needs to take account of the possibility of a *cline*, a gradation between two clear ends of a line (in this case, indisputable instances of Circumstantial Adjuncts and indisputable instances of Conjunctive Adjuncts); *then* seems to have some qualities of both, but to be closer to the Conjunctive end of the cline.

The book from which we took our extract continues with the passage in Text 3B. In the first sentence here we find another Conjunctive Adjunct: the time adverb *now*. In the subsequent sentence, we have the adverb *then*, and in the last sentence the adverbs *equally* and *afterwards*. *Now*, *then* and *afterwards* signal conjunction relating to time, and *equally* signals a kind of comparison. All are Conjunctive Adjuncts, and they can be contrasted with the other Adjuncts in the same text fragment.

### 3.4.3 Modal Adjuncts

The remaining Adjuncts in Text 3B can be split up into two sets. On the one hand we have the Circumstantial Adjuncts: *in Ringer's solution*, *into the solution*, *in the solution*, *out of bed*, and *to his lab*. On the other hand, we have: *normally*, *for a while*, and *repeatedly*. These three fall into a subclass of Adjuncts not yet mentioned, to which we give the label *Modal Adjuncts* (A$^{mod}$). The function of Modal Adjuncts is to indicate some aspect of the

> The experiment which now occurred to Loewi was to take a frog's heart, put it in Ringer's solution (a solution containing the salts which normally bathe cells, and which keep them alive for a while), and stimulate its vagus nerve repeatedly, in the expectation that some chemical substance would be liberated into the solution. Then to put the frog's heart in the solution and see if it slowed down. Loewi got out of bed, went to his lab, and did the experiment. It worked. Equally, if he stimulated the accelerator nerve, the solution would afterwards accelerate another heart.

**Text 3B**   (Taylor, *The science of life*[1]).

speaker/writer's attitude to the message or her comment on its relevance, reliability, interest and so on. Sometimes, it may be difficult to distinguish between a Modal and a Circumstantial Adjunct, or, indeed, even between a Modal and a Conjunctive.

Clearer examples of Modal Adjuncts are (34) to (37) from an earlier page of the same book:

(34) [. . .] the sodium ions which enter are *somehow* pumped out again.
(35) [. . .] it was *probably* the same substance [. . .]
(36) [. . .] one nerve cell does not *quite* touch another.
(37) These proved big enough for the voltage *actually* observed.

The adverb *probably* can be taken as the prototypical item realizing the function of Modal Adjunct. It represents the degree to which the speaker/writer is committed to the proposition being made. For this chapter, we are using as our main source a popular textbook, a history of biology. In texts of this type, there is a tendency to present propositions in a relatively unmodified way as scientific truths. We say 'relatively' because, as the samples just given demonstrate, the phenomenon is certainly not absent. However, in articles written by scientists reporting their own research, there tends to be a greater amount of 'hedging', that is, signals of a degree of caution in the making of claims. This can show up in the use of various modifiers such as *approximately*, *about*, *around*, usually as part of a Nominal Group, and also in the use of modal verbs like *may, might* and *could* in the Verbal Group, realizing the Finite. In addition, more significantly for our present discussion, the hedging can take the form of Modal Adjuncts like *probably*.

Modal Adjuncts have something in common then with modal verbs, hence their shared part of the label. On a scale of commitment to a proposition, we might have *certainly* at the positive end and *certainly not* at the negative end, with such items as *probably, possibly, conceivably* at various points along the line, along with expressions like *perhaps, maybe, indisputably, without doubt, imaginably, surely*.

Less obvious examples, perhaps, are the items which we identified in Text 3B: *normally, for a while*, and *repeatedly*. These tell us about the frequency, duration or regularity of the process. At the positive end of this scale we might have *always* or *invariably* and at the negative end *never, not once* or *at no time*.

Discourse analysts and scholars who are interested in how scientists write about their work have paid considerable attention to modality in text, and one thing that has emerged is that reports of scientific research in newspapers and popular magazines feature less hedging than do the reports in specialist scientific journals. In contrast, school textbooks, histories and biographies tend to resemble newspapers rather than specialist texts, in this respect if not in others. One good reason, perhaps, why there are fewer hedging expressions in our source text than in original research reports is that what is recounted here is seen with hindsight to be reliable information. Moreover, politeness factors (modesty and lack of encroachment into other people's space) that are significantly present when a scientist reports his or her own work do not apply when a historian reports it retrospectively. This is discussed further in Chapter 11.

Examples of other Modal Adjuncts that serve a similar purpose are *in our view*, *in my opinion*, *according to our calculations*, *on present evidence*. A similar expression found later in the same book is (38) (italics added):

(38) Diluted by a lot of Ringer's solution, it would, *one would expect*, be much too weak to exert any effect.

This expresses the author's caution with regard to the likelihood of the proposition even though it exploits the impersonal pronoun *one* to do so. If we remove the italicized words, we have a more strongly committed claim. Although this hedging device is a clause, it is a something like a fixed expression functioning as a simple Adjunct. (*See* Chapters 9 and 10 for a discussion of clause complexes.)

All these Modal Adjuncts have a similar function, namely that of hedging or modulating the proposition. As we have said, they have much in common in this respect with modal verbs (*may*, *might*, and so on), which function as Finites within the Mood of the clause. Thus, they can with greater delicacy be labelled *Mood Adjuncts* to distinguish them from the other subclass of Modal Adjuncts which we call *Comment Adjuncts*. For most purposes, however, it is not necessary to make such subtle distinctions.

*Comment Adjuncts* are typically realized by such adverbs as *frankly*, *fortunately*, *obviously*, and *regrettably*. These offer the speaker/writer's comment on the proposition, but that comment does not say anything about probability, frequency or generality. An example from later in our source text is (39) (italics added):

(39) *Oddly enough*, a case where the transmission actually was electrical was discovered soon after.

The Modal (Comment) Adjunct that begins it (*Oddly enough*), serves to indicate to the reader something of the author's surprise at the fact which he is reporting. Incidentally, the sentence also includes another Modal Adjunct, this time the Mood Adjunct: *actually*, and a Conjunctive Adjunct: *soon after*.

### 3.4.4  Adjuncts and conjunctions

As we have said, Adjuncts are normally realized by prepositional phrases, Adverbial Groups, and sometimes even Nominal Groups, but they are not realized by conjunctions. This is deducible from the statement made in Chapter 2 that conjunctions are not part of the structure of the clause. The word *then*, in this text, is not a conjunction but an adverb, as are *now* and *afterwards*; all function here as Adjunct.

As their name suggests, Conjunctive Adjuncts have a function similar to that carried out by conjunctions; they signal the rhetorical organization of the text, which places them as part of the textual metafunction. The distinction between *conjunctions* and *Conjunctive Adjuncts* can be a source of some confusion.

Conjunctions are a word class within the same system as *noun, verb, adjective, adverb, determiner, preposition,* and *numeral* (*see* Chapter 2) whereas Adjunct is a function in the clause and is realized by such word classes as adverbs and nominals as well as by prepositional phrases. In our analysis, conjunctions fall outside the clause structure SFPCA. Although they often seem to convey a similar meaning to that conveyed by conjunctions, Conjunctive Adjuncts differ from them grammatically. For instance, the conjunction always occurs at the beginning of the clause which it links or binds, whereas Conjunctive Adjuncts can occur at various points within the clause that they affect. Consider Example (40):

> (40)  He remembered that he had written down something of the greatest importance, but he could not decipher his own scrawl.

There are three clauses here: *He remembered* ‖ *that he had written down something of the greatest importance* ‖ *but he could not decipher his own scrawl*. The first two go together and we will ignore that relationship here and focus on the link signalled by *but*. The conjunction *but* indicates to the reader that there is an adversative relation between the two parts of the sentence, or rather that the second is in an adverse relation to the first. Now, suppose we reword this as (40a):

> (40a)  He remembered that he had written down something of the greatest importance. However, he could not decipher his own scrawl.

The adverb *however* here carries something akin to the force of *but* in the actual sentence, but, in addition to the change of lexical item, there is a grammatical change. Instead of a two-part sentence linked by a linking conjunction, we have two separate sentences with an adverb as Conjunctive Adjunct in the second. That this is not just an arbitrary labelling distinction is clear if we try to move the words in question. We can say in the same linguistic context (40b) or (40c):

> (40b)  He remembered that he had written down something of the greatest importance. He could not, however, decipher his own scrawl.
> (40c)  He remembered that he had written down something of the greatest importance. He could not decipher his own scrawl, however.

However, there is no other position for the conjunction *but* without a change of meaning. We do not, in Standard English, say (40d) or (40e):

> (40d)  *He remembered that he had written down something of the greatest importance, he could not but decipher his own scrawl.
> (40e)  *He remembered that he had written down something of the greatest importance, he could not decipher his own scrawl but.

Plainly, *however* and *but* behave grammatically in very different ways. That is why we classify them differently, assigning them different labels as word classes (*adverb* versus *conjunction*) and functionally (since *However* is an Adjunct and no comparable function can be assigned to *but*). That is why orthographic conventions prescribe a full stop (or a semi-colon) between the two clauses with *however* and permit a comma with *but*. The same can be said, *mutatis mutandis*, of the other items in Fig. 3.12.

| Conjunctive Adjunct (adverb) | conjunction |
|---|---|
| moreover, furthermore | and |
| however, nevertheless | but, yet |
| alternatively | or, whereas |
| meanwhile, simultaneously | when, while |
| thus, therefore, consequently | so that |

**Fig. 3.12**

Note that *yet* can be a conjunction, similar in meaning to *but*, or it can be a temporal adverb and hence function as Adjunct: (*He has not spoken yet*).

When analysing clauses into SFPCA, conjunctions are omitted from the analysis, but Conjunctive Adjuncts are included.

## 3.5   *Sample analysis*

The first three sentences are analysed in terms of SFPCA in Fig. 3.13. The first two sentences are clause complexes, that is, they consist of more than one clause (*see* Chapter 9), but this does not present any problems for analysis here. The first sentence also contains an embedded clause (*which he jotted down on a piece of paper*), but this is left unanalysed. Embedded clauses are discussed in Chapter 8. The fourth sentence in the paragraph contains multiple embedding of clauses, which does make for some difficulty in analysis, and so it is not analysed here, but similar structures are dealt with in Chapter 7. In future chapters, the superscript will normally be left out of such analyses because the labels C or A are usually sufficient without further detail.

## *Summary*

In this chapter, we deal with the five clause functions: Subject (S), Finite (F), Predicator (P), Complement (C) and Adjunct (A). A Nominal Group with a

| The night before Easter Sunday, 1920, | | Otto Loewi, an Austrian physiologist, | | | | | |
| A$^{cir}$ | | S | | | | | |
| awoke | in the night | with an idea which he jotted down on a tiny slip of paper, | | | | | |
| F/P | A$^{cir}$ | A$^{cir}$ | | | | | |
| and | then | went | back to sleep. | When | he | awoke | again | about six |
| | A$^{con}$ | F/P | A$^{cir}$ | | S | F/P | A$^{con}$ | A$^{cir}$ |
| he | remembered | that | he | had | written down | something of the | |
| S | F/P | | S | F | F/P | C$^{do}$ | |
| greatest importance, | | but | he | could not | decipher | his own scrawl | |
| C$^{do}$ continued. | | | S | F | P | C$^{do}$ | |
| The next night at 3 a.m. | | the idea | returned. | | | | |
| A$^{cir}$ | | S | F/P | | | | |

**Fig. 3.13**

Nominal Group in apposition is treated as a group complex. Two tests for Subject (Subject-Finite agreement and question tag formation) are followed through in detail and found partly satisfactory. The pronoun *it* can be a personal pronoun referring to some entity or a dummy, empty of content and filling only a grammatical role. When dummy-*it* occurs with an extraposed clause, we analyse the whole as a discontinuous Subject. Subject interacts with Finite in Mood and mood system choices are realized in the sequence of S and F. Complements subclassify as Direct Object Complement (C$^{do}$), Indirect Object Complement (C$^{io}$), Intensive Complement (C$^{int}$). Adjuncts subclassify as Circumstantial (A$^{cir}$), Conjunctive (A$^{conj}$) and Modal (A$^{mod}$). Finally we stress the difference between conjunctions and Conjunctive Adjuncts.

*Further study*

The lexical items *be* and *have* have given lot of trouble to linguists over the years, and there is still widespread disagreement about how to treat them. Part of the difficulty resides in the fact that each has very varied functions; sometimes they resemble auxiliaries like *can* and *may*, and sometimes they have characteristics of lexical verbs.

Halliday (1994) treats all finite instances of *be* (*am, is, are, was, were*) as Finite, even when they stand alone. Consider *was* in the sentences from our source text discussed above as Examples (9) and (12), repeated here:

(9)  It was a way of determining whether there is any chemical substance involved in nerve transmission.

(12) [...] it was a mystery why some nerves stimulate an organ and others depress it.

In (9) and (12), *was* is analysed as Finite alone, just as it is in its obviously auxiliary role in Example (10), repeated here:

(10) The nerve impulse was known to be electrical in nature [...]

Thus, finite forms of the verb *be* are exceptions to the general principle that we implied earlier, though we did not explicitly state it, that a finite verbal group made up of a single word consists of a fused Finite and Predicator (F/P). Thus, in equative and attributive clauses ('x is y') some form of *be* realizes the function of Finite and there is no Predicator at all.

There are no instances in *Introduction to Functional Grammar* of forms of *be* being analysed as F/P. An exception can be made, however, for the very rare use of *be* meaning *exist* as in (41):

(41) I think; therefore I am.

The analysis of this as a simple Finite rather than F/P is not entirely plausible, since it functionally parallels so closely comparable clauses with *exist*; see (41a).

(41a) I think; therefore I exist.

In (41a), the verbal group is clearly to be analysed as F/P; so it seems to follow that the same analysis could apply to *am* in Example (41).

The lexical item *have* is in some ways even more slippery than *be*. Perhaps its most frequent occurrence is as an auxiliary in present or past perfect constructions, such as (42):

(42) [...] he had written down something of the greatest importance [...]

However, there are other instances (not, unfortunately, in our source text fragment) where finite forms of *have* (*has, have, had*) might be construed as more like fused F/P. Again, though, Halliday (1994) is less ready to accord such an analysis than we might be. For example, on p. 80 we find:

*Mary has a cold, hasn't she?*

Here, Halliday analyses *has* as a simple Finite with no Predicator. However, in analysing

*Fred has coffee, doesn't he?*

where *has* means *takes*, Halliday does analyse *has* as a fused Finite and Predicator (F/P).

The auxiliary in the tag is evidently significant here. A possible logical case might go something like this:

Where *have* is the auxiliary, unfused Finite in the declarative clause, it is repeated in the tag (for example: *You have read it, haven't you?*). Where *have* is a fused Finite/Predicator (lexical verb), the tag auxiliary must be some form of *do*, as with all other fused F/Ps. If the tag has *have* rather than *do*, then the first *have* must be unfused Finite without a Predicator.

Unfortunately for this argument, not all English speakers say (43). Some say (43a):

(43)   Mary has a cold, hasn't she?
(43a)  Mary has a cold, doesn't she?

Are we to assume that for such speakers *have* is a fused F/P and for others (such as Halliday) it is a simple Finite? Possibly. It is probably the case that this use of *have* is a point of change in the language, moving towards a more fully lexical quality. There are variations in usage not only among individuals, but also on a large regional basis, for example, between America and Britain.

Of course, if *have* appears in a non-finite form, it is all or part of the Predicator. For example, in (44) we analyse *has* as Finite and *had* as Predicator and in (45) *had* is Finite and *been having* is Predicator.

(44)   Mary has had a cold.
(45)   He had been having difficulty with the proofs.

## Exercises

### Exercise 3.1

Analyse the following examples, labelling them for SFPCA. If you wish, you may try subclassifying Adjuncts and Complements, but identification as A or C will suffice.

1.  They cannot choose.
2.  The nature of the city around us changed.
3.  This required positive effort.
4.  We had friends in the suburbs.
5.  The other side is a dark pool.
6.  They were the tumultuous postwar years.
7.  The locations filled beyond capacity.

8.  The Ninomaru Palace itself is a national treasure.
9.  Industrialization brought a flood of people to the city.
10. Telephones are reserved for trivialities.
11. We had to spend so many evenings at home.
12. All over the city the divisions increased.
13. In Japan, the word 'duty' has special meaning.
14. Every appointment must be kept.
15. A new one was installed in the house.
16. He handed me the document.

17. The papers declared the strike a failure.
18. The castle was built in 1603.
19. In its day it served as a symbol of the power and authority of the Tokugawa military government.
20. No word may be carelessly spoken in front of the children.
21. The transoms are carved from massive cypress blocks.
22. We had been protected from criticism for years.
23. These have been designated Important Cultural Properties by the Japanese Government.
24. Now we too were singing songs in the bath.
25. The disciplines are never obliterated.

*Exercise 3.2*

Identify two Conjunctive Adjuncts and two Modal Adjuncts in the following text fragment.

> Since then, it has become clear that these 'recognition' systems are wide-spread in the body. [. . .] No doubt they explain why sperm of one species will not normally fertilize eggs of another species. Furthermore, certain diseases, including possibly arthritis, are due to the body making the mistake of treating part of its own tissue as if it were foreign.

*Exercise 3.3*

Explain in terms of SFPCA functions the joke mentioned earlier:

*Hotel guest*: Call me a taxi!
*Hotel porter*: All right. You're a taxi.

**Answers**

*Exercise 3.1*

Complements and Adjuncts are subclassified in the answers, but a simple C or A will suffice.

1.

| They | cannot | choose. |
|---|---|---|
| S | F | P |

2.

| The nature of the city around us | changed. |
|---|---|
| S | F/P |

3.

| This | required | positive effort. |
|------|----------|------------------|
| S | F/P | C$^{do}$ |

4.

| We | had | friends | in the suburbs. |
|----|-----|---------|-----------------|
| S | F | C$^{do}$ | A$^{cir}$ |

5.

| The other side | is | a dark pool. |
|----------------|-----|--------------|
| S | F | C$^{int}$ |

6.

| They | were | the tumultuous postwar years. |
|------|------|-------------------------------|
| S | F | C$^{int}$ |

7.

| The locations | filled | beyond capacity. |
|---------------|--------|------------------|
| S | F | A$^{cir}$ |

8.

| The Ninomaru Palace itself | is | a national treasure. |
|----------------------------|-----|----------------------|
| S | F/P | C$^{int}$ |

9.

| Industrialization | brought | a flood of people | to the city. |
|-------------------|---------|-------------------|--------------|
| S | F/P | C$^{do}$ | A$^{cir}$ |

10.

| Telephones | are | reserved | for trivialities. |
|------------|-----|----------|-------------------|
| S | F | P | A$^{cir}$ |

11.

| We | had to spend | so many evenings | at home. |
|----|--------------|------------------|----------|
| S | F/P | C$^{do}$ | A$^{cir}$ |

12.

| All over the city | the divisions | increased. |
|-------------------|---------------|------------|
| A$^{cir}$ | S | F/P |

13.

| In Japan | the word 'duty' | has | special meaning. |
|----------|-----------------|-----|------------------|
| A$^{cir}$ | S | F | C$^{do}$ |

14.

| Every appointment | must | be kept. |
|---|---|---|
| S | F | P |

15.

| A new one | was | installed | in the house. |
|---|---|---|---|
| S | F | P | A$^{cir}$ |

16.

| He | handed | me | the document. |
|---|---|---|---|
| S | F/P | C$^{io}$ | C$^{do}$ |

17.

| The papers | declared | the strike | a failure. |
|---|---|---|---|
| S | F/P | C$^{do}$ | C$^{int}$ |

18.

| The castle | was | built | in 1603. |
|---|---|---|---|
| S | F | P | A$^{cir}$ |

19.

| In its day | it | served | as a symbol of the power and authority of the Tokugawa military government. |
|---|---|---|---|
| A$^{cir}$ | S | F | A$^{cir}$ |

20.

| No word | may | be | carelessly | spoken | in front of the children. |
|---|---|---|---|---|---|
| S | F | P .. | <A$^{cir}$> | P *continued* | A$^{cir}$ |

Note: when one item interrupts another, as here A interrupts P, the symbol < > encloses the interrupting element.

21.

| The transoms | are | carved | from massive cypress blocks. |
|---|---|---|---|
| S | F | P | A$^{cir}$ |

22.

| We | had | been protected | from criticism | for years. |
|---|---|---|---|---|
| S | F | P | A$^{cir}$ | A$^{cir}$ |

23.

| These | have | been designated | Important Cultural Properties | by the Japanese Government. |
|---|---|---|---|---|
| S | F | P | C$^{int}$ | A$^{cir}$ |

| 24. | Now | we | too | were | singing | songs | in the bath. |
|-----|-----|-----|-----|------|---------|-------|--------------|
| | $A^{con}$ | S | $A^{con}$ | F | P | $C^{do}$ | $A^{cir}$ |

| 25. | The disciplines | are | never | obliterated |
|-----|-----------------|-----|-------|-------------|
| | S | F | $A^{mod}$ | P |

*Exercise 3.2*

Conjunctive Adjuncts: *Since then, furthermore.*
Modal Adjuncts: *no doubt, possibly.*

*Exercise 3.3*

The joke depends on the fact that in the hotel guest's meaning the pronoun *me* is Indirect Object Complement and *a cab* is Direct Object Complement (paraphrase: *Call a cab for me*); but the porter unexpectedly interprets (or pretends to interpret) *me* as Direct Object Complement and *a cab* as Intensive Object Complement (compare: 'Call me Ishmael').

**Note**

1.  Taylor, G.R. 1967: *The science of life*. London: Thames & Hudson (Panther Books).

# 4

# Information Structure and Thematic Structure

## 4.1 *Organizing ideas*

An extremely important aspect of a functional grammar is the way information is structured in communication. If we are explaining something to another person, whether in speech or writing, we instinctively try to organize what we say in a way that will make it easier for the hearer or reader to understand (unless, of course, we are deliberately trying to confuse).

Most of us are familiar with the way in which we structure large chunks of information in writing because this is something that is usually taught in school, especially for particular genres like *essays* or *business letters*, where we are encouraged to plan what we are going to write about, paragraph by paragraph.

Genres with which we are very familiar from childhood, like stories, come more naturally to us, and most children can tell a joke or even write a reasonably well-organized story without too much thought by the time they are eleven or twelve years old. That is not to say that conscious knowledge does not help us to construct stories better. Successful writers are often well aware of the ways in which they construct their texts even though they write sentences intuitively.

Spoken language too is sometimes carefully planned and sometimes totally spontaneous. The context makes a big difference to how we talk and how far we think in advance about what we are going to say. We can make a distinction between *prepared speech* and *unprepared speech*. Prepared speech, as, for example, in an after-dinner speech or a formal lecture, is similar to the letter or the essay, in that a lot of planning can go into the organization of ideas and the structure of the text. A speaker may write down the ideas in note form before the spoken event takes place, and politicians and other official speech-makers may have their whole speech written out in full, sometimes even prepared by a professional speech-writer. With an ordinary conversation, however, we rarely even think about what we are going to say, let alone how we are going to structure it; it just 'comes naturally'. Yet, when we study language, we can see that we do subconsciously impose a structure on our speech as part of the act of communication.

This structure is something which is built into the grammar of the language and happens at the level of the clause (although it affects longer stretches of text as well). All clauses have information structure and we make use of this in spoken as well as written language.

In a Hallidayan grammar, there are two parallel and interrelated systems of analysis that concern the structure of the clause. The first of these is called *Information structure* and involves constituents that are labelled *Given* and *New*. The second is called *Thematic structure* and involves constituents that are labelled *Theme* and *Rheme*.

These two types of structure are introduced in turn in Sections 4.2 and 4.3.

## **4.2**  *Information structure: Given and New information*

An independent clause is a clause that can stand alone as a complete sentence. Given and New information is found in both dependent and independent clauses and in combinations of the two, but for the sake of simplicity we will consider only independent clauses at this stage.

In order for a person to understand what someone says, he or she must be able to understand what the speaker is talking about. Another way of saying this is that an interlocutor must be able to 'use the sound uttered by another to locate some appropriate area within his own store of accumulated and generalized experience' (Moore and Carling, 1982: p. 168). This means that in order to communicate effectively the speaker must bring to the hearer's attention some element of shared or 'mutual' knowledge. This shared information is usually found at the beginning of a clause and is labelled Given information. Most clauses also include information that is the focus of the speaker's message, information that is considered New. The two elements together make up an *information unit*.

Thus, if a woman wants her friend to make tea and calls to him, 'The kettle's boiling', she is making the assumption that her friend knows what a kettle is and more particularly can identify the particular kettle referred to. That is to say that they share the knowledge about the kettle, and this knowledge is taken for granted in the statement. The main focus of the information (the New element) is *is boiling*, which is found at the end of the clause. The information unit is analysed as in Fig. 4.1.

| The kettle | 's boiling |
|------------|------------|
| Given      | New        |

**Fig. 4.1**

### 4.2.1    Given and New in written English

Text 4A is an extract from a computer manual. The text begins with the heading in the form of a question ('What is an Operating System?'). The function of a question is often to *ask for information* and here the writer of the manual

---

**What is an Operating System?**
An operating system runs a computer. It controls how the parts of a computer interact and organizes information in and out of the computer. Without an operating system, a computer cannot be used effectively. Some operating systems are DOS, CP/M, OS/2 and UNIX.

---

**Text 4A**    (Chua Chooi See, *DOS 5: a step by step guide*[1]).

uses a question that he imagines (quite reasonably) is in the mind of the reader who has opened this book. This is a common device in textbook writing and is used to establish the area of mutual knowledge. Having posed the question, the writer can then begin the first paragraph with the words 'operating system' presented as Given and the rest of the sentence, the explanation of what an operating system does, is New. In fact, every sentence in this text begins with a reference to this shared concept of operating systems (although the third sentence also includes the shared reference to *a computer*), so the text is a clear example of the principle that the New information is regularly presented in the second part of the clause.

> GIVEN elements in Text A:
> Sentence 1.    An operating system
> Sentence 2.    It
> Sentence 3.    Without an operating system, a computer
> Sentence 4.    Some operating systems

There are, however, two main exceptions to this general statement. One is at the beginning of a fresh topic of conversation or of a new section of a written text, where the whole of the information is new (although even there the speaker or writer is likely to identify or assume some 'shared' element). A classic example of a clause without a Given element is the opening of the Jane Austen novel *Pride and prejudice* seen in Text 4B.

In this case *It* carries no information at all (*see* discussion of the *empty it* in Chapters 3 and 8). The rest of the clause, of course, carries what is technically called the New information. This message may be something other than

---

It is a truth universally acknowledged, that a single man in possession of a good fortune must be in want of a wife.

---

**Text 4B**    (Austen, *Pride and prejudice*[2]).

'information' in the general meaning of the word; in the case of the quotation from Jane Austen, of course, it is an ironical comment on the social pressures on families in the early nineteenth century to find rich husbands for their daughters. The New information might be the expression of an opinion (*I really like Sydney*), or the refusal of a invitation (*I'm sorry I can't possibly come*), or a variety of messages other than informative ones.

The second exception comes when, by using ellipsis, we leave out the Given information and only express the New. Examples of this can be seen in the computer manual text above. The second sentence contains two clauses (a) and (b):

(a)  It controls how the parts of a computer interact
(b)  organizes information in and out of the computer

In the second clause (b), the information is all New. The subject of the verb *organizes*, which would normally carry the Given part of the clause, is omitted. However, the reader understands that the subject is also 'it' (referring to 'operating system'). The grammar of English allows ellipsis of this type in certain contexts where the meaning is clear.

Thus we can say that an information unit consists of Given, which is optional, and New, which is obligatory. This is summarized in the following diagram, where brackets indicate the optional element:

(GIVEN) ——— NEW

### 4.2.2   Given and New in spoken English

In real life (and in fiction and drama that imitate real life) language is always set in a social context. It is this context that usually provides the source of the Given information. The words that feature most commonly as Given in conversation are pronouns referring to the interlocutors: *I*, *we* and *you*. Proper nouns, the names of the people or places one is talking about, are also very common.

Look at the example (Text 4C) from a famous English play *The importance of being earnest* by Oscar Wilde. Immediately before the section

Algernon: Divorces are made in heaven. [Jack puts out his hand to take a sandwich. Algernon at once interferes.] Please don't touch the cucumber sandwiches. They are ordered especially for Aunt Augusta.

Jack: Well, you have been eating them all the time.

Algernon: That is quite a different matter. She is my aunt. Have some bread and butter. The bread and butter is for Gwendolen. Gwendolen is devoted to bread and butter.

**Text 4C**   (Wilde, *The importance of being earnest*[3]).

quoted, which takes place at tea time, Jack and Algernon have been discussing divorce, but then Jack does something which causes Algernon to change the topic of conversation. Notice that he does this by using an imperative clause.

In an imperative clause like *Please don't touch the cucumber sandwiches* all the information is effectively New. Part of the shared element is the unspoken *you*. This can be unspoken, because, as in most imperatives, the context makes clear who the request is directed at, in this case Jack. The word *please* is a conventional reduction of *If it please you* but here the meaning is more like *It would please me if you don't touch the cucumber sandwiches*.

In Text 4Ca, a version of the same text as C but with only the conversation reproduced, the information units have been separated by slashes (//) and the New elements in the information units have been presented in italics.

---

*Please don't touch the cucumber sandwiches.//* They are *ordered especially for Aunt Augusta.//*

Well, you *have been eating them all the time.//*

That *is quite a different matter.//* She *is my aunt.// Have some bread and butter.//* The bread and butter *is for Gwendolen. //* Gwendolen *is devoted to bread and butter.//*

**Text 4Ca.**

---

We can see that, with the exception of the imperative, all the clauses have Given elements that are referentially linked either to the interlocutors or to previously mentioned elements in the conversation. However, in this case, each clause begins with a different Given element, each taking up information from some idea that was presented as New in an earlier clause. In this way a speaker or writer can structure the clause so that the Given element is already understood by the listener. Thus *They* refers to the same cucumber sandwiches mentioned in the previous sentence. *That* refers to the whole of the information in the previous sentence (*You have been eating them all the time*), and *She* refers to the same person as *Aunt Augusta*. *Bread and butter* and *Gwendolen* both also have previous identical mentions. This type of organization is extremely common in everyday conversation, but it is also found in written texts in many contexts.

Where a speaker or writer constructs a clause in the way outlined above (with the Given information first and the New information second) the clause is said to be *unmarked*. This is a matter primarily of *intonation*, the way in which the different levels of pitch (or *tone*) are used in the language to express meaning.

In an unmarked declarative clause, the New information is said to have the most *communicative dynamism* (to use a term from the Prague School linguists) and is signalled intonationally by a falling tone.


### 4.2.3    Difficult cases of Given and New

Not all clauses are as clearly structured as the ones in our examples above. The letter in Text 4D, written by the English novelist D.H. Lawrence after his return to England from New Mexico, contains an interesting example of a difficult case in the first paragraph.

---

110, Heath St,
Hampstead,
7 December, 1923


Dear Bynner,
Here I am – London – gloom – yellow air – bad cold – bed – old house – Morris wallpaper – visitors – English voices – tea in old cups – poor D.H.L. perfectly miserable, as if he were in his tomb.

You don't need his advice, so take it: Never come to England any more.

In a fortnight I intend to go back to Paris, then to Spain – and in the early spring I hope to be back on the western continent.

I wish I was in Santa Fe at this moment. As it is, for my sins, and Frieda's, I am in London. I only hope Mexico will stop revolting.

De profundis,

D.H.L.

---

**Text 4D**    (Lawrence, Selected letters[4]).

The meaning of this letter is not difficult to decipher even though it was written a long time ago and was written to someone we do not know. Moreover, the rhetorical structure of it is quite clear:

Paragraph 1: The writer complains about life in London

Paragraph 2: The writer advises the reader to stay away from England

Paragraph 3: The writer explains his plans for future travel

Paragraph 4: The writer repeats that he is in London and wishes he was back on the American continent

What is happening, however, in this letter at the level of Information structure? How is the Given and New information organized? The first paragraph is particularly interesting because, after the first clause *Here I am*, the information is not presented in complete sentences. Every word and phrase represents new information: that is to say, the reasons why *poor D.H.L.* is *perfectly miserable*. He seems to have found it superfluous to his communicative requirements to present the Given information in each clause and so he has just left it out. It is certainly not difficult for us to guess what the Given elements would have been had he chosen to express them.

There are a number of different types of text which present mainly New information. One common genre is the shopping list, a list of words or phrases, sometimes written for others to follow but more often written for oneself as a simple reminder of what to buy.

> A Shopping List
>
> toothpaste
> soap
> rice
> eggs
> fish
> flour

We could claim that each item in a shopping list has a sort of implied clause, like (*We need*) *toothpaste*, or (*I want*) *some rice*, but we do not need to go as far as imagining some missing words to realize that the information in the list is the information that matters, that which holds the information focus.

A more formal text of this type, usually carefully prepared, is the encyclopedia or gazetteer entry, which conventionally often omits all but the new information. In Text 4E, the headword 'Cheetah' alone represents the Given information and the rest of the entry is New.

> **Cheetah** or 'hunting leopard', the large spotted cat of Africa and Southern Asia, the swiftest four-footed animal alive.

**Text 4E**   (Cook and Barker (eds.), *Pears' cyclopaedia*[5]).

## 4.3   *Thematic structure: Theme and Rheme*

We now turn to the second system of analysis involved in text organization, Thematic structure. Thematic structure, like Information structure, operates at the level of the clause. All clauses have thematic structure with the exception of expressions like 'Good morning' or 'Hi'.

In some ways, Thematic structure is similar to Information structure and in many clauses there is a parallel equivalence between Theme and Given on the one hand and between Rheme and New on the other. Some linguists conflate these concepts (*see* 'Further study'). However, in this chapter (following Halliday) we treat them as separate structures, and by the end of the chapter the difference between them as tools of analysis should be made clear.

A simple explanation of Theme in English is to think of it as *the idea represented by the constituent at the starting point of the clause*. This has been expressed by Halliday as 'the point of departure of the message', where he is thinking of the 'message' carried by one clause. In simple terms then, a clause begins with a realization of the Theme. This is followed by the realization of the Rheme, which can be explained as being *the rest of the message*:

THEME ———— RHEME

Another way of explaining this idea informally is to say that the Theme tells the listener or reader what the clause is *about*, but this explanation can sometimes be misleading. In this book, we distinguish between the idea of *topic* (or what the language user is speaking or writing about, a nonlinguistic issue) and Theme, the starting point of the message, realized in the clause, which is a linguistic category.

All clauses in English incorporate what is known as a *Topical* Theme (and sometimes other types of Theme as well, as we see in Section 4.3.4). The term *Topical Theme* does not imply that this Theme always represents the topic of the discourse in the popular sense of the term 'topic'. An after-dinner speaker may, for example, take as the topic (or 'theme' in the nontechnical sense) of a speech 'The Social Value of the Family' but this does not mean that any clause in the speech will *necessarily* have any part of that title as Theme of specific clauses. The Themes chosen by the speaker may, for example, refer to place (*in this country*) or time (*in the last century*); they may indicate when the speaker is about to express attitude (*in my opinion*) or give an example (*for example*); a Theme may even begin a rhetorical question (*What* are we going to do about the lack of values?). The last mentioned example is particularly interesting: the topic of discussion is 'lack of values' but the Theme is *what*, because the speaker's starting point here is the question he or she is asking about the Complement of the clause.

The so-called *Topical Theme* in any clause is the first constituent that is part of the meaningful structure of the clause. To put it another way, we can say that the Topical Theme always represents a *Participant, Circumstance* or *Process* (these terms are introduced in Chapter 6).

The Topical Theme is always realized by one of the following elements: Subject (S), Predicator (P), Complement (C), or Circumstantial Adjunct

(A). As we see later, in some interrogative clauses, the Finite (F) precedes the Subject and hence can be Theme, but in this case it is not a *Topical* Theme.

In Text 4F, each of the topical Themes is Subject of the clause it introduces. Themes are presented in bold type to assist recognition.

> **Europe**, after 1500, entered a time of far-reaching mechanical and scientific discovery and development. **Inland Africa**, by contrast, did not. **Inland peoples** continued with the steady but slow development of their own civilization.

Text 4F.

### 4.3.1 Nominal Groups as Theme

As we saw in Chapter 3 on SFPCA, declarative clauses frequently begin with the Subject and so it is usually the case (as in the examples in the box above) that the Subject of a clause is in Theme position. In the first clause of Text 4A, for example, the Subject is also the Theme, as shown in Fig. 4.2.

| An operating system | runs/a computer |
|---------------------|-----------------|
| Given | New |
| Subject | FP/C |

**Fig. 4.2**

When a subject is in Theme position in a declarative clause, it is said to be *unmarked*. Some further examples of clauses with unmarked Themes appear in Examples (1), (2) and (3), analysed in Fig. 4.3.

(1) The capital of Malaysia is Kuala Lumpur.
(2) Kuala Lumpur is the capital of Malaysia.
(3) It's the capital of Malaysia.

The starting points of the clauses are listed in the first column of Fig. 4.3. These constituents are all Nominal Groups.

| Theme and Subject | Rheme and FC |
|-------------------|--------------|
| 1. The capital of Malaysia | is Kuala Lumpur |
| 2. Kuala Lumpur | is the capital of Malaysia |
| 3. It | 's the capital of Malaysia |

**Fig. 4.3**

In the first example, we can assume that the speaker is engaged in discourse about, say, Malaysia or capital cities and so chooses to begin the clause with a reference to what has been previously discussed. In example (2), on the other hand, the chosen Theme is *Kuala Lumpur*. This would be the appropriate wording for, say, the first clause in a paragraph about the city. Example (3), which might be the response to the question 'Where is Kuala Lumpur?', shows how a pronoun might be chosen as Theme in certain contexts.

In the following examples, we see a contrast between a clause with a verb in the active voice and one with a verb in the passive voice:

(4) Ziggy played guitar.
(5) Guitar was played by Ziggy.

| Theme | Rheme |
|---|---|
| 4. Ziggy | played guitar |
| 5. Guitar | was played by Ziggy |

**Fig. 4.4**

Example (4), the opening line from the David Bowie song *Ziggy Stardust*, begins with the Theme as topic (*Ziggy*), which is followed by the Rheme (*played guitar*) which provides the first essential information about the character described in the song. Consider the change of focus in Example (5). Whereas (4), the original line, describes Ziggy's professional talent or general ability, the clause 'Guitar was played by Ziggy', with *guitar* in Theme position could only appear in a situation where a speaker or writer was describing the line-up in a band, as in 'Piano was played by John, drums by Ali, and guitar by Ziggy.' Thus, we can see that although there may be a semantic relationship between a clause with an active voice verb and its passive inversion, the selection of a different thematic structure changes the focus of the clause in significant functional ways.

In Examples (2), (3), (4) and (5) above, words acting as Subject and Theme consist of only one Nominal Group. In Example (1), however, there are two nominals (*the capital* and *Malaysia*) making up the Theme. Similarly, in the examples (6) and (7) below, two nominals together make the Theme of the clause (printed in italics).

(6) *Incorrect eating habits and insufficient exercise* disturb or alter the fat metabolism of the organism.
(7) *Assessment and evaluation* are increasingly based on the performance of communicative acts.

In fact, the Theme may be quite long or have a complicated structure, but we will not consider too many complexities at this stage.

### 4.3.2 Interrogatives, imperatives and exclamations

In Chapter 3, we discussed the structure of declarative and interrogative clauses in English, in terms of SFCPA. To recapitulate, we showed that while the declarative clause followed the S,F,P,C,A order of constituents, the interrogative reversed the order of the Finite and the Subject as in Example (8), where *had* is the Finite and *he* is the Subject, and in (9), where *what* is the Subject.

(8) Had he written down something of the greatest importance?
(9) What had he written down?

Since the starting point of the clause is different in interrogative clauses, it follows that the Theme-Rheme structure is different also. The Theme in the (unmarked) interrogative (8) is realized by the Finite and the Subject together, in this case *Had he*. In type (9), the Theme is realized by the word *What*.

Similarly, the imperative in (10) and exclamative moods in (11) and (12) incorporate typical Themes.

(10) Write it down.
(11) What neat writing you've got!
(12) How sweetly she sings!

In (10) the Theme is *write*, and in (11) the Theme is *what neat writing*, and in (12) the Theme is *how sweetly*.

We can say that each Mood has a typical unmarked thematic pattern, which is summarized in Fig. 4.5.

If we look in more detail at Theme in interrogative clauses with question words (for example, *who, what, where, when, why*) we can see that question words represent different elements from the SFCPA structure. In the question *Who wrote down the idea?*, the word *who* represents the Subject of the verb *wrote* (because the question is asking the name of the person who did the writing). In the alternative question *What did Loewi write down?*, *what* represents the Complement of the clause. In *When did he write it down?* and

| MOOD | THEME realized by |
|---|---|
| Declarative | Subject |
| Interrogative | Finite + Subject |
| Imperative | Predicator |
| Exclamative | Wh-word Complement OR Wh-word Adjunct |

**Fig. 4.5**

*Why did he write it down?*, *when* and *why* represent an Adjunct of time and reason respectively.


### 4.3.3    Marked Theme in declarative clauses

We said above that, in a declarative clause, the Theme is said to be unmarked where the Subject is the starting point of the clause. However, other elements are frequently found in Theme position in English clauses, and in these cases the Theme is *marked*. The most common element to appear as marked Theme is the Circumstantial Adjunct, as in the following examples from Russell's *History of western philosophy*,[6] p. 116 (each is the beginning of a consecutive paragraph).

> (13) After the war, the Spartans erected a memorial on the battlefield of Thermopylae [...]
> (14) For a long time, the Spartans proved themselves invincible on land [...]
> (15) Apart from war, the reality of Sparta was never quite the same as the theory [...]

In these clauses the Theme is realized by the prepositional phrases which are acting as Circumstantial Adjuncts (*see* Section 3.4.1): *After the war*; *For a long time*; *Apart from war*. Russell could have, had he wished, put each of these Adjuncts at a later position in the clause (as in, *The Spartans erected a memorial on the battlefield at Thermopylae after the war*), but the language allowed him to select the initial position. This flexibility of position makes it easier for a writer to present a Given element in Theme position, which can assist in making a text coherent.

A more unusual, but interesting, case of marked Theme, occurs where the first constituent in the clause is the Complement. Complements more usually follow the verb in declarative sentences (*see* Section 3.3), but occasionally, for special effect, we find them as Themes. This phenomenon occurs in conversation, often in response to questions concerning Complements, and also in English poetry, as in the following well-known example, where the Thematic Complement is in italics.

> (16) I strove with none; for none was worth my strife
> *Nature* I loved, and, next to nature, Art;
> I warmed both hands before the fire of life;
> It sinks, and I am ready to depart.
> (Landor, 1775–1864)

In (16), the more usual prose order would have been *I loved Nature*.

In (17) a lecturer is talking to a student about an assignment that he has just marked.

> (17) Oh yes, I dropped one of your pages, so some of the comments I've scrubbed out. They're all rubbish. Ignore them.

It can be seen that in the second clause (*some of the comments I've scrubbed out*) the Complement is in Theme position. The unmarked form of this clause would have been *I've scrubbed out some of the comments*.

A prose example of Complement as Theme can be seen in Text 4G. Notice that the clause in question consists of only three words (*Hard it is*), but a longer section of the text, with the complex series of clauses that follow, is reproduced since it makes it easier to understand the writer's stylistic intent in fronting the word 'hard'.

*Hard* it is, no doubt, to read in Stanley's pages of the slave-traders coldly arranging for the surprise of a village, the capture of the inhabitants, the massacre of those who resist, and the violation of the women; but the stony streets of London, if they could but speak, would tell of tragedies as awful, of ruins as complete, of ravishments as horrible, as if it were in Central Africa.

**Text 4G** (Booth, *In darkest England and the way out*[7]).

The Themes in all the marked examples we have looked at so far are still part of the ideational element of the clause, which is to say that they tell us something about the world that the writer is describing or discussing.

### 4.3.4 Multiple Themes

All clauses which have one thematic constituent, like those we looked at in Section 4.3.2, are said to have *simple* Themes (even though the thematic constituent may have more than one part to it, as in Examples (6) and (7) in this chapter. However, some clauses have more than one theme or what is known as a *multiple* Thematic structure. We consider these in this section.

The explanation of multiple Theme relates to the three metafunctions discussed in Chapter 1: *ideational, interpersonal, and textual*. Basically, every clause has a Theme which relates to the ideational function of language. This is the Theme which usually represents *what the clause is about*, or the *topic* of the clause. For this reason it is known as the Topical Theme. In all the examples of Simple Theme given above, where only one Theme was identified for each clause, the Theme is the Topical Theme.

However, in addition to the Topical Theme, some clauses also have a Textual and/or an Interpersonal Theme. When speakers in a conversation, for example, use expressions like *well*, or *oh* in order to indicate that they are about to continue an idea or refute an argument, they are commenting, in a sense, on the previous speaker's text. This would indicate that they are using a Textual Theme. When speakers address listeners directly, by using a name or a term of affection, they can be said to be using an Interpersonal Theme. In the example in Fig. 4.6, the speaker uses each type of Theme in turn, end-

| Well, | children, | the story | is about to continue |
|---|---|---|---|
| Textual Theme | Interpersonal Theme | Topical Theme | Rheme |

**Fig. 4.6**

ing with the Topical Theme, which, in this case, is an unmarked Subject expressing the main topic of the clause *the story*.

In the example in Fig. 4.6, the speaker addresses the children who are listening to the story. In a similar way, in the example in Fig. 4.7, the speaker (a lecturer in biochemistry) uses an Interpersonal Theme to address the students, but here the Topical Theme is a marked Circumstantial Adjunct: *last time*. The speaker begins with the phrase *last time* in order to get the students to recall the previous lecture. The Rheme is the New information that the lecturer wants the students to focus on.

| Morning, | ladies and gentlemen, | last time | I was talking about the concept of theory |
|---|---|---|---|
| Interpersonal Theme | Interpersonal Theme | Topical Theme | Rheme |

**Fig. 4.7**

In Example (16), discussed in the last section, we see two examples of multiple Theme, analysed in Figs. 4.8 and 4.9. The first clause begins with a Textual Theme (*Oh yes*, meaning something like 'There's something I must tell you') followed by Topical Theme (*I*). The second clause is particularly interesting. Here, we have a Textual Theme (*so*), followed, as we explained above, by a marked Topical Theme. This special ordering of the constituents, which is unusual but perfectly possible in English, allows the speaker to save the unexpected (new) information (in this case the fact that he has crossed out some comments he made on the student's work) until the end of the clause in Rheme position.

| Oh yes, | I | dropped one of your pages |
|---|---|---|
| Textual Theme | Topical Theme | Rheme |

**Fig. 4.8**

| so | some of the comments | I've scrubbed out |
|---|---|---|
| Textual Theme | Topical Theme | Rheme |

**Fig. 4.9**

## 4.4 *The interaction of Information structure and Thematic structure*

As we have seen in this chapter, it is possible to analyse clauses for both their Given-New structure and for their Theme-Rheme structure. We have seen that it is usually the case that the Given element is the same as the Theme, but this is not always so. In imperative clauses, for example, we draw a distinction between Theme and Given (*see* Fig. 4.10). A slightly more complex example can be seen in Figs. 4.11a and 4.11b.

| (*You*) | Have | some bread and butter |
|---------|------|----------------------|
|  | Theme | Rheme |
| Given | New | |

**Fig. 4.10**

| (*You*) | Please, don't touch the cucumber sandwiches |
|---------|---------------------------------------------|
| Given | New |

**Fig. 4.11a**

| (*You*) | Please | Don't | touch the cucumber sandwiches |
|---------|--------|-------|-------------------------------|
|  | Interpersonal Theme | Topical Theme | Rheme |

**Fig. 4.11b**

The fact that we have both *Thematic structure* and *Information structure* in the language makes it possible for a writer or speaker to choose to put New information in Theme position and Given information in Rheme position.

In spoken English, we can use special emphasis and intonation to indicate that we are presenting New information in Theme position instead of the more normal Rheme position. Take the case where a husband and a wife are arranging delivery of goods in a store. The shop assistant turns to the wife and asks for her name:

Could I have your name, please?

The expected answer would probably be simply the name or something like one of the following:

It's Ms Bloggs.
My name's Bloggs, Ms M. Bloggs.

Thus, where a full clause is Given, the New information (the information that the assistant is seeking) is in Rheme position. However, suppose the woman is going to be away and prefers her husband's name to be taken. She might say, with special emphasis on the first syllable of *husband*:

My husband's name is Mr T. Bloggs. Please phone him if there are any problems.

The first clause could be analysed as in Fig. 4.12. Here, the speaker is indicating with emphasis that she is introducing New Information in Theme position in addition to the expected New Information of the name.

| My HUSband's name | is Mr T Bloggs |
|---|---|
| Theme | Rheme |
| New | New |

**Fig. 4.12**

Another example (adapted from Firbas, 1972), demonstrates the difference between a clause spoken in different circumstances. The first is spoken when some children who are expecting their father to arrive hear his footsteps in the hall:

Daddy's COMing.

The alternative version is spoken when the children do not expect their father but unexpectedly recognize his steps or hear him calling:

DADdy's coming.

In the Hallidayan model, these clauses would be analysed differently, as in Figs. 4.13 and 4.14.

In written English prose, it is more difficult to vary the relationship of Theme and Given. In the vast majority of English written sentences, the two functions are realized by the same constituent, and, similarly, the Rheme and

| Daddy | 's COMing |
|---|---|
| Theme | Rheme |
| Given | New |

**Fig. 4.13**

| DADdy | 's coming |
|---|---|
| Theme | Rheme |
| New | Given |

**Fig. 4.14**

the Given information are realized by the rest of the clause. However, there are certain expressions in English which can be used to signal special cases. These include *x as well as y* and *not only x but also y*.

In Section 4.2 we discussed the role of Given and New in a letter written by D.H. Lawrence (Text 4D), and we observed that, after the initial clause, the first paragraph was largely New information. Since Lawrence is not using full clauses, it is difficult to assign a Theme-Rheme structure to the fragments of information that we find here. As we said above, Thematic structure does not apply to *minor clauses*. However, it is arguable that *Here* realizes the function of (marked) Theme in relation to all the minor clauses up to *tea in old cups*, and that we then have the new Theme *poor D.H.L.* In looking at the interaction of Theme and Rheme, it is important to take into account not only the particular clause that we are analysing but also context in which that clause is set. The context may involve issues like prior knowledge of speaker and hearer or the prior knowledge that a writer expects his or her readers to have on a particular topic. It may also involve the *co-text* (the rest of the text) since, if a writer or speaker has previously introduced a topic of discussion, that topic may later appear as Given information in Theme position in the clause.

## Summary

This chapter begins with a discussion of the way we organize information in discourse, but most of the chapter is concerned with the way information is ordered in the clause. In Section 4.2 we explained the principles of *Information structure*, first in written and then in spoken English, and looked at the ways in which speakers and writers usually present Given (or shared) information first in the clause and save New information until the end of the clause, where it has the most *communicative dynamism*. In 4.3 we discussed how Theme and Rheme combine to make up the *Thematic structure* of the clause and examined different ways in which the Theme of a clause is realized, including the difference between *marked* and *unmarked* Themes. We then examined the difference between Textual, Interpersonal and Topical Themes and looked at clauses with multiple theme. Finally, Section 4.4 dealt with the interaction of Information structure and Thematic structure.

## Further study

### The Prague School and Thematic Progression

Prague School linguists (for example Daneš, 1970, and Firbas, 1972) identify utterances as being ordered on the basis of Theme and Rheme, but do not distinguish Theme from Given. They describe sentences as 'theme followed by 'rheme' where the starting point of the utterance is shared information and as 'rheme followed by theme' where the starting point of the utterance is new information. The Prague school account is, therefore, substantially different from the account described in this chapter even though it is an attempt to capture the same features of the language.

One interesting contribution of the Prague School was the concept of *thematic progression* (usually attributed to Daneš, 1970; 1974). We discuss this further in Chapter 5.

Other approaches to Theme (and some possible problems of analysis) are discussed in Fries and Francis (1992) and Francis (1990).

## Markedness

*Markedness* is a concept which is useful in language study as a whole, not only with respect to issues that are discussed in this chapter. Markedness, in the sense in which we use the term here, concerns the probability of a grammatical occurrence in the language as a whole rather than in any particular use of the language in context. Clauses can be said to be *marked* (the unusual form) or *unmarked* (the usual form). In spoken English, when a clause is *marked* for information structure, special intonation or emphasis will indicate to the listener that shared (Given) information appears in the second part of the clause and New information in the first.

## *Exercises*

### *Exercise 4.1*

1.  Identify the Given and New information in the short biography of the novelist Kazuo Ishiguro (Text 4H).

---

**Kazuo Ishiguro**

Kazuo Ishiguro was born in Nagasaki, Japan, in 1954 and came to Britain in 1960. He attended the University of Kent at Canterbury and the University of East Anglia. He now lives in London. His first novel, *A Pale View of Hills*, was awarded the Winifred Holtby Prize by the Royal Society of Literature and has been translated into thirteen languages. His second novel, *An Artist of the Floating World*, won the Whitbread Book of the Year award for 1986: it has been translated into fourteen languages.

---

**Text 4H**    (from cover of Ishiguro, The remains of the day[8]).

2.  Write a brief encyclopedia entry for Kazuo Ishiguro, following the example for **Cheetah** (Text 4E), and then underline the Given information.

*Is this really given*

*Exercise 4.2*

1. Read Text 3A about Otto Loewi and look at the Theme of the first clause in each sentence. Make a note of any marked Themes.
2. Suggest reasons why the author uses clauses with marked Theme in this text.

*Exercise 4.3*

In the comedy *The importance of being earnest*, Jack wishes to marry Lady Bracknell's niece. In the famous conversation reproduced in Text 4I, Lady Bracknell is questioning Jack about his family background. We find here a number of utterances where shared information is re-iterated in a different guise. Read the conversation and imagine how an actor and actress might say the words in the italicized sections.

---

Lady Bracknell: Who was your father? He was evidently a man of some wealth.

Jack: I'm afraid I really don't know.  The fact is, Lady Bracknell, I said *I had lost my parents*. It would be nearer the truth to say that *my parents seem to have lost me.* . . . I don't know exactly who I am by birth.  I was . . . well, *I was found.*

Lady Bracknell: *Found!*

Jack: The late Mr Thomas Cardew, an old gentleman, found me and gave me the name of Worthing, because he happened to have a first-class ticket for Worthing in his pocket at the time. Worthing is a place in Sussex. It is a seaside resort.

Lady Bracknell: Where did the charitable gentleman who had a first-class ticket for this seaside resort *find you*?

Jack: In a hand-bag.

Lady Bracknell: *A hand-bag?*

Jack (very seriously): Yes, Lady Bracknell. I was *in a hand-bag.*

---

**Text 4I**    (Wilde, *The importance of being Ernest,*[3] Act One).

**Answers**

*Exercise 4.1*

1. The Given and New distribution in Text 4H is unmarked, with the Given information first in each clause. Two clauses consist of just New ele-

ments: *came to Britain in 1960* and *has been translated into thirteen languages*. The Given elements are: *Kazuo Ishiguro*; *He*; *His first novel, A Pale View of Hills*; *His second novel, Artist of the Floating World*; *it*.

2. An open-ended question. One possible answer might be:

**Kazuo Ishiguro**, novelist, born Japan 1954, educated in Britain and lives in London; awarded Winifred Holtby Prize for *A Pale View of Hills* and the Whitbread Prize for *An Artist of the Floating World* (1986).

Unless you have used full clauses, the only Given is likely to be *Kazuo Ishiguro*.

*Exercise 4.2*

1. The marked Themes in Text 3A are:

   The night before Easter, 1920
   When he awoke again about six
   The next night, at three a.m.
   Seventeen years before

2. The marked Themes tell us the *time* of the event reported in the Rheme; three are Circumstantial Adjuncts and one (*When he awoke again about six*) is a Temporal clause. They help the reader organize the order of the reported events. This type of Theme is common in stories and the use of it here gives a narrative effect. You may also have noticed the example of multiple Theme:

| For instance | the vagus nerves | slow down the rate of heartbeat. |
|---|---|---|
| Textual Theme | Topical Theme | Rheme |

*Exercise 4.3*

Actors can interpret lines in many ways, so there is more than one possible answer. Here is one. The difference between the first italicized clause and the second will probably have contrastive emphasis, in the first case on *parents* and the second case on *me*. Jack begins his announcement of his origins with *I was*, followed by a pause and a repetition of *I was*, keeping the audience waiting to the very end of the clause for *found*, giving it full prominence. In Lady Bracknell's two later speeches, she incorporates Given information in Rheme position (marked), expressing disbelief and amazement with her questions: *find you*? *A hand-bag*? Finally, Jack (*very seriously*) reverts to what is probably an unmarked declarative expression, spoken with a falling tone. (*See* Halliday, 1994: Chapter 8, for a discussion of tone and emphasis.)

# Notes

1. Chua Chooi See, 1992: *DOS 5: A  step by step guide*. Kuala Lumpur: Federal Publications.
2. Austen, Jane 1813: *Pride and prejudice*.
3. Wilde, Oscar 1895: *The importance of being Ernest*.
4. Lawrence, D.H. 1950: *Selected letters*. Harmondsworth: Penguin Books.
5. Cook, C. and Barker, I.M. (eds.) 1980: *Pears' cyclopaedia* (89th edition). London: Pelham Books Ltd.
6. Russell, B. 1961: *History of western philosophy* (2nd edition). London: George Allen & Unwin.
7. Booth, William 1890: *In darkest England and the way out*. In Hampton, C. 1984, *A radical reader*. London: Penguin.
8. Ishiguro, Kazuo 1989: *The remains of the day*. London: Faber and Faber.

# 5

# Grammar and text

## 5.1  *Text and texture*

In the last chapter we looked at the ways in which the grammar of English allows speakers and writers to structure information within the clause by making use of the two independent patterns: (a) the Theme + Rheme system of the clause and (b) the combination of Given and New information units. In this chapter, we consider how this type of patterning works in longer stretches of discourse and how the Thematic choices made by a language user can help to make a text coherent. In addition, this chapter seeks to explain how other elements of the language – cohesive devices – are combined with structural elements to give a sense of continuity to discourse.

In Section 1.7, we explained that one of the three metafunctions of language is the *textual function*, which relates what is said to ideas outside the actual discourse and which organizes the text itself. When we use language to talk about the language we are using and when we use language to link other pieces of language or help our ideas 'hang together', we are exercising the textual function.

A stretch of language which is coherent and 'makes sense' is said to have *texture* (originally discussed in Halliday and Hasan, 1976: pp. 2–3); *texture* is simply the quality of being a text, rather than a set of unconnected bits of language such as one might find in a collection of independent sentences used as exercises in a language text book.

This is illustrated in the two samples of language in Texts 5A and 5B. Of these, only Text 5B has texture, even though the individual sentences in Text 5A 'make sense' as separate items. In Text 5A, the sentences are not linked together in a logical way. Although we have called it a 'text' for ease of reference, in fact Text 5A, which is part of a translation exercise from an Italian language course book, is not really 'text' at all, since, by definition, a text has texture.

In Text 5A the pronouns (*me, him, them, her*) do not have any common referents with any other nouns or pronouns in the text. The reader does not know who the pronouns refer to in any sense. What is more we do not have any basis on which to decide whether or not *him* in sentence (1) refers to the

1. Give it to me, not to him.
2. Those two men with the oxen will arrive tomorrow.
3. I met them in town, this morning, but I did not see her.
4. That book was written by him.

**Text 5A** (Speight, *Teach yourself Italian*[1]).

same person as the *him* in sentence (4) or not. This kind of link between the sentences is not necessary since each one is a separate entity within the context of the larger actual text, a language teaching book. We can contrast this with the pronoun reference in Text 5B.

Wole Soyinka, dramatist and scholar, is a Nigerian. He was born in 1934, and has devoted his life to drama for the theatre, both as a dramatist and as a university teacher of drama and English in his own country. He is also an accomplished writer of stories, novels and poetry. His background and his professional life have made him uniquely able to write plays with an African setting which can absorb the conflict between past and present, tradition and novelty, tribal beliefs and the ideologies of the Western world today.

**Text 5B** (Lott, *A course in English language and literature*[2]).

Text 5B, which is the first half of a summary of the life of Soyinka from a book on language and literature, is coherent and textured. How cohesion is realized in language is discussed in detail in the next section.

## 5.2 *The textual component of the grammar*

Halliday (1994: Chapter 9, section 6) identifies the *textual component* of the grammar of English (and hence *texture*) as consisting of the features associated with two groups of resources: the *structural* and the *cohesive*. The first (the structural) is subdivided into the two areas we discussed in Chapter 4. The second (the cohesive) is subdivided into four further areas, as can be seen in the following diagram (from Halliday, 1994: p. 334):

Structural Component
1. Given and New: Information Structure and Focus
2. Theme and Rheme: The Thematic Structure

Cohesive Component
1. reference
2 ellipsis and substitution

3. conjunction
4. lexical cohesion

Text 5B provides a straightforward example of the textual component in operation. This text comes at the end of a book, which includes some extracts from a play by Soyinka, so the readers of the text already have some familiarity with the dramatist's name. The author is able to assume that the reader has already heard of Soyinka and takes *Wole Soyinka, dramatist and scholar* (two Nominal Groups *in apposition*, referring to the same person) as Theme of the first clause, presented as Given information. The subsequent clauses, with the exception of Clause 3 (discussed below) take up the same Given information either by referring to the dramatist as the Theme of each clause or as a crucial part of the theme. This is shown clause by clause below with the Theme given in italics:

Clause 1. *Wole Soyinka, dramatist and scholar*, is a Nigerian.
Clause 2. *He* was born in 1934.
Clause 3. *[he]* has devoted his life to drama for the theatre, both as a dramatist and as a university teacher of drama and English in his own country.
Clause 4. *He* is also an accomplished writer of novels, stories and poetry.
Clause 5. *His background and his professional life* have made him uniquely able to write plays, etc.

In Clause 5, the novelist is referred to in the possessive pronouns *his* and *his*, each standing in place of *Soyinka's*. We can express the Theme + Rheme structure of the text diagrammatically to show the *thematic progression* in the text. The diagram here shows that the first Theme is re-iterated in each clause, with additional elements in Clause 5. Each Rheme is fresh and equates with New information.

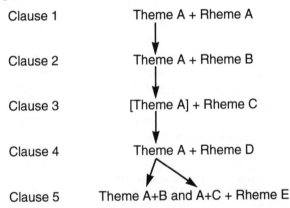

Clause 1          Theme A + Rheme A

Clause 2          Theme A + Rheme B

Clause 3          [Theme A] + Rheme C

Clause 4          Theme A + Rheme D

Clause 5     Theme A+B and A+C + Rheme E

The additional elements (*background*, signified by B, and *professional life*, signified by C) are also presented as Given information because the concepts are recoverable from the previous discourse.

Daneš (1974) identified a number of models of thematic progression including the one in Text 5B, where the Theme does not change for a section of the text. This is usually known as the *Continuous* or *Constant Theme Pattern*. We will use the term *Constant* in this book.

The use of *he*, in Clauses 2 and 4, is an example of the cohesive feature *reference*. Clause 3 fails to refer directly to Soyinka because the subject of the verb *has devoted* is omitted, but the reader understands that the person who has devoted his life to drama is the same as the person who *was born in 1934*. Here, the omission of any word (even a pronoun) to refer to Soyinka is an example of the cohesive feature named *ellipsis*. In Clause 4, we find the word *also*, which is an example of a *Conjunctive Adjunct*. Its function is to help the reader link the clause which refers to his general writings with the earlier clauses that refer only to dramatic writings.

In addition, Text 5B includes some clear examples of *lexical cohesion*. Lexical cohesion can occur between words which are members of the same semantic set, which is to say that they are associated in terms of meaning. The association concerned may be one of related or equivalent meaning or may be one of contrast. In Text 5B, the words listed in each of the four lines stand in a variety of meaningful relationships with each other, and each of these relationships helps the cohesive effect when they are used together in the same short stretch of written English:

1. dramatist – drama – theatre
2. writer – novels – stories – poetry – write – plays
3. scholar – university – teacher – professional
4. [Nigerian – country – African] – [English – Western]

Since each word in each line is joined in some meaningful relation to the following word, the words are said to form a *cohesive chain*. Any text may contain a number of cohesive chains. In the fourth chain given above the lexical items are all concerned with places and nationalities but since these fall into two linked groups, the African and the English, we have separated them with brackets.

Thus Text 5B can be said to be *cohesive* because the logical progression of the information through the text is helped both by the thematic structure and the use of the devices: *reference*, *ellipsis*, *conjunction*, and *lexical cohesion*.

In the remainder of this chapter, we look first in more detail at patterns of thematic progression and then at some of the uses of cohesive devices.

## 5.3   *Thematic progression*

As we have seen in Text 5B, thematic progression can be very straightforward. However, there are more complex options available and these we consider in this section.

### 5.3.1   The Constant Theme Pattern

The Constant Pattern, where a common Theme is shared by each clause and this Theme equates with Given information, is common in short passages of biographical information (5B) and sometimes in narratives which focus on the behaviour of one person. It is also frequently found in textbooks and descriptions of factual information focusing on a particular thing or concept.

Text 5C, from a booklet on survival in tropical forests, provides a further illustration of the Constant Pattern in use; here the Theme of each clause refers wholly (*it*) or partially (*its* length) to the main topic of the text, the saw-scaled viper.

---

The saw-scaled viper is found in dry sandy areas where there is little vegetation. Its length is about two feet, and it is sandy in colour with darker spots. It is aggressive and very poisonous. It may be found in the full blaze of the sun or beneath hot stones and in crannies heated by the sun.

---

**Text 5C**   (Ministry of Defence pamphlet, *Jungle survival*[3]).

However, there are other types of thematic progression that are equally common and equally cohesive.

### 5.3.2   The Linear Theme Pattern

The second type we look at in this chapter is the *Linear Pattern*. In this type, the Rheme of one clause is taken up as the theme of the subsequent clause. An example of this can be seen in Text 5D, which comes from a book about the natural world.

---

The stomach produces gastric juice, which contains dilute hydrochloric acid. The acid kills most of the bacteria in the food. [...] The partly digested food passes next into the duodenum, the first part of the small intestine. This is a coiled tube about eight metres long, which is as wide as a man's thumb.

---

**Text 5D**   (Martin, Larkin and Bembaum (eds.), *The Penguin book of the natural world*[4]).

The first sentence in Text 5D contains two clauses. The Rheme of the first clause (*gastric juice*) becomes the Theme of the second clause (*which*, a relative pronoun, standing in place of *gastric juice*). The Rheme of the second clause (*dilute hydrochloric acid*) is taken up as Theme of Clause 3 (*The acid*). The Rheme of Clause 3 (*the food*) becomes the Theme of Clause 4 (*The partly digested food*). Finally, the Rheme of Clause 5 (*the duodenum*, *the first part of the small intestine*) is summarized in the word *This*, which is the Theme of the first clause in the final sentence.

Diagrammatically, this pattern can be represented as follows:

Clause 1.    Theme A + Rheme B

Clause 2.                 Theme B + Rheme C

Clause 3.                 Theme C + Rheme C

### 5.3.3   The Split Rheme Pattern

The third common type of thematic progression dealt with here is known as the *Split Rheme Pattern*.

This pattern occurs when the Rheme of a clause has two components, each of which is taken in turn as the Theme of a subsequent clause. An example of this can be seen in Text 5E, which is taken from a chapter in a geography textbook discussing population distribution in 1970.

---

The only other considerable region of dense population in the world lies in Japan. This country shows a remarkable fusion of both densely populated rural and urban communities. Japanese peasant farmers, who constitute 45 per cent of the total population, practise a typical monsoon Asian subsistence economy, whereas the millions of people living in vast industrial cities such as Tokyo and Osaka have much in common with counterparts in Europe and North American.

---

**Text 5E**   (Lowry, *World population and food supply*[5]).

If we analyse this passage clause by clause and mark the Themes of the clauses in italics, as we did for Text 5B, we get the following.

Clause 1.   *The only other considerable region of dense population in the world* lies in Japan.

Clause 2.   *This country* shows a remarkable fusion of both densely populated rural and urban communities.

Clause 3.   *Japanese peasant farmers* practise a typical monsoon Asian subsistence economy

Clause 4.   *who* constitute 45 percent of the total population

Clause 5.   *whereas // the millions of people living in vast industrial cities such as Tokyo and Osaka* have much in common with counter-parts in Europe and America.

Clause 2 has two co-ordinated components in its Rheme, indicated by the word *both*: (1) *densely populated rural communities* and (2) (*densely populated*) *urban communities*. The first, referring to rural communities, is taken up as Theme of Clause 3 (*peasant farmers*) and also as the Theme of Clause 4 (*who*). The second, referring to urban communities, is taken up as Topical Theme of Clause 5 (*the millions of people living in vast industrial cities such as Tokyo and Osaka*).

The Split Rheme Pattern can be represented diagrammatically as follows.

Clause 1.  Theme A + [Rheme B + Rheme C]

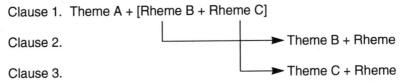

Clause 2.                                                                    ➤ Theme B + Rheme

Clause 3.                                                                    ➤ Theme C + Rheme

### 5.3.4   Derived Themes

We have looked so far at three common types of thematic pattern that help in the structure of coherent texts, but, as a glance at almost any book will show, they do not account for all the thematic patterns that can be identified.

In a longer text, a variety of topics for discussion might be introduced by an author at, say, the beginning of a chapter. Later in the course of the chapter, the author might refer back to any one of the topics or aspects of the topics and use it as Theme. As a result, we often find texts where two or more independent Themes alternate within the text. A straightforward, typical example of this type of thematic structure can be seen in Text 5F, which is a short narrative section from Ted Hughes' story The Iron Man. At this point in the story a farmer's son, a boy called Hogarth, meets the Iron Man for the first time.

---

And now the Iron Man was coming. Hogarth could feel the earth shaking under the weight of his footsteps. Was it too late to run? Hogarth stared at the Iron Man, looming, searching towards him for the taste of the metal that had made that inviting sound.
Clink, Clink, Clink! went the nail on the knife.
CRASSSHHH!
The Iron Man had fallen into the pit. Hogarth went close. The earth was shaking as the Iron Man struggled underground. Hogarth peered over the torn edge of the great pit.

---

**Text 5F**   (Hughes, *The Iron Man*[6]).

In this text, with the exception of the interspersed representation of the sounds of clink and crash, we find an alternating pattern of Themes: *The Iron Man* and *Hogarth*. *The earth* also appears as Theme, being picked up from the Rheme in the second quoted clause.

In many texts, it can be difficult to analyse thematic progression even where it is fairly straightforward unless we take into account the notion of *Derived Themes*. The term is used to describe expressions in Theme position which are cohesively linked in meaning, but not necessarily in form, to a topic which has been stated earlier in the text.

In long educational texts, such as science and geography textbooks, elaborate structures can be signalled by the writer early in a section or chapter. These structures then serve as a way of introducing New information which can be taken up as Theme of subsequent clauses. In, for example, *The Penguin book of the natural world*[4] (Section 112), there is a chapter on rodents. After the heading *The animal kingdom*; *the gnawing rodents*, the writer begins with the sentence:

> *Rodents, gnawing animals, usually of small size, are the largest order of mammals, making up two fifths of all mammal species.*

After a general description of the physical characteristics of rodents, the author continues by introducing what are to become his subsequent Themes as New information in Rheme position:

> *The order can be divided into three main groups: squirrels, rats and porcupines.*

Each of the groups (squirrels, rats and porcupines) then becomes a (derived) Theme in turn. The paragraph on rats is typical of many such paragraphs in the book and is given in Text 5G. The Derived Themes in the paragraph are all subcategories of rat-like rodents. In fact the author continues to describe this type of rodent in a continuation of the passage, beginning the next two sentences with *the spiny mouse* and *lemmings*.

In this text the Themes chosen by the author relate closely to the overall topic of the paragraph: *the rat-like rodents*, which is also the Theme of the

---

The rat-like rodents include hamsters, lemmings, voles and gerbils, as well as rats and mice. The black rat is found in buildings, sewers and rubbish yards, but has been largely replaced by the bigger, more aggressive, brown rat. Voles are mouse-like rodents that live in the grasslands of Europe and Asia; water voles, or water rats, build complex tunnels along river banks. The house mouse often lives inside buildings and is a serious pest because it eats stored food. The field mouse, on the other hand, very rarely comes near human dwellings.

---

**Text 5G** (Martin, Larkin and Bernbaum (eds.), *The Penguin book of the natural world*[4]).

first sentence. In a similar way the Theme *the rat-like rodents* relates to the Chapter heading *Rodents*.

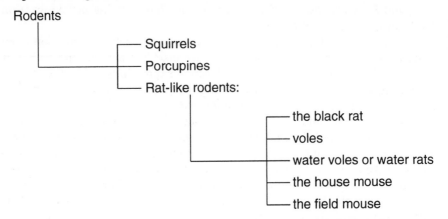

Each of the subordinate themes here are said to be *derived* from the *hypertheme* 'rodents'. In this particular book, there is an even higher level of hypertheme, *the animal kingdom*, which is subsequently used by the authors to allow them to introduce new Themes such as *sea mammals* and *flesh eaters*.

We now leave discussion of thematic progression and return to the cohesive features of text outlined in Section 5.2.

## 5.4    *Cohesive ties*

As we mentioned above, cohesive ties can be classified into four main types: reference, ellipsis and substitution, conjunction, and lexical cohesion. In Section 5.2, in Text 5B, we saw all four in operation simultaneously, working together with the thematic and information structure of the text, and this is how they are normally used by speakers and writers. Now, however, we deal briefly with each type of cohesive tie in turn.

### 5.4.1    Reference

As we have seen in the text examples above, reference can be cohesive when two or more expressions in the text refer to the same person, thing or idea. Thus, for example, in Text 5B *Wole Soyinka*, *he*, *his* and *him* all refer to the same person, and in Text 5C *saw-scaled viper*, *its* and *it* all refer to the same creature.

An essential characteristic of cohesive reference is that, on second and subsequent mention, the person or thing referred to is not *named* but is indicated by means of a pronoun, demonstrative (*this*, *these*, etc.) or comparative term. As we have seen in the sections on thematic progression, the repetition of nominals may also have a cohesive function, but there is a special characteristic that is produced by the use of unnamed reference. When readers or listeners come across a pronoun or a determiner, say, they are forced to mentally identify the linked nominal in order to make sense of the text. This has a very strong cohesive force.

The term *reference*, as used by Halliday and Hasan (1976), is an extension of the term as used in philosophy and some types of semantics to mean an act of referring to entities outside the discourse ('in the real world' as it were, although we need to remember that 'real world' can include imaginary worlds, such as we find in fiction or myth). Reference in this sense is not necessarily textually cohesive. For example, when out walking at night, a person might point to the moon and say to a companion, 'Look at that'. In this case, *that* refers to an entity which is identifiable in the situation of utterance. The word *that* here is an example of noncohesive *exophoric reference* or reference *outside the text*.

If, on the other hand, the speaker says, 'Look at the moon' and the companion replies, 'I can't see it' or 'Where is it?', with *it* referring to the previously mentioned moon, co-referentiality is established between the pronoun *it* and *the moon*, and cohesion is established. The latter is known as *endophoric reference* or reference to something within the text (in this case the short exchange about the moon).

Strictly speaking, of course, it is speakers or writers who *refer* to entities, using expressions for the purpose, but as a shorthand device we often talk about words or expressions referring *to each other* and say that endophoric reference occurs when *two or more expressions refer* to the same entity.

Endophoric reference is classified into *cataphoric* and *anaphoric reference*. *Cataphoric* is 'forward pointing', in the sense that in a text the unnamed expression, usually a pronoun or demonstrative, appears first and the named expression appears second, as in Example (1) from a computer manual, where the cohesive tie is indicated in bold type.

(1) To see how it works, type VER and press ENTER. You will see **this** on your screen:
    **MS-DOS Version 6.00**

*This* forms a cohesive tie with the message *MS-DOS Version 6.00*. In this case of cataphoric reference, the reader does not fully understand the sense of *this* until he or she has read on to the next line in the text.

The second type of endophoric reference, and by far the most common, is called *Anaphoric* reference. This type is 'backward looking' in the sense that the named item appears first and the pronoun appears second. It is, therefore, similar to all the examples discussed in Text 5B above.

In terms of grammatical realization, there are three main types of cohesive reference: *personal reference*, *demonstrative reference* and *comparative reference*. What is known as *personal reference* (although it does not always involve people) is dependent on the use of personal pronouns (masculine, feminine and neuter). As we saw in Chapter 2, pronouns can be used anywhere in the clause that a nominal group can be found. Possessives are also commonly referential and can be used as Modifier or Head in a Nominal Group. *Demonstrative reference* is dependent on the use of Determiners (*this, these, that* and *those*) and adjuncts (*here, now, then, there*), and *comparative* reference uses adjectives like *same, other, identical, better, more* or their adverbial counterparts *identically, similarly, less,* and so on, to forge links with previously mentioned entities.

We end this section on reference with one example of each type of referential tie. In each of our examples, the tie operates across adjoining sentences, but referential ties can stretch over a number of sentences in a text and often do so both in conversation and in written texts.

> (2) Personal reference
> **West African dwarf sheep** are found roaming about the towns and villages in many southern parts of West Africa in small flocks. **They** thrive and breed successfully in areas of trypanosomiasis risk. **Their** coat colour is either predominantly white with irregular black patches, or black marked with white patches.
> (3) Demonstrative reference
> Be careful of **wasps, bees and hornets. These** are dangerous pests.
> (4) Comparative Reference
> Beecher Stowe gives a moving **account** of the horrors of slavery. Clemens' treatment of the issue in the classic novel *Huckleberry Finn* is **lighter** but more **subtle.**

## 5.4.2  Substitution and ellipsis

Substitution is used where a speaker or writer wishes to avoid the repetition of a lexical item and is able to draw on one of the grammatical resources of the language to replace the item. In English, there is a set of words available for this purpose.

The main difference between reference and substitution is that, as we have explained, in the case of referential cohesion, the tie exists between two or more references to the same concept. With substitution we do not have co-referentiality, but rather a substitute for a *word* or *group of words*. The difference should be clear from Examples (5) and (6).

> (5) Reference
> Would you like **this cake**? I bought **it** this morning.
> (6) Substitution
> Would you like **this cake**? Or do you prefer the other **one**?

In the case of reference, *this cake* and *it* refer to the same object, but in the case of substitution only *this cake* refers to a particular cake. *One* replaces the word *cake* but refers to the general class of cakes. The presence of the word *other* ensures that it refers to a different cake. Nevertheless, the receiver of the message can only interpret *one* in terms of the previous mention of *cake*, and this forms a cohesive tie.

There are three types of substitution in English: *nominal, verbal* and *clausal substitution*, and each type has its own set of substitute words.

In nominal substitutes, *one, ones* and *same* can stand in place of Nominal Groups and Head Nouns (not necessarily the whole of a Nominal Group), as in Examples (7), (8) and (9):

(7) 'Would you like **some sandwiches**?'
    'Please pass the **ones** with cucumber in.'
(8) 'I'm having **chicken and rice**.'
    'I'll have **the same**.'
(9) In an experiment, some children were given six cardboard **discs** each in a different colour. They were then asked to choose the colour they liked best. The majority chose **the blue one**.

The words *one* and to a lesser extent *same* resemble pronouns, but there are certain crucial differences between substitutes and other pronouns. First, *one* has a plural form in *ones*, but only a third person form unlike personal pronouns. Second, it can be used with Deictics (articles and determiners) and Numeratives: a *red one, the blue one, some old ones, five new ones*.

In verbal substitutes, any nonfinite form of the verb *do* (plus, sometimes, additional words like *it* or *that*), can stand in place of the lexical verb in a Verbal Group, as in Example (10).

(10) 'We met in Brazil. Do you remember?'
     'Yes, we must have done.'

*Done* here stands in place of *met in Brazil*.

The third type, clausal substitution, is extremely common both in speech and in written prose. Here, the words *so* and *not* stand in place of an entire clause except for the subject, and the reader or listener can only interpret the meaning of the substitute in terms of what has previously been expressed in full. Example (11), a conversation between two people from the play *The importance of being earnest*, includes two examples of *so* substituting for full clauses.

(11) 'I do mean something else.'
     'I thought so.'
     'And I would like to take advantage of Lady Bracknell's temporary absence [...].'
     'I would certainly advise you to do so.'

The equivalent negative expression to *so* is illustrated in Example (12).

(12) 'Well, I don't intend to get killed if I can help it.'
     'I suppose not.'

An interesting point about substitution is the grammatical distinction between the use of the substitute *not* following a verb like *think, suppose, guess* and the ordinary negative form of the verb, as in *I don't suppose*. Students of English as a second or foreign language can be easily confused by the distinction between say *I think not* and *I don't think*, sometimes interpreting the former as an ordinary negative form and, by analogy, producing clauses like *\*I want not* when they wish to say *I don't want*.

In the same cohesive class as substitution, we find *Ellipsis*, or the omission of words, groups or clauses (referred to by Halliday as 'substitution by zero'). Ellipsis takes place in similar grammatical environments to substitution. Thus, we have *nominal, verbal* and *clausal ellipsis*.

The grammar of Nominal Ellipsis permits the omission of Head Nouns in a Nominal Group as in Example (13) where *two* in the final clause means *two cucumber sandwiches*. The Classifier and the Head Noun are not realized, leaving the Numerative as Head of the Nominal Group.

> (13) 'Have you got the cucumber sandwiches cut for Lady Bracknell?'
> 'Yes, sir.'
> (Algernon inspects them and takes two.)

Verbal Ellipsis is common in all short form answers and responses as is exemplified in (14) where there are two examples of Verbal Ellipsis in responses (indicated with [E]). In both cases the tie is with *save you* in the first sentence of the verbal exchange. In these instances, it is the lexical verb that is omitted.

> (14) 'I'll help you. I'll save you.'
> 'You can't [E].'
> 'I can [E].'

In (14) the finite in the Verbal Group is realized both negatively and positively. It is also possible to omit the finite and realize the lexical verb as in (15).

> (15) *The boys were filling the bags, the men* [E] *moving them to the dikes.*

Example (16) illustrates Clausal Ellipsis; the word *don't* stands in place of *don't open the door.*

> (16) Get up quick and open the door. If you don't, they will break it down.

### 5.4.3   Conjunction

*Conjunction* is the term used to describe the cohesive tie between clauses or sections of text in such a way as to demonstrate a meaningful relationship between them. It is also possible to perceive this process as the linking of ideas, events or other phenomena. This 'linking' or 'joining' is achieved by the use of *Conjunctive Adjuncts*, which are sometimes called *cohesive conjunctives* (for example, *then, for this reason, on the other hand*). These are words or expressions that have two textual functions: they indicate *conjunc-*

*tion* and, at the same time usually indicate the type of relationship that operates between the elements being joined (for example, relationships of *time, reason, cause*).

In Chapter 3, we discussed the difference between Conjunctive Adjuncts and *conjunctions* (*linkers and binders*), pointing out that, although they have a lot in common semantically, they have different grammatical characteristics. We can see this illustrated in Example (17), where a linking conjunction (*but*) points out a contrastive relationship between two propositions within one sentence, and (17a), where a similar relationship is expressed in separate sentences with the use of a Conjunctive Adjunct (*however*).

(17)   Most of us are aware that plants contain chemical substances of various kinds that can be extracted and used for the benefit of mankind, but what most people don't know is that plant extracts have been used for centuries and have therefore stood the test of time.

(17a)  Most of us are aware that plants contain chemical substances of various kinds that can be extracted and used for the benefit of mankind. However, what most people don't know is that plant extracts have been used for centuries and have therefore stood the test of time.

The nature of the relationships that can be expressed by the use of Conjunctive Adjuncts are many and lack of space prevents a full account here, but four classes of cohesive conjunction, each of these with numerous subclasses, were identified by Halliday and Hasan (1976), who provide a fuller account:

1. Additive
2. Adversative
3. Causal
4. Temporal

Some common types are illustrated in (18) and (19). In (18), an extract from an academic paper on management, there are two examples, the first Additive-Exemplification and the second Adversative-Contrastive.

(18)   It is easy to identify theoretical conflicts in management accounting. **For example**, contingency theorists argue that the type of management accounting system which is appropriate to an organization is dependent on a number of organization-specific variables. **By contrast**, the emphasis in much of the management accounting research published between the late 1950s and the mid-1970s was on the development of specific normative models which were allegedly suitable for use in a wide variety of organizations without any context-specific adaptation.

In (19), there is an example of a Causal-Result relationship and also Temporal-Sequential relationship. The Conjunctive Adjuncts are indicated in bold type.

(19)   There is a severe shortage of mathematics teachers in Britain and America. **As a consequence of this**, far too many people leave school without any

interest in pursuing the study of subjects like engineering that rely on mathematical concepts. Two possible solutions are available. **Firstly**, it should be a priority to train more teachers; **secondly**, teachers' salaries should be made competitive with other jobs in order to attract young people to the profession.

It can be seen from (18) and (19) that Conjunctive Adjuncts provide a useful guide to the rhetorical paths that a writer is following. They have been compared to signals or signposts that indicate the direction of argument.

### 5.4.4    Lexical cohesion

*Lexical cohesion* refers to the cohesive effect of the use of lexical items in discourse where the choice of an item relates to the choices that have gone before.

We have already seen in the analysis of Text 5B (Section 5.2) that words that are associated in meaning can form cohesive chains and, moreover, a text may well have more than one cohesive chain running through it. We now look in a little more detail at the types of associative meaning that are possible between lexical items.

One important type of lexical cohesion, probably the one with the strongest cohesive force, is repetition (or *re-iteration*) of the same item. Thus, if a person's name is mentioned more than once (as is the name Hogarth in Text 5F) the reader will recognize the link in a chain of information connected with that person. Synonyms and near synonyms can have the same effect as can other words which refer to the same person. In other parts of the book from which Text 5F was taken, for example, Hogarth is referred to as *the boy* and *the farmer's son*. Where the cohesive chain has the same referent, it is termed *an identity chain*. This type of chain is arguably the strongest type of lexical cohesion and it has much in common with reference.

Nevertheless, for cohesion to occur, it is not necessary for each word in a chain to refer to the same entity or even to have the same word class. All the words related to the root *pollen* play a part in the cohesion of (20).

> (20)    A flower cannot produce seeds until it is pollinated and its ovule fertilized. Pollination is the transfer of pollen from the male parts (stamens) to the female parts (stigmas) of a flower. If pollen is carried to the stigma of the same flower, it is called self-pollination.

Example (20) also includes examples of re-iteration, of *flower* and *stigma*. Later in the same text, we find further use of the word *seeds* and also reference to *plants*, a word which stands in a superordinate relationship with *flower*, and then to *grasses*, a word in a subordinate relationship to *plants*.

Near-synonyms can sometimes be quite difficult to pin down in a text. However, a good example of how they are used came in a newspaper report of floods in France and Holland, which reported the fact that many families had been forced to leave their homes. This short piece contained the words *left, exodus, abandoned, deserted, evacuated, moved*, all of which entail the core meaning of *leave*.

As well as synonyms, words from mutually exclusive categories (such as *male* and *female* or *hot* and *cold*) or words with opposite and contrastive meanings (*antonyms*) can have a cohesive effect.

Another type of lexical relationship which is often cohesive is termed *collocation*. *Collocation* covers two or more words which can be said to 'go together' in the sense of frequency of occurrence. If words commonly occur in the same text and we are frequently exposed to their co-occurrence, we come to expect them together. Traditionally, for example, children's stories with a Princess in them usually ended up with a Prince in them as well, although the *Prince and Princess* collocation is an example of an association that may well be changing with more egalitarian approaches to children's literature.

One aspect of collocation that we need to remember is that words collocate differently in different registers. The word *cone*, for example, collocates with *angle, cross-section, base* and *circle* in a geometry textbook, but with *ice cream* in the context of a children's holiday. Similarly, the word *data* would collocate with *bank, processing*, and *storage* in the field of Computer Applications, but *spoken* and *written* in Applied Linguistics.

The last, but one of the most important, types of lexical cohesion concerns the use of *general nouns*. These are nouns that have very general all-embracing meanings; they form a class of high level superordinates. The most extreme examples of words that can be used as general nouns (although they are not always used in this way) are the words *person, people, place, thing* and *idea*. With these words, a speaker or writer can create a cohesive link with almost any previously mentioned entity, as for example in (21) where *the ideas* acts as an all-embracing word that coheres with much of the substance of the previous text.

(21) The ideas outlined above should provide the basis for the practical analysis of texts.

A special class of general nouns, which have been called *summary nouns* or *anaphoric nouns (A-nouns)*, are words used to summarize or refer back to sections in a text (usually a lecture or written text). These are extremely important in academic writing where they can be used as a device to introduce a new topic in an argument, as we can see in the examples in (22).

(22) a. This explanation has been challenged by [. . .]
  b. The controversy outlined in the first section is [. . .]
  c. However, serious questions have been raised about even the few proposals outlined above [. . .]

It has been suggested that any noun which can be used to refer to other sections of the discourse (*metadiscursively*) can take on the quality of an anaphoric noun, but it seems usual for these nouns to be used together with pre-modifying anaphoric devices like Deictics (*the, this, these*) or post-modifying expressions which refer the reader to the text (such as *outlined above, in the previous chapter, given earlier*).

In short, lexical cohesion involves meaningful connections in text that are created through the use of lexical items and that do not intrinsically involve reference, substitution, ellipsis or conjunction.

## Summary

This chapter has tried to make the case that texts have texture as a result of a complex interaction of linguistic resources which are used by writers and speakers to provide cohesion. These resources include the Information Structure (organization of Given and New information) and the Thematic Structure (Theme and Rheme) at clause level and also the way in which thematic patterns (thematic progression) are built up from clause to clause through a text. The thematic structure of the text is supported by the cohesive component of the grammar, which consists of reference, ellipsis and substitution, conjunction and lexical cohesion. Although we may analyse each of these elements separately, there is likely to be a blending of many cohesive elements in any stretch of genuine discourse except in very short or abbreviated texts.

## Further study

The major work in the area of cohesion is Halliday and Hasan (1976), which still provides the fullest account of cohesive ties in English. Halliday (1994) has a concise summary that makes links to other aspects of the grammar. Halliday and Hasan (1989) deals with aspects of text and cohesion from an explicitly social semiotic perspective.

Hoey (1983, 1991) develops Halliday and Hasan's account to investigate how cohesive features combine to organize long stretches of text. In his earlier work, he considers cohesion in relation to some important patterns of rhetorical organization. In his later work, he looks in detail at cohesive chains and the significance of repetition. Hoey continues to make important contributions to functional theory, including ideas on the role of the sentence (as distinct from clause), which he suggests may be 'a part grammatical, part textual phenomenon'.

Two excellent monographs on lexical cohesion are Tadros (1981) and Francis (1986), the origin of work on anaphoric nouns. Readers who are interested in the complexities of lexical relations (so-called *sense relations*) will find detailed accounts in Lyons (1977: Chapter 9) and Hurford and Heasley (1983).

On text analysis, we can recommend Mann and Thompson (1992). This unusual book includes examples of twelve analyses of the same text by distinguished linguists. Six of the papers are concerned with lexico-grammatical analysis and include an analysis by Halliday that perceptively demonstrates how the grammar of English works in creating meaning in text and how lexical and grammatical choice can 'give the text its distinctive flavour' (p. 356). A further example of text analysis by Halliday (Halliday and Martin, 1993: Chapter 5), focusing on the textual organization of a piece of writing by Charles Darwin, demonstrates how the interaction of Given and New with Thematic progression underpins the rhetorical value of the discourse.

Although much of what has been discussed in this chapter is applicable to spoken discourse, space has prevented any detailed discussion of spoken text, and most of the examples of spoken interaction have been taken from drama (Oscar Wilde) rather than natural conversation. Halliday's and Hasan's own works are, of course, essential reading, particularly Halliday (1994: Chapters 8 and 9; 1989) and Halliday and Hasan (1989).

A good introduction to spoken discourse can be found in Coulthard (1985), which includes the role of intonation, and more advanced studies are reported in Coulthard (1992). Brazil et al. (1980) also discuss intonation in discourse, especially its application to language teaching.

Much has been written on the question of how far cohesive elements can account for coherence in discourse, and how far straight linguistic description can help us understand it. Such discussions, in the areas of philosophy and pragmatics, relate to some of the matters we have discussed in Chapters 4 and 5. Of particular interest is work on the shared assumptions (*mutual knowledge*) of speakers and hearers and socially acquired 'models' people have of discourse structure, lexical classification or word associations (*frames and schemata*). Other work is concerned with the psychological processes involved in comprehension (for example, so-called *top-down* and *bottom-up text processing*) and the psychological conditions necessary for human communication to take place at all (*communicative principles* or *maxims*). Introductions can be found in Brown and Yule (1983), Leech (1983) and Mey (1993), and more complex discussions in Moore and Carling (1982) and Downes (1984).

This chapter has touched on issues of discourse analysis, some of which are taken further in Chapter 11. Interesting discussions of aspects of discourse, including applications to language teaching, can be found in Widdowson (1979: Chapters 7, 8, 9 and 10; 1984: Chapters 4 to 9; 1990: Chapter 6). The last-mentioned includes a salutary reminder that 'language learning is essentially learning how grammar functions in the achievement of meaning and it is a mistake to suppose otherwise' (p. 97).

## Exercises

### Exercise 5.1

1.  Identify the derived themes in the following text and say where they are derived from.
2.  Find two examples from the text of Nominal Groups without nouns as Head. Are these Elliptical groups? Give reasons for your answer.
3.  Comment on the cohesive ties formed by the following pronouns: she (Sentence 2); they (Sentence 4).
4.  List two lexical chains in the text.

> Once upon a time, there lived a rich merchant who had three beautiful daughters. The youngest was the prettiest of the three and she was also good and kind to everyone. Her elder sisters were also quite attractive but they were neither good or kind. They were greedy and extremely selfish.

**Text 5H.**

### Exercise 5.2

The following extract (Text 5I) on the subject of time and the calendar has a somewhat complex Thematic Pattern. Try to identify the type of thematic progression used by the author. Is it Constant, Derived, Linear or Split Rheme or a combination of more than one pattern? (Note: Ignore the clause beginning *the earth*.)

> The two basic periods upon which our system of time-keeping depends are the year and the day. These are determined by two quite distinct notions. The year depends upon the time the earth takes to travel round the sun in a circular path [. . .] The day depends principally upon the time taken for the earth to rotate around its axis.

**Text 5I**    (Land, *The language of mathematics*,[7] p. 55).

### Exercise 5.3

Identify the type of substitution or ellipsis in each of the following pairs of sentences.

1.  Outside the sleet had turned to rain. The car radio said more was forecast.
2.  Is the contract severable? If so, is the agreement valid?
3.  The French government has declared a national emergency. Fifteen people have been killed; five are missing.
4.  The answer to this problem can be reached by two paths: the short one and the long one. Both in my judgement are satisfactory.

*Exercise 5.4*

Find two short texts of different genres (for example a letter and report, or a sports report and a recipe) and compare the ways texture is created in each text.

**Answers**

*Exercise 5.1*

1. The derived Themes are *The youngest* and *Her elder sisters*. They are both derived from *Three beautiful daughters*.
2. The two Nominal groups without nouns as Head are *the youngest* and *the prettiest*. They are both examples of Elliptical Nominal Groups. The Head Nouns (*daughter* in each case) have been omitted.
3. *She* forms a tie with *the youngest (daughter)* and *the prettiest (daughter)*. *They* (final sentence) forms a tie with *her elder sisters*.
4. beautiful – prettiest – quite attractive
   good – kind – greedy – selfish

*Exercise 5.2*

The Theme and Rheme of the first clause refer essentially to the same concepts: *the two basic periods* and *the year and the day*, the latter being an example of a split Rheme. The Theme of the second clause, *These*, refers to both the Theme and the Rheme of the first clause. So we have either (or both!) Constant and Linear progression. The third clause has the Theme *the year*, which progresses linearly from the Rheme of Clause 1 and the final clause has the Theme *The day* which also progresses linearly from the split Rheme in Clause 1. The clause beginning *the earth* is rankshifted (*see* Chapter 8), so we do not discuss this here.

*Exercise 5.3*

1. Nominal ellipsis.
   The car radio said more [E: *rain*] was forecast.
2. Clausal substitution.
   *So*, in the second sentence, stands in place of '(if) *the contract is severable*'.
3. Nominal ellipsis.
   Fifteen people have been killed; five [E: people] are missing.
4. There are 2 parts to this answer.
   (a) There are two examples of substitution.
   *One* stands in place of *path* in the phrases *the short one/path* and *the long one/path*.

(b)  There is one example of Ellipsis.
Both [E: *paths*] in my judgement are satisfactory.


*Exercise 5.4*

This is an open-ended question so there are many possible answers. Have you considered the thematic progression in each text? Were there any problems in the analysis? If so, why?

What type of cohesive ties could you identify? Some texts are very rich in cohesive ties, but other texts rely largely on the context to make a text coherent.

Remember that sometimes models of grammar are difficult to apply. If this is so, maybe you need to find out more details of the model by more advanced reading (*see* 'Further study' above) or maybe you have hit upon an unusual text.


## Notes

1.  Speight, K. 1943: *Teach yourself Italian*. London: English University Press Ltd.
2.  Lott, Bernard 1986: *A course in English language and literature*. London: Edward Arnold.
3.  Ministry of Defence pamphlet 1967: *Jungle survival*. PAM (AIR) 214,
4.  Martin, E. Larkin, S. and Bernbaum, L (eds) 1976: *The Penguin book of the natural world*. Harmondsworth: Penguin.
5.  Lowry, J.H. 1970: *World population and food supply*. London: Edward Arnold.
6.  Hughes, Ted 1986: *The Iron Man*. London: Faber & Faber.
7.  Land, Frank 1960: *The language of mathematics*. London: John Murray.

# 6

# Process and Participant

Jerry took the money, picked up a hat from the table and strolled out. Half
an hour later he returned and gave some of the bills to Thaler.
  [...]
  Presently something hit the door.
  Jerry opened the door and we went down three steps into the back yard.
It was almost full daylight. There were ten of us in the party.
  'This all?' I asked Thaler.
  He nodded.
  'Nick said there were fifty of you.'
  'Fifty of us to stand off that crummy force!' he sneered.
  A uniformed copper held the gate open, muttering nervously:
  'Hurry it up, boys, please.'
  I was willing to hurry, but nobody else paid any attention to him.
  We crossed an alley, were beckoned through another gate by a big man
in brown, passed through a house, out into the next street, and climbed
into a black automobile that stood at the kerb.
  One of the blond boys drove. He knew what speed was.
  I said I wanted to be dropped off somewhere in the neighbourhood of
the Great Western Hotel. The driver looked at Whisper, who nodded. Five
minutes later I got out in front of my hotel.
  'See you later,' the gambler whispered.
  The last I saw of it was its police department licence plate vanishing
around a corner.

**Text 6A**    (Hammett, *Red harvest*,[1] pp. 52–3).

## 6.1    *Meanings: the clause as representation*

Without getting bogged down in philosophical debate about the nature of
reality, we can say for practical purposes that language is a means of representing the world. Or perhaps, more precisely, a means of representing
'worlds', perceived or imagined. Language encodes our experience, and

thereby plays a crucial role in our involvement with other people, animal life in general, inanimate matter and, indeed, in Douglas Adams' memorable phrase, 'Life, the Universe and Everything'.

The extent to which language determines, rather than simply represents, experience is one of the major questions in philosophy and in linguistics, but we do not propose to go into it here. Suffice it to say that when we speak of language as 'representing' real-world events, or imaginary ones, we are not ruling out the probability that language itself has a central formative role in human experience, nor are we challenging the indisputable fact that it is also part of the reality which it is said to represent. (*See* the discussion of Whorf in Chapter 12.) It is purely for ease of discussion that we take the practical line of saying that we have on the one hand experience and on the other hand language, which symbolically represents it.

There is more than one kind of meaning present in language. The expression 'What does it mean?' can be a different question on different occasions. When we say that *Sint saat new?* means *What time is it?*, we are substituting one encoding for another, English for Amharic. We are, in effect, matching up the two and judging them to be in some sense equivalent. Something similar is going on when we say that Example (1) (below) means the same as (1a): we are claiming that one is a paraphrase of the other, though in the second case instead of matching two expressions from different languages we are matching two grammatically distinct expressions from the same language, English. We are talking about their ideational function and ignoring textual and interpersonal considerations.

(1)   [We] were beckoned through another gate by a big man in brown [. . .]
(1a)  A big man in brown beckoned us through another gate.

The difference between (1) and (1a) is that the first expression in the pair is in the active voice and the second is in the passive. We have touched on this relationship already in our discussion of Subject in Chapter 3. Let us look at it again in the context of this new example.

Some people have difficulty with the claim that two sentences like (1) and (1a) *mean* the same thing. They say that there is a difference; they are not precisely interchangeable. This perception is quite sound. As we have seen in the discussion of Theme and Rheme (Chapter 4), with regard to the way that the text is being packaged, there is a big difference in the writer's actual choice of the passive version (1) and the grammatically possible choice which he did not take up (1a). In the actual text, the clause corresponding to (1) is elliptical. Because it occurs in a series of clauses with the same Subject, *we*, the Subject is omitted, as it is for all the clauses in the series except the first. We can say that *we* is 'understood' to be the Subject of each of the clauses in the series (2).

(2)   We crossed an alley,
      [we] were beckoned through another gate by a big man in brown,
      [we] passed through a house, out into the next street,
      and [we] climbed into a black automobile that stood at the kerb.

Out of context, it might seem that the choice between the active and passive clauses is virtually unconstrained, but in context there is not the same freedom. The author could not have used the passive voice here without making a number of other changes. To some extent, then, the choice is, as it were, determined for the author by his other choices; it is a consequence of his decision to present a series of closely linked, consecutive events in this particular form. It is tied up with his decision to make the group of which the narrator is a part the focus of the narrative at this point. In short, it is in large part a question of the textual metafunction and thematic choice.

It might be as well to stress here again that when we talk about 'choice' or the writer's 'decision' or 'opting' for something, there is no commitment to the view that this must be a conscious procedure. In the case of a professional writer, there is no doubt a great deal of explicit awareness of the merits of alternative forms of expression, frequently involving hesitation over a particular choice or the rewriting of a word, a phrase, a sentence or large chunks of text. To a certain extent, self-consciousness about language probably operates in all human beings in certain circumstances; but for much of the time we speak without reflecting on questions of form, vocabulary, and so on. Our use of these terms like 'choice' is neutral with regard to whether the language user is conscious of making a choice.

So the kind of meaning we are concerned with in this chapter is the kind in which Active and Passive are seen as in some sense substitutable for each other. That is a very approximate way of putting it. It is rather that there is a systematic relationship between the Active form and its Passive counterpart, and part of that relationship is to do with the representation of 'real world' relationships mentioned above. This is the *ideational* metafunction, the *clause as representation* as Halliday (1994) puts it. Active-passive relations are far from being the whole picture; they simply provide a convenient jumping-off point.

In order to discuss these issues, it is necessary to bring into play a set of technical terms distinct from SFPCA, which concern more syntactic considerations. Hence we have the term Actor (briefly mentioned in Chapter 2) and several more, which will be introduced in this chapter.

## 6.2 *Processes*

Text 6A is the end of a chapter recounting a shoot-out between corrupt police and a group of gangsters in whose predicament the narrator has become embroiled. In this extract, the police are then bribed to let the gang escape. In this short text, we have a linguistic representation of numerous human actions, including speaking, and a few other phenomena that are not exactly actions. As befits a thriller, there is a great deal going on, plenty of action.

Looking more closely at the linguistic representation of these imaginary events and the people and things involved, analysing them in terms of what is represented, we shall use the terms Process and Participant. The Process centres on that part of the clause that is realized by the Verbal Group, but it can also be regarded as what 'goings-on' are represented in the whole clause. The Participants are the entities involved in the Process. In the case of this text, they are mostly humans; they happen to be male, adult and American, but gender, age and nationality are less important for the particular Processes involved than the fact that they are human, or at least animate. They include: *Jerry, you, he, Thaler, we, more men, us, ten of us, I, fifty of you, fifty of us, that crummy force, a uniformed copper, nobody else, a big man in brown, one of the blond boys, the driver, who, the gambler*, and (repeatedly) *I*. Of course, in many instances the same individuals are referred to by different forms; for example, *Jerry* and *he*; and in some cases the same item refers to different individuals; for example, in the second sentence, *he* refers to *Jerry*, but in the sentence *He knew what speed was*, *he* refers to *the blond boy*.

However, not all the Participants are human or even animate. In the first clause in the text fragment, Example (3) below, there are two Participants *something* and *door*, both inanimate.

(3) Presently something hit the door.

Also, in other clauses we find the inanimate Participants: *the money, a hat, some of the bills, the office, the back gate, an alley, that* (referring to *a black automobile*), *the car, it, its police department licence plate* and even the abstract entities *any attention* and *speed*.

The term Process as a technical term in Systemic Functional grammar has a slightly different meaning from its everyday usage. As we have said, it is used in two senses: (i) to refer to what is going on in the whole clause, and (ii) to refer to that part of the proposition encoded in the Verbal Group. This is a little confusing perhaps, but that is how the terms are used by Halliday. Processes can be subdivided into different types, and it is here that the difference between the technical and nontechnical senses of the term are highlighted. For instance, not only is (4) described as a Process but so are (5) and (6).

(4) Jerry opened the door.
(5) It was almost full daylight.
(6) There were ten of us in the party.

In order to discuss this aspect of language satisfactorily, it is necessary to distinguish between these two types of Process and several others and to label them accordingly. Different types of Participant, too, have to be distinguished from each other with different labels. And different types of Process generally involve different types of Participant.

In Chapter 2, we discussed the misleading practice of describing verbs as 'doing words'. In the days when grammar was widely taught, teachers would use this term and illustrate it with examples like (4) above.

It is quite reasonable to describe *opened* in Example (4) as a 'doing word', but to focus exclusively on such verbs leaves out of account many structures where the term could not reasonably be applied: for example *was* and *were* in Examples (5) and (6). It is also potentially misleading to apply the term 'doing word' to *saw* or *was* in the last sentence in the text, repeated here as Example (7).

(7) The last I saw of it was its police department licence plate vanishing around a corner.

One implication of this too-narrow labelling is that all clauses represent physical actions, which is plainly false. It is evident that it is not the case, even in our text, which is selected from a genre in which action is highly prized. Clearly, although *What did Jerry do?* might be a question which triggers the response *Jerry opened the door* (or, more probably, *He opened the door*), there is no similar question involving *do* that could be the trigger for *It was nearly daylight*; *There were ten of us in the party*; *I saw the last of it*; or *He knew what speed was*. Systemic Functional Grammar distinguishes carefully between these different Processes.

## 6.3   *Material Process*

The prototypical action-type clause beloved of traditional school grammars is classified in our grammar as a *Material Process clause*. Material Processes actually could be said to involve 'doing words'. In an action-oriented narrative such as the one from which this text fragment is taken, such Processes tend to occur frequently, though they are by no means the only type.

The first sentence in the text consists of three clauses, Examples (8), (9), (10), with ellipsis of the Subject (*Jerry* or *he*) in the second and third clause. There are three Processes and all three are Material.

(8)   Jerry took the money,
(9)   [Jerry] picked up a hat from the table
(10)  and [Jerry] strolled out.

### 6.3.1   Actor and Goal

In (8) *Jerry* is explicitly the performer of the action described by the Process *took*. We therefore label *Jerry* as *Actor*. In the imaginary world of this narrative, Jerry did something to the money; he *took* it. It is Jerry who performs the action and the money that undergoes the action. The label we give to *the money* in this clause is *Goal*. Unfortunately, this term is not as self-explanatory as the label *Actor*, but it is one that is in widespread use in semantics. A similar analysis applies to Example (9); the elliptical Subject *Jerry* is Actor;

*a hat* is Goal. (*From the table* is not a Participant but a Circumstance, which is discussed later in this chapter.)

However, Examples (8) and (9) differ grammatically from (10) and from (11) (below) in one important respect.

(11) Half an hour later he returned.

In (10) and (11) we have again a Material Process, but this time there is only one Participant in each: the elliptical *Jerry* in (10) and *he* in (11). (The expression *Half an hour later* is a Circumstance.) Here there is no Goal involved in the Process. The Process realized by the verb *returned* is not extended from the Actor *he* to any other entity. In Chapter 3, we introduced the notion of *transitive* and *intransitive* clauses. Examples (10) and (11) are intransitive.

*Transitive* clauses involving Material Processes include, among others, Examples (3), (4) and (8), repeated here, and (12).

(3)   Presently something hit the door. (Actor: *Something*; Goal *the door*)
(4)   Jerry opened the door. (Actor: *Jerry*; Goal: *the door*)
(8)   Jerry took the money. (Actor: *Jerry*; Goal: *the money*)
(12) A uniformed copper held the back gate open. (Actor: *a uniformed copper*; Goal: *the back gate*).

The choice between active and passive voice is significant for SFPCA functions since the item which is Complement in the active is Subject in the corresponding passive, but the items retain the same roles of Actor or Goal regardless of voice. This is evident in Fig. 6.1, where Examples (3), (4) and (8) and their passive equivalents are labelled for SFPCA and also for participant roles.

*Active*

| Presently | something | hit | the door |
|---|---|---|---|
| | Jerry | opened | the door |
| | Jerry | took | the money |
| **A** | **S** | **F/V** | **C** |
| | **Actor** | **Process** | **Goal** |

*Passive*

| Presently | the door | was | hit | by something |
|---|---|---|---|---|
| | The door | was | opened | by Jerry |
| | The money | was | taken | by Jerry |
| **A** | **S** | **F** | **P** | **A** |
| | **Goal** | **Process** | | **Actor** |

**Fig. 6.1**

In the original text, the clauses analysed above are in the active voice. We have supplied the corresponding passive form. Example (1) is passive in the original; we supply the corresponding active form in Fig. 6.2.

*Passive*

| We | were | beckoned | through another gate | by a big man in brown. |
|---|---|---|---|---|
| S | F | P | A | A |
| Goal | Process | | | Actor |

*Active*

| A big man in brown | beckoned | us | through another gate. |
|---|---|---|---|
| S | F/P | C | A |
| Actor | Process | Goal | |

**Fig. 6.2**

Intransitive clauses in a Material Process include Examples (13), (14) and (15).

   (13)  We went down three steps into the back yard. (Actor: *we*)
   (14)  One of the blond boys drove. (Actor: *One of the blond boys*)
   (15)  Five minutes later I got out in front of my hotel. (Actor: *I*)

Intransitive clauses have no corresponding passive clauses and in the examples considered have only the Actor role as Subject (compare Fig. 6.3).

| Half an hour later | he | returned. |
|---|---|---|
| | Jerry | strolled out. |
| | One of the blond boys | drove. |
| A | S | F/P |
| | Actor | Process |

**Fig. 6.3**

## 6.3.2 Beneficiary

In Example (16) we have a Material Process with three Participant roles.

   (16)  [he] gave some of the bills to Thaler.

The Process, in the narrow sense of the term, is realized by the verbal expression *gave*. The elliptical Subject *he* is Actor; it is not expressed in the clause but it is plainly understood, carried over, as it were, from the first clause. This is a straightforward case of ellipsis as it is 'fully recoverable'; that is, we know exactly what the referent of the 'gap' is. It has to be *he*. By now, it should be clear that *some of the bills* is Goal. So what is the third element: *to Thaler*?

The label for this Participant is Beneficiary. In Chapter 3 we discussed clauses of this type, which are called ditransitive clauses. In the SFPCA dimension, they typically feature two Complements, more delicately distinguished as Direct and Indirect Object Complements ($C^{do}$ and $C^{io}$). These involve verbs such as *give*, *send*, *offer*, *buy*, *take*, and so on. In terms of our present interest, the Process involves two Participants other than the Actor.

There is an optional alternative sequencing for the Goal and Beneficiary in such clauses. With no significant change of ideational meaning, (16) could take the form of (16a).

(16a) He gave Thaler some of the bills.

The label Beneficiary is self-explanatory with regard to the example we are talking about. The character Thaler in the story literally benefits from the Process (though admittedly the money was his in the first place). The label cannot always be interpreted so literally, however. If the proposition is negated, it does not affect the label given to the Participant. In the invented clauses (16b) and (16c), the Beneficiary label still attaches to Thaler.

(16b) He didn't give some of the bills to Thaler.
(16c) He gave no money to Thaler.

Moreover, in the real world – or in fictional worlds – you can give things to people that they benefit from and things that are of no benefit at all; they may even be harmful. You can promise someone a punch on the nose, hand them cigarettes, give them an earful of abuse, or offer them a poisoned chalice. As far as the labelling of the Participants is concerned, the relative benefit or damage is of no significance; the receiver is still labelled Beneficiary. A similar analysis applies to the parental threat *I'll give you something to cry about*, and comparable threats.

The term Beneficiary is not unusual in having a different range of application from its nontechnical sense. Within the framework of the grammatical description, these are technical terms and must be used with the meanings ascribed to them for the purpose of the analysis. This is no stranger than the fact that in the register of computers the word *window*, though it shares something of the meaning of the everyday term, has a more specific technical meaning limited to the computer.

In active voice clauses the Beneficiary is usually the Indirect Object Complement, but in passive clauses it is often the Subject (*see* Fig. 6.4).

### 6.3.3   Range

English (together with some other languages) has a tendency to nominalize (that is, to express in noun form) certain events which might be seen as essen-

| he | gave | Smith | some cash |
|---|---|---|---|
| S | F/P | C$^{io}$ | C$^{do}$ |
| **Actor** | **Process** | **Beneficiary** | **Goal** |

| Smith | was | given | some cash |
|---|---|---|---|
| S | F | P | C$^{do}$ |
| **Beneficiary** | **Process** | | **Goal** |

**Fig. 6.4**

tially actions and which often have a non-nominal synonym (*see* Chapter 11). These nominalizations are often coupled with a verb which has little lexical meaning, a verb which is semantically almost empty in this context, usually *take* or *have*. Such verbs are sometimes said to be *delexicalized* because they have lost their full lexical content and become almost 'dummies'. Thus we can say *I dined before I came* or, nominalizing, *I had dinner before I came*, and in informal conversation we would usually prefer the second expression. Similarly, we have *bathe* versus *take a bath* or *have a bath*; *wash* versus *have a wash*; *swim* versus *have/take a swim*; *drink* versus *have/take a drink*; *look at* versus *have/take a look at*; *rest* versus *have/take a rest*; and so on. The members of each of these pairs may not be exactly synonymous and there are often stylistic/register differences, but you will probably agree that up to a point they mean the same thing. You will perhaps also agree that, functionally speaking, there is a difference between the role of *the money* in *Jerry took the money* and the role of *a bath* in *I took a bath*. English encodes them in a grammatically similar way, but it seems desirable at the semantic level of Process and Participant to make some distinction between them. The term coined by Michael Halliday for items like *a bath* in *I took a bath* is Range.

There is a very close relation between Range and Goal. As with many other categories in grammar, this is not a clear-cut distinction with a sharp dividing line between the two categories; one merges into the other. Since the examples in the text are peripheral rather than clear cases, we will postpone discussion of them and go outside for our first examples.

The most clear-cut example of Range, as we see it, is where the Process and the Participant are blended together, as in the expressions already mentioned. Of course, in a more literal use of the words *I took a bath* (for example, as uttered by a burglar whose larceny extends to ripping out the plumbing), the analysis would be Goal. In the case of the burglary situation, the verb *take* retains its lexical meaning of 'seize, transfer to one's possession' instead of being a delexicalized dummy. This time it does resemble *Jerry took the money*. (The rule-of-thumb test seems to be whether the utterance in question is an answer to the question 'What did he/you/etc. do to X?' In the second case, where the thief is talking about his crime, his utterance could be construed as an answer to some hypothetical question *What did I do to a bath?* In the first case, where the speaker is referring to his or her personal hygiene, no such question is conceivable.

A similar sort of role to that of *a bath* in the personal hygiene example seems to attach to *a song* in *She sang a song*, and also to *a terrible death* in *Don Giovanni died a terrible death*, or *the good fight* in *Fight the good fight*. Thus, these too are classified as Range. In these instances, we find not 'empty' verbs like *have* or *take* but verbs which share semantic features with the head noun in the Range element: *die* has a lot in common with *death*; *sing* with *song*.

This is a fairly limited set of items, however, and the relationship still holds for items which are not so obviously related. For example, the italicized items in the following are all Range: she sang *the national anthem*; she hummed *a tune*; the band played *'Waltzing Matilda'*; Run *the straight race*; Did Pele play *football?*; he counted off *a hundred or two*.

One example of Range in the Hammett extract is *any attention* in Example (17).

(17)  Nobody else paid any attention to him.

*Pay attention* is a fairly clear example of a metaphorical expression which has become idiomatic. Lexically and grammatically, the structure resembles a clause with a Goal, but the semantic evidence suggests that *any attention* is Range; on either analysis, *to him* is Beneficiary.

In the extract, we also find the clause: *We crossed an alley*. In Functional-Systemic grammar, *an alley* is classed as Range. This seems to us a more peripheral case than the ones we have already considered. Again the question test, rough though it is, seems to bear out this decision. It doesn't seem to be quite right to say *What did we do to an alley? We crossed it*. The argument is that *an alley* is not so much the recipient or sufferer of the action as the scope of the action, hence we label it Range.

## 6.4  *Mental Process*

Some processes involve not material action but phenomena best described as states of mind or psychological events. To these we give the label *Mental Processes*. Mental Processes tend to be realized through the use of verbs like *think, know, feel, smell, hear, see, want, like, hate, please, repel, admire, enjoy, fear, frighten*.

In Example (18), we cannot construe the Process as an action and so we can deduce that it is not a Material Process.

(18)  He knew what speed was.

The clause could not serve as an answer to the question *What did he do?* In this respect it differs from the clause immediately preceding it: *One of the blond boys drove.* (What did one of the blond boys do? He drove; but not: What did he do? He knew what speed was.) Knowing is not doing.

Another example of Mental Process is *wanted* in Example (19).

    (19)  I wanted to be dropped off somewhere in the neighbourhood of the Great Western Hotel.

Simpler examples can be found elsewhere in the same source, Examples (20) to (24).

    (20)  He didn't see me.
    (21)  I heard the shots.
    (22)  I knew the number.
    (23)  You didn't want it this morning.
    (24)  I dislike your manner.

### 6.4.1  Senser and Phenomenon

In all these examples the Subject is the one who experiences the Process. For obvious reasons, this Participant is labelled *Senser*. That which is experienced is given the label *Phenomenon*. The examples cited all have the same Participant roles in the same order: Senser, Mental Process, Phenomenon, as demonstrated in Fig. 6.5.

| Senser | Mental Process | Phenomenon |
|--------|----------------|------------|
| He | didn't see | me. |
| I | heard | the shots. |
| I | knew | the number. |
| You | didn't want | it. |
| I | dislike | your manner. |

**Fig. 6.5**

It happens that in all these examples the Senser is realized as Subject and the Phenomenon as Complement, but this is not always the case. Firstly, even with the same verbs, a change of voice would make the Phenomenon the Subject. For stylistic and rhetorical reasons, passive counterparts of these clauses are not very plausible, at least in this context, but they are hypothetically possible. For example, *he didn't see me* has the passive counterpart *I wasn't seen by him*; and *I heard the shots* could be paraphrased as *the shots were heard by me*. This reverses the order of the Participants as seen in Fig. 6.6.

In fact, we would be more likely to come across these structures with the Senser omitted (*I wasn't seen*; *the shots were heard*) because one common

| Phenomenon | Process | Senser |
|---|---|---|
| I | wasn't seen | by him |
| The shots | were heard | by me |

**Fig. 6.6**

motivation for using the Passive Voice is that it permits us to omit certain participants. Thus it might be possible to find in a different context the clauses in Fig. 6.7.

It is largely coincidental that all the Sensers in the examples above are also realized as personal pronouns. The grammar permits nominal groups of any degree of complexity to function as Senser. Thus *he* in *He didn't see me* could be replaced with *Donald, the person I mentioned, my husband,* or many another Nominal Group, without affecting the fact that it is still Senser.

There is one constraint that you should be aware of, however. The Senser must by definition be a sentient being: a human or at least animate creature (except in metaphorical or fantastic uses). The Senser has to be animate since only animate beings (people and animals) can think, feel or perceive, though, of course, in metaphor and in fairy stories and the like such Processes may be attributed to inanimate entities. Phenomenon may be animate or inanimate.

It is not only in Passive clauses that the Phenomenon may show up as Subject. The situation worded as Example (24) I dislike your manner could be represented without too much change of meaning as Example (25).

(25)  Your manner displeases me.

Both clauses express a Mental Process, and in both we have two Participants: a Senser and a Phenomenon. One difference is that in (24) the role of Senser is realized as Subject (*I*) and the role of Phenomenon as the Complement (*your manner*), whereas in (25) the roles are reversed. Similarly, the clause *I like it* has the potential alternative *It pleases me* (*see* Fig. 6.8).

There are several pairs of verbs in English which permit rough 'parallel' representations of this type. Assuming an active voice clause, with verbs on

| Phenomenon | Process |
|---|---|
| I | wasn't seen. |
| The shots | were heard. |
| The number | was known. |
| It | wasn't wanted. |
| Your manner | was disliked. |

**Fig. 6.7**

| I | dislike | your manner. |
|---|---|---|
| I | like | it. |
| **S** | **F/P** | **C** |
| **Senser** | **Mental Process** | **Phenomenon** |

| Your manner | displeases | me. |
|---|---|---|
| It | pleases | me. |
| **S** | **F/P** | **C** |
| **Phenomenon** | **Mental Process** | **Senser** |

**Fig. 6.8**

the left the Senser is Subject and the Phenomenon is Complement; with verbs on the right the Phenomenon is Subject and the Senser is Complement:

| like | please |
|---|---|
| dislike | displease |
| enjoy | amuse, delight |
| pity | move, touch (in the emotional sense) |

### 6.4.2   Phenomenon realized as clause

One example of Phenomenon realized as a clause can be found in Example (18), *He knew what speed was*, where *he* is Senser, *knew* Process and *what speed was* is Phenomenon.

There are numerous examples of clause as Phenomenon in the source novel, usually involving the verb *know*. The fragment in Text 6B exploits *know* to breaking point.

In all these instances, the Phenomenon is realized by a full clause. This is fairly common in the type of Mental Process that involves 'knowing' (with verbs like *know, guess, suspect, deduce, calculate*).

The clause complex *He knows that Thaler came here* can be analysed as in Fig. 6.9, where it is compared with Example (18) and a simpler example.

Since the Phenomenon *that Thaler came here* is a clause in its own right, it too expresses a Process, this time a Material Process with *Thaler* as Actor.

---

Noonan knows that Thaler knows about the cheque. He knows that Thaler came here while Willson was here, but didn't get in. He knows that Thaler was hanging around the neighbourhood when Willson was shot. He knows that Thaler and a woman were seen bending over the dead man.

---

**Text 6B**    (Hammett, *Red harvest*,[1] p. 32).

| He | knows | that Thaler came here. |
|---|---|---|
| He | knew | what speed was. |
| He | knew | everything. |
| **Senser** | **Process** | **Phenomenon** |

**Fig. 6.9**

Of course, the clauses realizing Phenomenon also have their internal Process and Participant roles, as do all clauses. We will not pursue this here, but we return to such structures in Chapters 9 and 10.

## 6.5    *Relational Process*

Relational Processes are typically realized by the verb *be* or some verb of the same class (known as *copular verbs*); for example, *seem, become, appear* (as in *She appeared cheerful*) or sometimes by verbs such as *have, own, possess*. In SFPCA terms, they typically have a Subject and an Intensive Complement. The semantics of Relational Processes is very complicated, and different sets of Participant roles can be associated with different, more delicate categories of Relational Process. Out of context, it is often difficult, frequently impossible, to subclassify Relational Processes precisely.

### 6.5.1    Attributive Process

A common type of Relational Process ascribes an attribute to some entity as in (26).

(26) She was hungry again.

In Example (26) we have an Attribute (*hungry*) and a Carrier of the attribution (*she*); the Process is locally focused on *was* (past tense form of the verb *be*, the most central copular verb).

Text 6C is made up entirely of Relational Processes.

> She was in a ward on the third floor, alone. The other four beds were empty. She could have been a girl of twenty-five or a woman of fifty-five. Her face was a bloated spotty mask.

**Text 6C**    (Hammett, *Red harvest*,[1] p. 83).

These are analysed in Figure 6.10.

We find two examples of Relational Process in Example (27). Both are instances of attribution.

| Carrier | Process | Attribute |
|---|---|---|
| She | was | in a ward on the third floor. |
| The other four beds | were | empty. |
| She | could have been | a girl of twenty-five or a woman of fifty-five. |
| Her face | was | a bloated spotty mask. |

**Fig 6.10**

(27) I would rather have been cold sober, but I wasn't.

The Carrier (*I* ) and the Attribute (*cold sober*) are the same in both clauses, but in the second clause the Attribute is 'understood' instead of being explicit; that is to say, it is another instance of ellipsis: *but I wasn't [cold sober]*.

Also classed as a kind of Attributive Relational Process are certain possessive structures, such as (28).

(28) I had a little money.

Here *I* is the Carrier (Possessor) and *a little money* is the Attribute (Possessed).

Other copular verbs which appear in attributive Relational Processes include:

| | | |
|---|---|---|
| *feel* | as in | *I feel sick.* |
| *look* | as in | *He looked the picture of misery.* |
| *remain* | as in | *Kyoto remained the capital for many years.* |
| *smell* | as in | *The durian fruit smells disgusting.* |
| *sound* | as in | *You sound a little strange.* |
| *taste* | as in | *The coffee tasted delicious.* |

## 6.5.2  Identifying Process

An additional function for Relational Processes is identifying, as in Example (29). The key roles here are *Identified* and *Identifier*.

(29) Quint is his name.

Here the Participant roles are respectively *Quint* (Identifier) and *his name* (Identified). It is clear from the context that these are the functions. The speaker could have reversed the sequence without changing the functions.

(29a)  His name is Quint.

Example (29a) would be the more usual ('unmarked') order: *Identified*, *Identifier* respectively.

Since *Quint* can scarcely be anything but a personal name in English, the structure is fairly unambiguous with regard to the Participant roles. However, with a hypothetical, decontextualized sentence such as *Carpenter is his name*, we could have either a parallel structure to the real one about Quint or a reversed structure with *Carpenter* as the Identified and *his name* as Identifier (as in *Carpenter is his name not his profession*). In spoken English the intonation, as well as the context, offers clues to the roles and so the ambiguity, if any, is present only in the written form.

## **6.6**    *Verbal Process*

Speaking is certainly a kind of action, and to some extent it would not be unreasonable to treat it as Material Process. On the other hand, it has some features of Mental Process, especially if we believe that verbalization of thoughts is a kind of inner speech. A case can be made for postulating a new category of Process: *Verbal Process*.

Consider Example (30).

(30) I said: 'If there isn't, I'll have to take him down to the City Hall.'

In this example, we have the person who produces the utterance, to whom we give the self-explanatory title of *Sayer*; the Verbal Process itself, realized here as *said*; and the representation of the words actually spoken, which in this context we label *Quoted*. The function *Quoted* is realized as Direct Speech. The wording is identical to that initially uttered by the Sayer, or at least, it is presented as though it were identical.

Somewhat different from this is the Verbal Process where the words of the Sayer are transposed in line with the perspective of the speaker or writer who is reporting the speech. This involves Indirect (Reported) Speech, as in (31).

(31) I said I wanted to be dropped off somewhere in the neighbourhood of the Great Western Hotel.

Here *I* is Sayer and *I wanted to be dropped off in the vicinity of the Great Western Hotel* is *Reported*. (The Reported element itself contains clauses and so it could be further analysed in terms of Process and Participant, but we will not go into that here.)

There are various ordering possibilities with this type of Process, particularly with the direct speech form. The most neutral ('unmarked') ordering is Sayer–Process–Quoted, but we can have Sayer following Quoted, as in Example (32), or even interrupting Quoted, as in (33).

(32) 'That's nice,' the grey-moustached sleuth on my left said.
(33) 'I don't think I meant to kill him,' he repeated, 'though I took the gun with me.'

In some texts, we find the sequence Quoted–Process–Sayer as in Example (34).

(34) 'I would be staggered if the judges did not agree to a stay of the ratification process,' said Mr Martin Howe. (*Observer* 18.7.93)

In modern English, with the sequence Quoted–Process–Sayer, Sayer must be a full Nominal Group with a noun as Head (often a proper noun) and not a pronoun. Only in more old-fashioned or whimsical texts will you find Sayer realized as a pronoun in this sequence, as in Example (35), from an eighteenth-century novel.

(35) 'Hold a moment,' said she.

In addition to the Sayer and the Quoted or Reported, there is a third Participant in some of these examples: the person to whom the verbalization is addressed. In Material Process terms, this would be the Beneficiary, but since we have set up a separate system for Verbal Process, we call this Participant the *Receiver*. An example of this is *her* in (36).

(36) I asked her if she had heard him.

The typical verb for Verbal Processes is *say*, but there are many others. Probably the most important are *ask* and *tell*, for, although *say* can be used with all types of Quoted (statements, questions, orders), we need to distinguish among these when the speech is Reported. Thus, with Example (37), the author might easily have substituted *said* for *asked*.

(37) 'Where did the shots come from?' the chief asked.

However, in reported questions (indirect speech) such as (36), we cannot use the reporting verb *say*. Direct Speech equivalents of (36) include (36a) and (36b).

(36a) 'Did you hear him?' I asked (her).
(36b) 'Did you hear him?' I said (to her).

Example (36c) is not a valid option however.

(36c) *I said to her if she had heard him.

In fact, there is an additional area of meaning open to the writer/speaker who produces a Verbal Process clause, particularly one involving Quoted; this is in the choice of the lexical verb selected to encode the Verbal Process. In contradistinction to the neutral *say*, a large number of verbs can be exploited, each carrying some extra element of meaning.

Sometimes this meaning can relate to the *speech act* realized: just as we can have *ask* to indicate a question or *tell* to indicate a command, so we can use such verbs as *urge, explain, remind, challenge, beg, promise, congratulate, grumble, agree, report* to convey other subtleties of what Speech Act theorists call *illocutionary force*. All these are exploited in Quoting structures in the source novel.

Incidentally, as well as expressing a question (eliciting information), with Reported (but not normally with Quoted), *ask* can also serve to realize a request for goods or activity. In such cases the Reported often takes the infinitive form; see Example (38) (italics added).

(38)  I went to the phone and asked the girl *to send the house copper up.*

In Text 6A, we find Example (39).

(39)  'See you later,' the gambler whispered.

This typifies another kind of meaning that can be conveyed by the choice of lexical verb, a meaning connected with the nature of the actual delivery of the speech: such things as the tone, quality or volume of voice. Other examples in the same text fragment are *sneer* and *mutter* in (40) and (41).

(40)  'Fifty of us to stand off that crummy force!' he sneered.
(41)  [. . .] muttering nervously: 'Hurry it up, boys [. . .]'

From many other examples in the novel, we might mention: *lisped, growled, snarled, barked, bawled, babbled on, gasped.* Sometimes this aspect of the meaning overlaps with the illocutionary force already mentioned. For example, whereas *whisper* (in this text, at least) comments only on the voice quality, the choice of the word *sneer* tells us something of the Sayer's intention as well as of the manner of his delivery. The choice of *babble*, on the other hand, does not indicate illocutionary force, but rather, as well as commenting on the manner of delivery, conveys something of the narrator's judgement on the quality of what was being projected.

Another way of adding such extra information is by an Adjunct, as in the example *muttering nervously*, where the writer conveys more than a plain use of *saying* could achieve not only by choosing a non-neutral verb, *muttering*, but also by adding a Circumstantial Adjunct *nervously*. Adjuncts generally realize the function *Circumstance*, which is discussed below.

Finally, in this section on Verbal Process, we will mention two other potential Participants: *Verbiage* and *Target*.

The term Verbiage is used in this context to label items like *the truth* in (42).

(42)  I told her the truth.

Here the expression *the truth* represents what the Sayer said but instead of representing it as a quotation of the actual words used (Quoted) or a report of the proposition expressed in those words (Reported), it rather refers to what is said by classifying it in terms of its character as an expression. In fact, just as Sayer is a specialized form of Actor, so Verbiage is really Range within the framework of a special set of terms for Verbal Process. This can be seen more readily in such expressions as *ask a question, state your case, talk my language, speak English, tell (someone) the facts.* Verbiage can also be a clause that is not a projection of speech or thought, as in Example (43), italics added.

(43)  He told me *what I wanted to know.*

Target is a fairly peripheral Participant and does not occur with direct or indirect speech, except incidentally. It is the person or thing which is 'targeted by the process' (Halliday, 1994: p. 141), as in Example (44).

(44)  Former party officials criticized *party leadership*.

Lexical verbs often having a Target include: *describe, explain, praise, flatter, blame, condemn, castigate*.

## 6.7  *Other Processes*

Halliday classes the Processes Material, Mental and Relational as major processes and the others as minor. In addition to Verbal Process, already discussed, the minor processes include *Existential Process* and *Behavioural Process*.

Existential Process has only one Participant, the *Existent*. This type of Process has two main forms of grammatical realization. (i) With a copular verb and an empty *there* as Subject: Examples (45) and (46).

(45)  There were ten of us in the party.
(46)  There were fifty of you.

(ii) With a copular verb, the Existent as Subject and usually a Circumstantial Adjunct: Example (45a).

(45a)  Ten of us were in the party.

This looks very similar to a Relational Process, and indeed the same wording in a different context could be relational. For example, in describing a group of twenty people, half of whom were members of the Socialist Party, one might say *Ten of us were in the party* where *Ten of us* would function as Carrier and *in the party* as Attribute (compare *Ten of us were party members*; or *Ten of us were Socialists*).

When we have only the Existent without any explicit circumstance, the semantically empty Subject *there* is almost obligatory. This is not a Participant since it is simply a sort of place-holder or syntactic marker. An exception is the unusual type of structure typified by the second clause in the well-known proposition of the French philosopher, Descartes (already mentioned): *I think; therefore I am*. Similarly, *Ghosts do not exist* is a negative Existential Process: *Ghosts* (Existent) *do not exist* (Existential Process). As with most other grammatical phenomena, negation does not affect the Participant role label.

As far as clearly defined, discrete classification of Processes is concerned, the bottom of the barrel is *Behavioural Process*. This is the grey area between Material and Mental Processes. As with Existential Process only one Participant is normally required, but this one is labelled *Behaver*.

Example (47) could be a candidate for the label Behavioural Process, but it could equally be argued that it is a Material Process.

(47) [...] the car slid away.

A more straightforward example of Behavioural Process (though not a finite clause) is (48).

(48) [...] its police department number plate vanishing around a corner.

## 6.8   *Circumstance*

In the last section, we touched on the third component of the clause as representation: *Circumstance*. This is the name given (in the context of this dimension of analysis) to those elements which carry a semantic load but are neither Process (in the narrow sense) nor Participant. In some respects, Circumstances, as the name suggests, are more peripheral than Participants, being concerned with such matters as the settings, temporal and physical, the manner in which the Process is implemented, the people or other entities accompanying the process rather than directly engaged in it. Typically, the SFPCA function of Circumstance is Adjunct and the grammatical realization is adverb or prepositional phrase.

In the first clause in our main source text, the Circumstance is realized by the adverb *Presently*. This tells us something about the timing of the Process in relation to the other events described previously. In *we went down three steps into the back yard*, there are two Circumstances *down three steps* and *into the back yard*, both telling the reader about the location of the Process. In the elliptical, non-finite clause *muttering nervously: 'Hurry it up boys'*, the Circumstance is realized by the adverb *nervously*, a Circumstantial Adjunct of Manner, telling us about how the Sayer performed the Verbal Process.

In subsequent clauses, *out into the next street, into a black automobile that stood at the kerb* (and, in the embedded clause within that, *at the kerb*); *somewhere in the neighbourhood of the Great Western Hotel*; and *around a corner* are all Circumstances which give information about the spatial location of the Process. *Five minutes later* is a Circumstance concerned with location in time.

## *Summary*

In this chapter, we have dealt with the semantics of the clause: the Process and Participant, and, more briefly, the Circumstance. Processes can be sub-classified into the major ones: Material, Mental and Relational; and the minor ones: Verbal, Existential and Behavioural.

The Participants central to the various Processes are as follows.

Material:      Actor, Goal, Beneficiary, Range.
Mental:        Senser; Phenomenon.
Relational:    Carrier; (Attribute – not exactly a Participant); Identified; Identifier.
Verbal:        Sayer; Quoted/Reported (one or the other); Receiver; Verbiage, Target.
Existential:   Existent.
Behavioural:   Behaver.

The voice system (active-passive) allows us to choose among certain Participants for the Subject function. For example, in a Material process, the active voice has Actor as Subject whereas the passive voice allows Goal or Beneficiary to be Subject. Similarly, in Mental Processes, Senser and Phenomenon may alternate as potential Subject, depending on voice. Different lexical verbs (for example: *fear/frighten*) also affect the choice of Senser or Phenomenon as Subject. Passive voice also allows us to omit Participants that would be stated in the active voice; for example: Actor in Material Processes; Senser in Mental Processes.

Circumstances are typically Adjuncts, but not all Adjuncts are Circumstances. In passive voice Material Processes, for example, Actor may show up as Adjunct.

In some instances, the distinction between Participant types is very subtle, one notable case being Goal versus Range, and another the Participants in Relational Processes. Also there are some overlaps: in particular, Behavioural Process overlaps considerably with other Processes.


*Further study*

As always, the first reference for further details here is Halliday (1994: Chapter 5). In addition to more detailed treatment of the areas discussed in our chapter, Halliday outlines 'another interpretation' of transitivity and voice: the 'ergative interpretation' (1994: section 5.8), which perceives the semantics in terms of causative relations.

The classic work on this topic is to be found in Halliday's 'Notes on transitivity and theme' (1967, 1968). It is interesting to compare Halliday's account with that of Fillmore (1968), which has interesting similarities although it emerges from a very different linguistic tradition. Fillmore's account treats as a single phenomenon the two perspectives separated out by Halliday as *transitivity* and *ergativity* and deals with data from a wide range of languages.

On nominalization, raised by us in relation to Range, see Halliday's discussion of grammatical metaphor (1994: Chapter 10; also Halliday and Martin, 1993).

## *Exercises*

### *Exercise 6.1*

The following are all Material Processes. Label the Process and label Participants as Actor, Goal, or Beneficiary.

1. Neurotoxins will kill the insects.
2. A fungus destroyed the coffee plant leaves.
3. You can write him a note.
4. Sufficient water should be added.
5. A better crumb structure gives the soil more stability.
6. Standing crops can be trampled by wild animals.
7. Ignition is provided by battery, coil and distributor.
8. Remove the gudgeon pin.
9. Someone had found the fugitives a suitable hiding-place.
10. The prisoners were offered small concessions.

### *Exercise 6.2*

The following are all Mental Processes. Label Process and the Participants Senser and Phenomenon.

1. He saw the whole room.
2. Perceptual relationships were seen correctly.
3. The subject observed slight after-effects for months.
4. They were also noticed by the researcher.
5. Must we envisage the question in a purely intellectual sense?
6. Considerable discomfort may be experienced.
7. Does this explanation convince anyone?
8. The next report fascinated all of us.

The following are Mental processes with a clause in a Participant role. Label them, treating the italicized clauses as single elements.

9. We soon realized *that the planners had erred.*
10. I knew at all times *exactly what the President was doing.*

### *Exercise 6.3*

For each of the following: (a) identify the type of Process as Material, Mental, or Relational; (b) identify the Subject and assign its Participant label.

1. The side suspension arm may be removed.
2. The patient experienced the usual side-effects.
3. Hormones can be injected into animals.
4. India has a number of such dams.
5. Eight days later the outskirts of Melbourne were struck by a raging firestorm.
6. This was definitely bad news.

7. I want results.
8. Chemicals are spread on the land.
9. He absolutely hated the large formal dinners.
10. Why was he so anxious?
11. Herbivores can digest fibres.
12. People didn't like it.
13. Such a man would see enemies everywhere.
14. One of the witnesses before the committee was Nobel-winning economist Paul Samuelson.
15. I eventually fascinated reporters.
16. Hunt became a special projects man.
17. They could be rotated independently.
18. Not a sound was heard.
19. The only important risk is the moral one.
20. I remember the humorous aftermath of our first formal state banquet.

## Exercise 6.4

(a) Analyse the following examples of Verbal Processes, labelling the Process and Participants (Sayer; Quoted; Reported; Verbiage; Receiver.)
(b) Rewrite the first example (1) as direct speech and label your rewrite as in (a).
(c) Rewrite the second example (2) as reported (indirect) speech and label as in (a). Do not analyse the quoted or reported clauses.

1. He asked me if the money was traceable.
2. Dean said, 'That's the good news.'
3. Then he said, 'Can we meet again soon?'
4. Someone suggested we should do it differently.
5. The informants told the police everything.

## Exercise 6.5

Some of the following are Existential processes; some are not. (a) Identify the Existential Processes. (b) Identify the Existent in each.

1. There was little understanding of acoustics.
2. On either side of this structure are beige curtains.
3. There they heard further stories.
4. There is no ventilation.
5. There will not be many traitors.
6. There we come to a new dilemma.

## Exercise 6.6

Explain the following old joke in terms of Process and Participant.

Comedian A: My dog's got no nose.
Comedian B: Your dog's got no nose? How does he smell?
Comedian A: Terrible.

## Answers

*Exercise 6.1*

1.

| Neurotoxins | will kill | the insects. |
|---|---|---|
| **Actor** | **Process** | **Goal** |

2.

| A fungus | destroyed | the coffee plant leaves. |
|---|---|---|
| **Actor** | **Process** | **Goal** |

3.

| You | can write | him | a note. |
|---|---|---|---|
| **Actor** | **Process** | **Beneficiary** | **Goal** |

4.

| Sufficient water | should be added. |
|---|---|
| **Goal** | **Process** |

5.

| A better crumb structure | gives | the soil | more stability. |
|---|---|---|---|
| **Actor** | **Process** | **Beneficiary** | **Goal** |

6.

| Standing crops | can be trampled | by wild animals. |
|---|---|---|
| **Goal** | **Process** | **Actor** |

7.

| Ignition | is provided | by battery, coil and distributor. |
|---|---|---|
| **Goal** | **Process** | **Actor** |

8.

| Remove | the gudgeon pin. |
|---|---|
| **Process** | **Goal** |

9.

| Someone | had found | the fugitives | a suitable hiding-place. |
|---|---|---|---|
| **Actor** | **Process** | **Beneficiary** | **Goal** |

10.

| The prisoners | were offered | small concessions. |
|---|---|---|
| **Beneficiary** | **Process** | **Goal** |

*Exercise 6.2*

1.

| He | saw | the whole room. |
|---|---|---|
| **Senser** | **Process** | **Phenomenon** |

2.

| Perceptual relationships | were seen | correctly. |
|---|---|---|
| **Phenomenon** | **Process** | **Circumstance** |

3.

| The subjects | observed | slight after-effects | for months. |
|---|---|---|---|
| **Senser** | **Process** | **Phenomenon** | **Circumstance** |

4.

| They | were <also> noticed | by the researcher. |
|---|---|---|
| **Phenomenon** | **Process <Circumstance>** | **Senser** |

5.

| Must <we > envisage | the question | in a purely intellectual sense. |
|---|---|---|
| **Process <Senser>** | **Phenomenon** | **Circumstance** |

6.

| Considerable discomfort | may be experienced. |
|---|---|
| **Phenomenon** | **Process** |

7.

| Does <this explanation> convince | anyone? |
|---|---|
| **Process <Phenomenon>** | **Senser** |

8.

| The next report | fascinated | all of us. |
|---|---|---|
| **Phenomenon** | **Process** | **Senser** |

9.

| We | soon | realized | that the planners had erred. |
|---|---|---|---|
| **Senser** | **Circumstance** | **Process** | **Phenomenon** |

10.

| I | knew | at all times | exactly what the President was doing. |
|---|---|---|---|
| **Senser** | **Process** | **Circumstance** | **Phenomenon** |

*Exercise 6.3*

 1. Material. The side suspension arm: Goal.
 2. Mental. The patient: Senser.
 3. Material. Hormones: Goal.
 4. Relational. India: Carrier.
 5. Material. The outskirts of Melbourne: Goal.
 6. Relational. This: Carrier.
 7. Mental. I: Senser.
 8. Material. Chemicals: Goal.
 9. Mental. He: Senser.
10. Relational. He: Carrier.
11. Material. Herbivores: Actor.
12. Mental. People: Senser.
13. Mental. Such a man: Senser.
14. Relational. One of the witnesses before the committee: Identified.
15. Mental. I: Phenomenon.
16. Relational. Hunt: Carrier.
17. Material. They: Goal.
18. Mental. Not a sound: Phenomenon.
19. Relational. The only important risk: Identified.
20. Mental. I: Senser.

*Exercise 6.4*

1.

| He | asked | me | if the money was traceable. |
|---|---|---|---|
| **Sayer** | **Process** | **Receiver** | **Quoted** |

2.

| Dean | said, | 'That's the good news.' |
|---|---|---|
| **Sayer** | **Process** | **Quoted** |

3.

| Then | he | said, | 'Can we meet again soon?' |
|---|---|---|---|
| **Circumstance** | **Sayer** | **Process** | **Quoted** |

4.

| Someone | suggested | we should do it differently. |
|---|---|---|
| **Sayer** | **Process** | **Quoted** |

5.

| The informants | told | the police | everything. |
|---|---|---|---|
| **Sayer** | **Process** | **Receiver** | **Verbiage** |

(b)

| He | asked | me, | 'Is the money traceable?' |
|------|---------|----------|---------------------------|
| **Sayer** | **Process** | **Receiver** | **Quoted** |

Various alternative answers include (omitting the Receiver): He said, 'Is the money traceable?' It is also possible to start with the Quoted: 'Is the money traceable?' he asked/said.

(c)

| Dean | said | (that) that was the good news. |
|------|--------|-------------------------------|
| **Sayer** | **Process** | **Reported** |

Note: Other 'saying' verbs are possible, of course, including: *declared, stated, commented, conceded, pointed out, observed,* and many more. With a Receiver, we could have said, for example, *Dean told us that that was the good news.*

## Exercise 6.5

1. little understanding of acoustics.
2. beige curtains.
4. no ventilation.
5. many traitors. Note: The item *there* in the Existential processes is a dummy Subject. In 3 and 6 it is an adverb of place. 3 is a Mental Process and 6 a Material Process.

## Exercise 6.6

This is another joke based on ambiguity. Comedian B is asking about the dog's ability to smell things. In the intended meaning (the most obvious meaning) of his question, the Process is Mental and *he* (that is, the dog) is Senser. Comedian A, ignoring the relevance of the question, surprisingly interprets it as an entirely new topic concerning the odour possessed by the dog. In this reading of the question, the Process is Relational and *he* (the dog) is Carrier. Comedian A treats the verb *smell* as a copular verb.

*Comedian B's intended meaning*

| How | does <he> smell? |
|------|-------------------|
| **Circumstance** | **Mental Process <Senser>** |

*Comedian A's interpretation*

| How | does <he> smell? |
|------|-------------------|
| **Attribute** | **Relational Process <Carrier>** |

*Comedian A's answer (without ellipsis)*

| He | smells | terrible |
|---|---|---|
| **Carrier** | **Relational Process** | **Attribute** |

## Note

1.  Hammett, Dashiel 1975 (originally published by Cassell & Co. 1950): *Red harvest*. London: Pan Books.

# 7

# Structure of the Nominal Group

## 7.1   *Head and Modifier revisited*

In Chapter 2, we looked briefly at the make-up of groups. To recapitulate with new examples, let us begin by looking at Example (1).

(1)   Electricity is supplied to most homes through an underground cable.

The first Nominal Group here is *electricity*. It is made up of a single word, a noun. The noun stands alone without modification of any kind, and so we have a Nominal Group consisting of only a Head noun. This is the simplest kind of Nominal Group.

The second Nominal Group, *most homes*, is only slightly more complicated, with a Head, *homes*, and a Modifier *most*. Since the Modifier comes before the Head, we can call it a *Premodifier*.

The third, *an underground cable*, also has a Head, *cable*, and is premodified, this time by the determiner *an* and the noun *underground*.

Modification does not always precede the Head, however. Consider the first Nominal Group in Example (2):

(2)   In houses thirty or more years old it is still possible to find two or more fuse boxes.

The Nominal Group *houses thirty or more years old* has *houses* as Head and *thirty or more years old* as Modifier. Since the Modifier follows the Head this time, we can label it *Postmodifier*.

Take another example:

(3)   In modern homes the mains switch and the fuses are contained in a box called a consumer unit.

You will perhaps have identified the Nominal Groups here as *modern homes*, *the mains switch, the fuses* and *a box called a consumer unit*. The Heads are respectively *homes, switch, fuses* and *box*. The Modifiers are, in order of occurrence, *modern, the, the mains* and *called a consumer unit*, the last being a Postmodifier.

The function of Modifier can be realized by various word classes, most frequently by determiners, adjectives and numerals as Premodifier. In Example (4) with the Nominal Group *these two unusual botanical specimens*, we have a determiner followed by a numeral followed by two adjectives all serving to modify the Head, which is realized by the noun *specimens*.

(4)  These two unusual botanical specimens proved invaluable.

In Example (5) we find a prepositional phrase, *from lower socioeconomic classes*, as Modifier of the head *people*, this time a Postmodifier.

(5)  Poor health is more common in people from lower socioeconomic classes.

As we can see from the examples already given, however, the function of Modifier can often be realized by a noun (*fuse* in *fuse boxes*, *mains* in *mains switch*, and *consumer* in *consumer unit*). Common examples of noun as Modifier are found in such everyday expressions as: *art gallery, barn door, biology book, coffee cup, football field, history lesson, sports stadium, telephone number*; but they seem to be particularly characteristic of scientific and technical terminology: *accelerator pedal, animal husbandry, claw hammer, data base, land animals, input stacker, socket outlet, quantification models, systems engineering.*

The field of mechanical engineering is especially rich in expressions of this kind. In a motor-vehicle maintenance manual, we frequently find samples of three- or four-word combinations. Opening a manual at random, we can find, for example: *the castor tie rods, the crownwheel centre line, the distributor clamp plate, the distributor drive shaft, the cylinder head bolts, stub axle bearings*, as well as the occasional four-item term (not counting the determiner), such as *the scuttle panel grille sealing*, and occasionally even longer items like *the timing chain tensioner cylinder retaining bolts*.

The problem of deciding what exactly constitutes a word creeps in at this point. The terms just listed are the names of specific identifiable items in a motor-car engine. One might argue that these are, in effect, unanalysable terms like *wheel* or *brake*; it just happens that in English we write them as separate words. In the text where we found these terms, *crownwheel* is written as one word though it clearly combines the two elements *crown* and *wheel*. This might have been written as two words just as *clutch plate* or *drive shaft* are in the same manual. It is obviously the case that it is sometimes difficult to draw a hard and fast line between words and groups of more than one word. This difficulty is reflected in the orthographic uncertainty in written English about whether to write *word processor, wordprocessor* or *wordprocessor*; *ball game, ball-game* or *ballgame*; and so on. We shall not pursue this particular conundrum, but, as far as convenient, we shall continue to treat items as words on the basis of whether they are written as separate items.

The scope of these modifiers is not always predictable from their form. We often have to fall back on specialist knowledge to interpret the items. Is *the cylinder head gasket*, for example, *the gasket* relating to *the cylinder head* or *the head gasket* relating to the *cylinder?* Or doesn't that distinction mean anything? Without some knowledge of internal combustion engines, we might be at a loss for answers, though a thoughtful examination of the rest of the text in which the nominal occurs usually helps. In fact, in this case, it is the first interpretation that is right, and, once we are aware of that, we can see that there is a hierarchical relationship in which *cylinder* modifies *head* and *cylinder head* modifies *gasket*.

## 7.2   *Logical and Experiential functions*

In the Nominal Group *these two new light switches*, the items *these, two, new* and *light* are all classed as Modifiers in relation to the Head *switches*, and are to that extent functionally similar. However, it is fairly obvious that, from other points of view, they need to be considered as significantly different from each other. One way in which they differ is in the sorts of things they say about the switches, or in Hallidayan terms, in their *Experiential* function.

The Ideational function can be divided into two functions: *Logical* and *Experiential*. Head and Modifier fall within the Logical function. We will continue by considering the Experiential function within the Nominal Group.

### 7.2.1   Deictic

The function of the word *these* is, in a manner of speaking, to point out, and the label we give to such items is *Deictic*, a term derived from the Greek for *pointing*. In Nominal Groups, the Deictic function is realized by determiners: for example, demonstratives *this, that, these* and *those*, and also by the article *the*, which Halliday identifies as a weak form of demonstrative. In such cases the function is fairly literally one of 'pointing', but, as always with technical terms of this kind, the label must not be taken too literally. Deictics can also be possessive nouns or pronouns: for example, *Sony's* in *Sony's latest model*; *your* in *your home*. Further, they can be nonspecific items such as the indefinite article *a/an, some, each, every, neither, both, all*.

### 7.2.2   Numerative

The item *two* is a *Numerative*. Numeratives can be realized by numerals such as *two* or *second* (in *the second switch*) or by such expressions as *many, several, few*, and *lots of*. In Example (2), the electricity manual data discussed above, we have *two or more fuse boxes*, where *two or more* functions as Numerative.

## 7.2.3   Classifier and Epithet

The items *new* and *light* (in *these two new light switches*) realize two other functions: *Epithet* and *Classifier*. The function of a Classifier is to put the modified item into a subclass of such items: for example, in *bus station* the Classifier *bus* puts the item *station* in a subclass of stations, distinguishing it from *railway station* (or *train station*), or more broadly from such items as *petrol station* (or *gas station*); *supply* in *supply cable* distinguishes the type of cable from other types, and the same is true of *fuse* in *fuse box*. These are Classifiers. Hence, in *these two new light switches*, we can label *light* as Classifier. (Note: this is not the adjective *light* relating to weight, colour or brightness as in *a light load* or *a light colour* but the noun *light*.)

If we speak of the *noisy station, a new cable* or *the wrong box*, the items *noisy*, *new* and *wrong*, though they may help to define the scope of the terms *station*, *cable* and *box* respectively, do not identify a subcategory of stations or cables in the same sense that *railway* or *supply* or *fuse* do. The Classifier identifies a subclass: *bus* in *a bus station* pinpoints a feature that is distinctive and classificatory. However, *noisy* or *new* indicate features or characteristics of the station that do not put it into a subset of types of station; they just tell us something about the characteristics of this particular station. Hence our decision to find a different label, and the label used is Epithet. Thus, *new* in *these two new light switches* is Epithet.

Out of context, many expressions are ambiguous with regard to this functional distinction between Classifier and Epithet. Take the nominal group *some dancing girls*, for example. This string of words can be used to refer to some girls who earn their living by dancing (*dancing* as Classifier) or some girls who happen to be in the process of dancing (*dancing* as Epithet). In the motor-vehicle maintenance text already referred to, we find examples that are grammatically comparable to the first sense of *dancing girls*, but not the second, in such terms as *retaining bolts*. Here *retaining* realizes the function Classifier; retaining bolts are bolts which have the permanent task of retaining, that is, holding something in place. Compare from the same source: *blanking pieces, cooling system, connecting rod, locking disc, steering axis.*

An example from a less specialized register is the well-known 'ambiguous' Nominal Group, *a Spanish teacher*. Where this means a teacher who has Spanish nationality, *Spanish* is Epithet; but where it means a teacher of Spanish, *Spanish* is Classifier. In the first sense, we are speaking about a teacher who has the characteristic or quality of being Spanish; in the second, we refer to a teacher belonging to a subclass of teachers, namely Spanish (language) teachers, as distinct from science teachers, mathematics teachers, and so on.

Of course, when such 'ambiguous' expressions occur in real utterances, there is rarely any confusion about meaning. The context usually provides sufficient information to make it clear what is intended. Furthermore, in spoken English, the distinction between Epithet and Classifier is often reflected by differences in intonation.

Incidentally, there is a further grammatical distinction between the two meanings of the word *Spanish* in these two different uses. In the Epithet instance, *Spanish* is an adjective; in the Classifier instance, *Spanish* is a noun (the name of the language). As we have already said, however, the adjective versus noun distinction does not necessarily correspond to that of Epithet versus Classifier. Indeed, in our previous example *some dancing girls*, the item *dancing* is a form of verb in both the Classifier and the Epithet uses. Adjectives can certainly function as Classifiers: *electric* in *electric light, electric cable, electric shock*, for example; or *fast* in *fast food*.

In so far as there is a simple criterion for distinguishing Epithet from Classifier, it is that the structure with Epithet can normally be paraphrased as a clause with *be*, for example, *the switches are new*, whereas the Classifier cannot – *the switches are light* has no connection with light switches in this sense. *The teacher is Spanish* can only apply to the Epithet reading of *the Spanish teacher* and not to the Classifier reading. As is often the case, though, the test is not absolutely watertight.

### 7.2.4 Thing

In *these two new light switches*, the main item with regard to the experiential function is *switches*. This rejoices in the undistinguished name of *Thing*. This is the experiential label that Halliday's grammar assigns, and the usual warning applies against taking technical terms too literally. In this sense, Thing may be a material inanimate thing, an animal, a person, a substance or even an abstract concept. It is simply the name given to one of the six possible functions that occur in the structure of the Nominal Group. It specifies the class of the thing referred to. Classifier, as we have said, specifies the subclass. This is why, as we have said, it is sometimes difficult to say whether certain combinations should be treated as one word or two; for example, *word processor* Classifier + Thing or *wordprocessor* Thing. The label Thing applies not only to the inanimate noun *cable* in *supply cable*, but equally to the animate *girls* in *some dancing girls* or *teacher* in *a Spanish teacher*, as well as the abstract noun *wizardry* in *statistical wizardry* or *beliefs* in *eighth-century religious beliefs*.

### 7.2.5 Qualifier

The sixth function in the nominal group is *Qualifier*. This is the experiential label for the Postmodifier in, for example, *the electrical resistance of the insulation*, where *resistance* is Thing, and *of the insulation* is Qualifier. We can say that Qualifier conflates with Postmodifier.

Very frequently in English, the Qualifier function is realized as a prepositional phrase (as in all but one of the Qualifiers in Fig. 7.1). In *The Wind in the Willows*, the Thing is *Wind* and the Qualifier is *in the Willows*; in *the square on the hypotenuse*, the Thing is *square* and *on the hypotenuse* is Qualifier. Further examples of Nominal Groups containing prepositional phrases as Qualifiers are as follows (the Thing is printed in bold and the Qualifier is in italics): a **fire** *with an under-floor air supply*, the **packing** *between the hearth and the surround*, a **light** *over the front door*, the **polarity** *throughout the wiring*.

By far the most frequent preposition in Qualifiers is *of*. For example: the centre **line** *of the crownwheel*, **adjustment** *of the bearings*, **rotation** of *the differential*, an **area** *of up to 20 square metres*, the most economical **use** *of cable*.

This usage is by no means restricted to technical texts, as witness: a **bill** of sale, the **king** *of France*, the **story** *of Tina*, the probable **owner** *of the car*, the **capital** *of Romania*, the **price** *of coal*.

Fig. 7.1 represents a number of Nominal Groups analysed for experiential and logical functions.

| Premodifier | | | | Head | Postmodifier |
|---|---|---|---|---|---|
| Deictic | Num. | Epithet | Classifier | Thing | Qualifier |
| these | two | new | light | switches | |
| the | two | regular | domestic | flights | available |
| the | many | large | oil | companies | in operation |
| the | first 128 | standard | ASCII | characters | in common |
| | several | dirty | | ones | |
| the | | complete | | dismantling | of the gearbox |
| the | | | keyboard | layouts | |
| a | | careful | | study | of this matter |
| an | | effective | prediction | scheme | |

**Fig. 7.1**

Prepositional phrases in Nominal Groups are an instance of *embedding*, where one structure is, as it were, enclosed in another; in this instance the embedded element is the prepositional phrase. In Chapter 8, we look at another form of embedding within the Nominal Group, namely that of the clause.

### 7.3   *Postmodifier/Qualifier versus Adjunct*

A prepositional phrase has two major roles: as Postmodifier/Qualifier in a Nominal Group and as Adjunct in a clause. In Example (6) the prepositional phrase with *for* is a Postmodifier; in Example (7) the prepositional phrase with *for* is an Adjunct.

(6) Nearby is Chendor Beach, a popular nesting ground *for the giant leatherback turtles.*

(7) [...] a section of the road is closed from 7.00 pm to midnight *for the Saturday Night Market.*

In (6) the Nominal Group *a popular nesting ground for the giant leatherback turtles* is in apposition to the proper noun *Chendor Beach.* The ideational make-up is in Fig. 7.2.

| a | popular | nesting | ground | for the giant leatherback turtles |
|---|---|---|---|---|
| **Premodifier** | | | **Head** | **Postmodifier** |
| **Deictic** | **Epithet** | **Classifier** | **Thing** | **Qualifier** |

**Fig 7.2**

However, in (7) the prepositional phrase is operating at a different rank. Instead of being an embedded element in a Nominal Group, it realizes a function at the rank of clause, namely Adjunct. It provides information about the Circumstance of the Process. It does not postmodify *midnight.*

In Example (7) we have further examples of prepositional phrases both as Postmodifier (*of the road*) and as Adjunct (*from 7.00 pm to midnight*).

A crude test for distinguishing between Adjunct and Postmodifier depends on the fact that usually the Adjunct can readily be moved whereas the Postmodifier cannot. Hence, (6a) is not a possible paraphrase of (6) but (7a) is a paraphrase of (7).

(6a) *For the giant leatherbacked turtles* nearby is Chendor Beach, a popular nesting ground.

(7a) *For the Saturday Night Market,* a section of the road is closed from 7.00 pm to midnight.

Sometimes ambiguities can arise as a result of these two potential functions for the prepositional phrase. Indeed this type of ambiguity has been a favoured example for those grammarians who are preoccupied with such matters. Examples like (8) (an invented example) are often adduced to illustrate this point.

(8) Michael reads books on trains.

On one interpretation, we have as Complement of the clause a Nominal Group *books on trains,* where *books* is Head and *on trains* is Postmodifier (paraphrasable as *books about trains*). On the other interpretation, we have as Complement a Nominal Group consisting of an unmodified Head *books* and a Circumstantial Adjunct *on trains,* which tells us about the location of the process. We can represent this as in Fig. 7.3.

| Michael | reads | books on trains. |
|---------|-------|------------------|
|         |       | Head [Postmodifier] |
| **S** | **F/P** | **C** |

| Michael | reads | books | on trains. |
|---------|-------|-------|-----------|
| **S** | **F/P** | **C** | **A** |

**Fig. 7.3**

Sometimes this structural ambiguity exists but without any significant practical effect.

   (9)  Malaysia Airlines (MAS), the national carrier, operates an extensive network of domestic routes within the country.

Whether we interpret *within the country* as Postmodifier of *routes* or as a Circumstantial Adjunct telling us where MAS operates the routes has no significant effect on our understanding of the situation.

## 7.4   *Recursion*

We have said that a prepositional phrase is composed of a Preposition Group and a Nominal Group. The Preposition Group is usually a simple preposition, that is to say an unmodified Head, though it can be modified. With maximal information, the Nominal Group *the square on the hypotenuse* can be represented in tree diagram form as in Fig. 7.4 on p. 143.

It frequently happens that a prepositional phrase postmodifying a Head noun in a Nominal Group contains within itself another prepositional phrase postmodifying a Head noun, as in *the solution to the problem of inflation*. This is a Nominal Group with the noun *solution* as Head. The Postmodifier is the prepositional phrase *to the problem of inflation*. The preposition here is *to* and the Nominal Group is *the problem of inflation*. This Nominal Group (*the problem of inflation*) is also analysable in the same terms: the Head is the noun *problem* and the Postmodifier is the prepositional phrase *of inflation*. This prepositional phrase can in turn be analysed into preposition *of* and Nominal Group *inflation*. Represented as a tree diagram (omitting the Experiential labels) this gives Fig. 7.5 (*see* p. 144).

Sometimes the embedding goes beyond the two levels seen in the previous example. In (10), there are three stages of embedding.

   (10)  It proved to be the first of many steps on the road to ruin.

In this example, the Complement of *be* is the Nominal Group *the first of many steps on the road to ruin*. Using brackets [ ] to show the prepositional phrase boundaries, the Nominal Group in question can be represented as (10a):

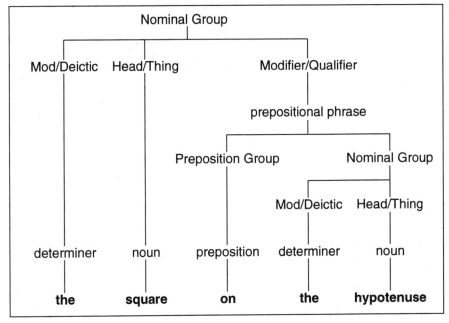

**Fig. 7.4**

(10a)  the first [of many steps [on the road [to ruin]]]

This can be represented in tree diagram form with relevant labelling (*see* Fig. 7.6 on p. 145).

## 7.5   *Paratactic Nominal Group complexes*

Sometimes two or more groups are combined as a single constituent to jointly fulfil a function such as Subject or Complement. We discussed an example of one such structure in Chapter 3, curtailed and renumbered here as (11) and italics added.

(11)  The night before Easter Sunday, 1920, *Otto Loewi, an Austrian physiologist*, awoke in the night [. . .]

At that point we contented ourselves with describing *an Austrian physiologist* as a Nominal Group in apposition to *Otto Loewi* and pointing out that the whole bundle realized the function of Subject. This implies that these two Nominal Groups are in some sense a single item, a super-Nominal Group, as it were. The term we use for this type of combination is a *paratactic group complex*. (Parataxis involves the linking of equal elements and is discussed further in Chapter 9.)

A paratactic group complex can also be formed by explicitly linking two

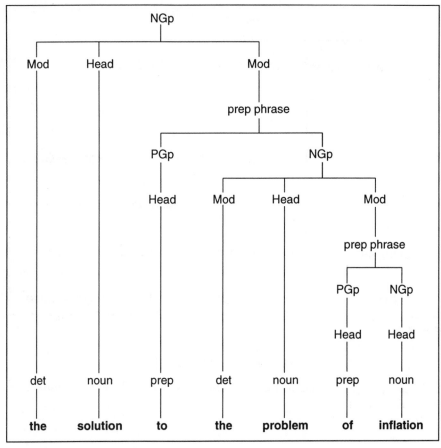

**Fig. 7.5**

or more groups together with a binding conjunction (*and, or*). Example (12) provides three instances of this.

> (12)  For lunch and dinner, plain or specially prepared rice is often eaten with side dishes of delicious chicken curry, 'rendang' and a variety of others.

In (12), *lunch and dinner* constitute a Nominal Group Complex in a prepositional phrase as Adjunct; *plain or specially prepared rice* realizes the function of Subject, and in *delicious chicken curry, 'rendang' and a variety of others*, three Nominal Groups make up a complex in a prepositional phrase.

In Halliday's model, groups with adjective as Head are classed as Nominal Groups; there is no such construct as an Adjectival Group. Not all Systemic Functional linguists accept this point, but we are not going to debate it here. Thus a group complex like those italicized in (13), and even (14) and (15), is classed as a Nominal Group Complex. (Of course, adjectives realizing Modifier are not groups of any kind but only dependent elements in the Nominal Group.)

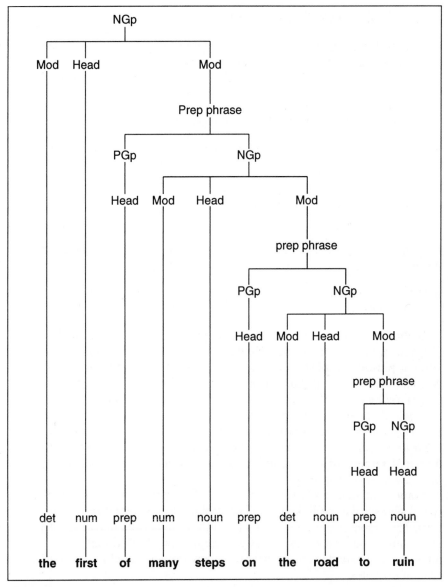

**Fig. 7.6**

(13) Such publicity positioned Chang as the surgeon chosen by Australia's *richest and most famous*.

(14) My position in this debate is *enthusiastic, cautious and sceptical*.

(15) Exhortations to the public to avoid heart disease by exercise, avoiding smoking, and making dietary changes are *banal, dull, often depersonalized, and frequently tinged with moralism and puritanism*.

## **7.6**   *Other kinds of group complex*

Although this chapter is about the Nominal Group, it is worth mentioning here that complexes exist in groups other than Nominal. For example, (16) contains an Adverbial Group Complex (italics added) realizing the function of Adjunct.

> (16) The affected eye should be bathed *regularly and carefully*.

Example (17) has a Verbal Group Complex, and (18) Preposition Group Complexes.

> (17) He neither *seeks nor assumes* formal leadership.
> (18) *Up and down* the City Road
>      *In and out of* the Eagle [. . .]

Prepositional phrases (which it must be remembered are not classed as groups in Halliday's model) can also form complexes as in (19).

> (19) He decided that *with no children of his own and with no position on the staff of a major hospital* his ideas might not outlive him.

Note that linked Nominal Groups in a prepositional phrase (i.e., with a single preposition) are examples of a Nominal Group Complex and not of a prepositional phrase complex. See, for example, (12) above, which contains two Nominal Group Complexes in prepositional phrases: *for lunch and dinner* and *of delicious chicken curry, 'rendang' and a variety of others*. A preposition which takes a Nominal Group Complex to complete the phrase is *between*: for example, *between the dark and the daylight, between Scylla and Charybdis, between the devil and the deep blue sea*. It can also take a simple Nominal Group, of course, for example *between them, between the lines, between the two extremes*.

Somewhat awkwardly for the neatness of the grammatical model, prepositional phrases can be linked with Adverbial Groups to realize Adjunct as in (20). They have in common the fact that they could each independently realize Adjunct, but the grammar assigns them crucially different labels: group and phrase. There does not appear to be any obvious label for this particular type of complex.

> (20) Data are often presented *partially and without proper analysis*.

A different kind of Verbal Group Complex (*hypotactic* not *paratactic*: see Chapter 9) is found with verbs such as *want, like, start, continue, pretend*, which combine with other verbs within a single clause as in (21).

> (21) She *began to practise medicine* on her own in a small way.

We return briefly to such structures in Chapter 10.

## Summary

In this chapter, we have looked in some detail at the Nominal Group. After recapitulating the Logical structure of the Head-Modifier analysis, we moved on to outline the Experiential functions that are realized in the Nominal Group: Deictic, Numerative, Epithet, Classifier, Thing and Qualifier. Qualifier and Postmodifier conflate; they are frequently realized by a prepositional phrase. A prepositional phrase may have another prepositional phrase embedded within it (as Postmodifer/Qualifier of the Nominal Group) and this phenomenon can be repeated. Groups can be combined as paratactic group complexes by linking or by apposition.

## Further study

### Head

In *Introduction to Functional Grammar*, Halliday has a detailed discussion of the relation between Thing and Head. Although these two usually conflate there are exceptions. In elliptical constructions elements other than Thing can be Head; for example: Epithet: She took the *yellow* and left the *white*. Numerative: The *second* is more interesting. Deictic: *This* is my story. However, Halliday discusses examples of mismatch between Thing and Head even when Thing is present (1994: section 6.2.6).

### Prepositional phrases with 'of'

We mentioned that *of* is the most frequently occurring preposition in English. This information comes from Sinclair (1991), who calculates that *of* occurs more than twice as often as any other preposition. Sinclair's observations, which are based on a massive collection of English text, the Cobuild corpus, challenge some of the standard grammatical descriptions. As we have seen, prepositional phrases realize two main functions: Adjunct in a clause and Postmodifier/Qualifier in a Nominal group. Sinclair points out that it is generally assumed that the most typical (that is, frequent) function of prepositional phrases as a whole is as Adjunct, and for most prepositions (*in*, *on*, *up* and so on) this is true. However, he notes that although *of* does, like other prepositions, show up with this function (for example: 'convict these people *of negligence*'), such occurrences are relatively rare, and the overwhelming majority of phrases with *of* are Postmodifiers. He also notes that, unlike most prepositions, *of* has no basic spatial sense (of direction or position); compare *up*, *on*, *in*, *over*, *under*. On grounds of distribution and typicality, Sinclair goes on to suggest that perhaps *of* should not be classified as a preposition at all, but belongs to a class of its own. To date, this position has not gained widespread acceptance, but the argument is a powerful one.

## Exercises

### Exercise 7.1

Analyse the italicized Nominal Groups in the following examples in terms of the experiential functions: Deictic, Numerative, Epithet, Classifier, Thing and Qualifier.

1. *The three red wires* will have been joined in *one terminal.*
2. *Car factories* produce *millions of cheap vehicles.*
3. *Domestic manufacture of goods* underwent *several significant changes.*
4. *Rapid, extensive technical development* replaced *older concerns.*
5. *The disastrous slump* was caused by *three unforeseen factors.*
6. There has been *much economic dislocation.*
7. *The available financial statistics* do not support *the many optimistic claims made.*
8. *The first dam on the Indus* was completed in 1932.
9. *This vast forested river basin* extends over some 700 million hectares.
10. *A broken brake cable* can easily be repaired.

### Exercise 7.2

Label the italicized prepositional phrases in the following examples as either Postmodifier in a Nominal Group or as Adjunct.

1. Hit the new pin *with a hammer.*
2. Jung also rejected his view *of childhood amnesia.*
3. Kandinsky took great pains to elucidate his artistic system *in theoretical terms.*
4. The genes located along a DNA module are present *at all times.*
5. His approach *to this action* was based on two basic dominant ideas.
6. The downturn was caused by over-investment, the result of imperfections *in the investment process.*
7. They were tired of the woman *with the handbag.*
8. Don't come *between me and my work.*
9. The distinction *between factives and nonfactives* is significant for prediction.
10. You can take a horse *to water,* but you can't make him drink.

### Exercise 7.3

Identify the group complexes (and prepositional phrase complexes) in the following and label them according to type (Nominal Group Complex, Verbal Group Complex, etc.)

1. In this sense, there is no past and no future.
2. He failed utterly and completely.
3. This may be a result of pay or poor working conditions.

4. Low carbohydrate diets and low protein diets are especially detrimental.
5. I neither criticise nor condone this behaviour.
6. Equally exciting is Chinese New Year, a major festival.
7. Attach the frame above and below the aperture.
8. The money went on the payment of debts and as gifts to relatives.
9. It seemed to shrink and grow alternately.
10. I want an answer here and now.

*Exercise 7.4*

Read the fragment in Text 7A from a Do-It-Yourself manual and answer the questions which follow it.

---

**Window Choices**
Replacement windows and patio doors can be timber (softwood or hard-wood), aluminium or plastic (unplasticized polyvinyl chloride – uPVC). All are available made-to-measure to fit exactly into an existing opening, but wooden made-to-measure windows are less easy to come by than aluminium and uPVC ones.

---

**Text 7A**   (*Which? Book of home improvements and extensions*[1]).

1. List all the Nominal Groups in the first sentence.
2. In two places the writer has used brackets to separate a Nominal Group from another Nominal Group. How do you interpret the bracketed group in relation to the other one?
3. Comment in general on the Group Complexes in the first sentence.
4. How do you perceive the relation between *unplasticized polyvinyl chloride* and *uPVC*.
5. In the first sentence of the text, the author introduces the types of materials that can be used for replacement windows and patio doors. Later in the text, he uses the names of these materials as Classifiers. Identify all the Classifiers in the text and indicate which are introduced (as Thing) in the first sentence.
6. From your reading of Chapter 5 you will know that *ones* is a substitution. Comment on the way it functions in this text.

**Answers**

*Exercise 7.1*

1.

| The | three | red | wires | | one | terminal |
|---|---|---|---|---|---|---|
| Deictic | Numerative | Epithet | Thing | | Numerative | Thing |

2.

| Car | factories |
|---|---|
| Classifier | Thing |

| millions of | cheap | vehicles |
|---|---|---|
| Numerative | Epithet | Thing |

3.

| Domestic | manufacture | of goods |
|---|---|---|
| Classifier | Thing | Qualifier |

| several | significant | changes |
|---|---|---|
| Numerative | Epithet | Thing |

4.

| Rapid, | extensive | technical | development |
|---|---|---|---|
| Epithet | Epithet | Classifier | Thing |

| older | concerns |
|---|---|
| Epithet | Thing |

5.

| The | disastrous | slump |
|---|---|---|
| Deictic | Epithet | Thing |

| three | unforeseen | factors |
|---|---|---|
| Numerative | Epithet | Thing |

6.

| much | economic | dislocation |
|---|---|---|
| Numerative | Classifier | Thing |

7.

| The | available | financial | statistics |
|---|---|---|---|
| Deictic | Epithet | Classifier | Thing |

| the | many | optimistic | claims | made |
|---|---|---|---|---|
| Deictic | Numerative | Epithet | Thing | Qualifier |

8.

| The | first | dam | on the Indus |
|---|---|---|---|
| Deictic | Numerative | Thing | Qualifier |

| the | Indus |
|---|---|
| Deictic | Thing |

9.

| This | vast | forested | river | basin |
|---|---|---|---|---|
| Deictic | Epithet | Epithet | Classifier | Thing |

10.

| A | broken | brake | cable |
|---|---|---|---|
| Deictic | Epithet | Classifier | Thing |

*Exercise 7.2*

1. Adjunct. 2. Postmodifier. 3. Adjunct. 4. Adjunct. 5. Postmodifier.
6. Postmodifier. 7. Postmodifier. 8. Adjunct. 9. Postmodifier. 10. Adjunct.

*Exercise 7.3*

1. no past and no future: Nominal Group Complex.
2. utterly and completely: Adverbial Group Complex.
3. pay or poor working conditions: Nominal Group Complex.
4. Low carbohydrate diets and low protein diets: Nominal Group Complex.
5. criticise nor condone: Verbal Group Complex.
6. Chinese New Year, a major festival: Nominal Group Complex.
7. above and below: Prepositional Group Complex.
8. on the payment of debts and as gifts to relatives: prepositional phrase complex.
9. seemed to shrink and grow: Verbal Group Complex.
10. here and now: Adverbial Group Complex.

*Exercise 7.4*

All except 1 are open questions and the answers given here are only suggestions.

1. Replacement windows; patio doors; timber; softwood; hardwood; aluminium; plastic; unplasticized polyvinyl chloride; uPVC.
2. In *timber (softwood or hardwood)* the linked Nominal Groups in brackets form a Complex; they expand on the meaning of *timber* by specifying that it can be of either type; timber must be either softwood or hardwood. In *plastic (unplasticized polyvinyl chloride – uPVC)* the bracketed pair of Nominal Groups similarly expand on the meaning of *plastic* by specifying the type of plastic in question. *Plastic* is a superordinate, general term and *unplasticized polyvinyl chloride* is both a specialized (as used by specialists in the field) and more specific term (a hyponym of *plastic*).
3. The Subject function is realized by a paratactic Nominal Group Complex *replacement windows and patio doors*. The Complement is realized by a paratactic Nominal Group Complex *timber (softwood or hardwood), aluminium or plastic (unplasticized polyvinyl chloride – uPVC)*. This is a particularly complicated Group Complex because it contains complexes within it. That is to say it is possible to identify a hierarchy of groupings within it. *Softwood and hardwood* form a complex which immediately combines with *timber*. *uPVC* forms a complex with *unplasticized polyvinyl chloride* and together they combine with *plastic*. Together with *aluminium* (the only simple Group) they all form a larger complex realizing Complement.
4. uPVC forms a complex with *unplasticized polyvinyl chloride*. It expands

on *unplasticized polyvinyl chloride* by offering an alternative (abbreviated) name. It could have been bracketed but it seems that, as the whole complex is in brackets, the author decided to use a dash to avoid confusion.

5. *Wooden*, made-to-measure, *aluminium*, *uPVC*. (Italicized items introduced in the first sentence; *wooden* only obliquely.)

6. The preceding clause suggests that *ones* is a substitution for *made-to-measure windows* rather than just *windows*. *Aluminium* and *uPVC ones are* two distinct groups though linked in a complex; *aluminium* and *uPVC* are not joint Modifiers of *ones* because they are mutually exclusive so aluminium must be Classifier as Head.

## Note

1.  Thomas, Jill and Holloway, David (eds) 1983: *Which? Book of home improvements and extensions.* London: Consumers' Association and Hodder & Stoughton.

# 8

# Rankshifted clauses

## 8.1   *Rankshifted clause as Postmodifier/Qualifier*

In Chapter 7 we looked at some forms of modification of the Head in Nominal Groups (and, briefly, other groups). In this chapter we consider, among other things, the way in which clauses can fulfil a similar function. In Example (1) the function of Qualifier/Postmodifier is realized by a clause (italics added).

(1)  The main supply cable goes to a sealed unit *that holds the service fuse.*

What we see here, then, is a clause which is functioning as part of a Nominal Group within another clause. This is a further example of *embedding* (discussed in Chapter 7 in connection with prepositional phrases). In systemic terminology it is also known as *rankshift* because, in terms of the rank scale (see Chapter 1), an item of one rank (clause) is being used as the whole or part of an item of a lower rank (group). *That holds the service fuse* retains its intrinsic qualities as a clause (with its own SFPCA functions), but it is simultaneously a Postmodifier in a Nominal Group inside another clause.

We call the clause which is inside another clause the *embedded* (or *rankshifted*) clause.
We call the clause which contains the embedded clause the *superordinate* clause.

In (1), then, the Nominal Group containing the relative is *a sealed unit that holds the service fuse.* This is presented in (1a) with the rankshifted clause in italics and the Head noun in bold print:

(1a)  a sealed **unit** *that holds the service fuse.*

When we look at it from the Experiential point of view, in the Nominal Group (1a) the italicized clause functions as Qualifier of the Thing *unit.* In terms of the Logical function, it is Postmodifier of the Head *unit.* Because, in this particular case, it is part of a constituent of another clause, it can be treated in this way (as in Fig. 8.1) as though it were a simple element in that clause without regard to its internal structure.

| a | sealed | unit | that holds the service fuse |
|---|---|---|---|
| **Deictic** | **Epithet** | **Thing** | **Qualifier** |
| **Premodifier** | | **Head** | **Postmodifier** |

**Fig. 8.1**

Ignoring any further subtleties, an analysis of the superordinate clause in terms of SFPCA is shown in Fig. 8.2. However, because the Adjunct contains a Nominal Group whose Postmodifier is also a clause, this clause too can be analysed in terms of the criteria we have just applied to the superordinate clause. Without regard to the fact that it functions as part of another clause, it can be examined in terms of its own SFPCA structure, or other characteristics, and the groups within it can be analysed in terms of their own structures.

| The main supply cable | goes | to a sealed unit that holds the service fuse. |
|---|---|---|
| **S** | **F/P** | **A** |

**Fig. 8.2**

An analysis of the embedded clause in (1) gives us the following labelling:

[[that | holds | the service fuse]]
[[ S | **F/P** |     C      ]]

Putting the two together in one diagram, we have Fig. 8.3. (The use of double square brackets [[ ]] enclosing a clause is a convention symbolizing a rankshifted clause.)

What we have done here is first analyse the superordinate clause in terms of its functions, represented on the third line of Fig. 8.3. We then shift to a more delicate stage of analysis (second line of the figure) to analyse the rankshifted clause embedded within the Nominal Group.

Let us now look at another example.

(2) The circuit should be tested with some device which reliably indicates the presence of mains voltage.

Here, the rankshifted clause is (2a):

| The main supply cable | goes | to a sealed unit | [[that | holds | the service fuse.]] |
|---|---|---|---|---|---|
| | | | [[ S | F/P | C          ]] |
| **S** | **F/P** | **A** | | | |

**Fig. 8.3**

(2a)  which reliably indicates the presence of mains voltage

In analysing for clause structure, Example (2), like the first example, needs to be treated as having two strata, as indicated in Fig. 8.4, where the labelling of the superordinate clause is represented on the third and sixth lines and the labelling of the embedded clause is represented on the fifth line of the figure.

| The circuit | | should | | be tested | | with some device | |
|---|---|---|---|---|---|---|---|
| | | | | | | | |
| S | | F | | P | | A ... | |
| [[which | reliably | | indicates | | the presence of mains voltage.]] | | |
| [[ S | A | | F/P | | C | | ]] |
| *A continued* | | | | | | | |

**Fig. 8.4**

Analysed for its experiential and logical structure, the Nominal Group *some device which reliably indicates the presence of mains voltage* can be represented as in Fig. 8.5.

| some | device | which reliably indicates the presence of mains voltage |
|---|---|---|
| **Deictic** | **Thing** | **Qualifier** |
| **Premodifier** | **Head** | **Postmodifier** |

**Fig. 8.5**

## 8.2    *The defining relative clause*

All the rankshifted clauses discussed so far are known as *defining relative clauses* (also known as *restrictive relative clauses*). Full defining relative clauses contain a *relative pronoun*. This may be a Wh-pronoun (*who, whom, which, whose, where, when*), or it may be *that*. In some relative clauses, however, the relative pronoun can be omitted entirely, and sometimes other elements are omitted to give what some linguists call a *reduced relative clause*. (A different type of relative clause, called a nondefining – or nonrestrictive – relative, is discussed in Chapter 9.)

Two significant considerations in the grammar of relative clauses are: the grammatical function of the group in which the clause is embedded; and the grammatical function of the relative pronoun inside the embedded clause itself.

Any common noun, and some pronouns, in English can be modified by a defining relative clause. The Nominal Group which contains the relative clause may realize any function normally open to Nominal Groups: for example, it may be Subject, Direct Object Complement, Intensive Complement, part of an Adjunct or part of a prepositional phrase functioning as Modifier in a Nominal Group. In Examples (3), (4), (5) and (6), the Nominal Group containing the relative clause is italicized and its grammatical function given in parentheses; the relative clause itself is enclosed in double brackets.

(3) *Any circuit* [[*that is to be worked on*]] must be dead. (Subject)
(4) Soil variations greatly affect *the plants* [[*which can be grown*]]. (Direct Object Complement)
(5) The circuit should be tested with *some device* [[*which reliably indicates the presence of mains voltage*]]. (Complement of preposition in an Adjunct)
(6) It's *a job* [[*that can be done all in one go*]]. (Intensive Complement)

More significantly, perhaps, within the relative clause, the relative pronoun can realize any of the functions open to a Nominal Group. In the previous examples, although the Nominal Groups containing the relative clause have different functions, the relative pronoun is the Subject of the rankshifted clause in every example. It does not always have to be so, however.

In Examples (7), (8), (9) and (10) the relative clause is in double brackets and the relative pronoun is in italics; the function in parentheses is that of the relative pronoun within the rankshifted clause:

(7)  The men [[*who* founded modern science]] had two merits. (Subject)
(8)  Suddenly, the work [[*that* the Greeks had done from pure love of theory]] became the key to warfare and astronomy. (Direct Object Complement)
(9)  In 1900, de Vries finally brought out the book [[in *which* he put forward his 'mutation theory']]. (Complement of preposition in Adjunct)
(10) It is most passionate in those [[*whose* lives are most exposed to catastrophe]]. (Possessive Premodifier of Head in Subject)

In (10) the Nominal Group *whose lives* is Subject of the relative clause, but the relative pronoun itself, *whose*, is Modifier, not Head of its group.

This is not the complete range of possible functions for the relative pronoun, but it gives some idea of the possibilities. The relative pronoun can itself function as Adjunct (realized as *where* or *when*). In (11) the relative clause is bracketed and the relative pronoun italicized.

(11) I remember those first days [[*when* Kissinger was in the White House]].

In a nonrelative clause the function of the Direct Object Complement is usually signalled by its position in the clause. The relative clause in Example (8) corresponds to the (constructed) nonrelative clause (8a).

(8a) The Greeks had done the work from pure love of theory.

In (8a) the Direct Object Complement is in its normal place after the Predicator. When this same proposition is expressed as a relative clause, as in the actual example, (8), the relative pronoun *that* comes at the beginning of the clause even though it is the Complement: *that the Greeks had done from pure love of theory*. The requirement for the Object Complement to follow the Predicator is overridden by the requirement that wh-words and *that* come at the beginning of the clause. Of course, there are other reasons why we do not always place the Complement after the Predicator as we have indicated in the discussion of Theme and Rheme in Chapter 4, and it is arguably for thematic reasons that the relative or interrogative pronoun always comes first in its clause.

In sentences of this kind, some languages (unlike English) permit a pronoun in the Complement position as well as the relative marker at the beginning. This is why we sometimes find foreign speakers of English saying (or, in this case, more probably writing) such things as (12).

(12) *The work that the Greeks had done *it* from pure love of theory became the key to warfare and astronomy.

To speakers of such languages, English seems to miss out a crucial element. English teachers who condemn this error as 'illogical' are mistaken. True, there is a kind of logic in the omission, but the inclusion is no less logical. To understand this is not, of course, to recommend the practice.


**8.3** *Omitted relative pronoun*

Even more tricky for the foreign learner is the relative clause which omits the relative pronoun entirely (but without any further ellipsis). We cannot omit the relative pronouns from Examples (13) and (14).

(13) The men [[ *who* founded modern science]] had two merits [. . .]
(14) Here they met the woman [[ *whose* ideas were to change their lives]].

However, instead of writing (8) (repeated below), the author (Bertrand Russell) could, if he wished, within the options offered by English grammar, have written (8b).

(8) Suddenly, the work [[*that* the Greeks had done from pure love of theory]] became the key to warfare and astronomy.
(8b) Suddenly, the work [[the Greeks had done from pure love of theory]] became the key to warfare and astronomy.

In fact, in Example (15) (brackets added), the same author did take this zero-pronoun option when he chose to write:

(15) Socrates was guilty of not worshipping the gods [[the State worshipped]].

Similar examples (brackets added) from our other sources are (16) and (17).

(16) The nerves [[we have just discussed]] are efferent nerves.
(17) The sorts of improvements [[you might want to make to an existing system]] include adding sockets, installing fixed equipment and re-organizing lighting.

Here there is no relative pronoun *which* or *that*, but the meaning is the same as if *which* or *that* had been included. Such clauses are often called *contact clauses*. Writers often take this option, but when speaking (as opposed to writing), people are more likely to omit the relative pronoun where the grammar permits than to include it. The following example is from a recording of a group discussion in a hospital.

> (18)  Is there anything else [[you'd like to do]] – before you go on to order any barium investigations?

In the exercises at the end of this chapter, you are asked to think about the *grammatical* limits to the possibility of omitting the relative pronoun.

## 8.4   *Relative with preposition*

We now return to an example that we discussed earlier, Example (9), repeated here.

> (9)  In 1900, de Vries finally brought out the book in which he put forward his 'mutation theory'.

In this example, the relative pronoun *which* is the complement of the preposition *in* in a prepositional phrase functioning as Adjunct. The corresponding nonrelative clause would be: *he put forward his 'mutation theory' in the book.*

In principle, the grammar permits four choices here. One is the choice that the author made, where the preposition is placed before the relative pronoun. The others, which he did not choose, are as follows.

> (9a)  In 1900, de Vries finally brought out the book [[*which* he put forward his 'mutation theory' in]].
>
> (9b)  In 1900, de Vries finally brought out the book [[*that* he put forward his 'mutation theory' in]].
>
> (9c)  In 1900, de Vries finally brought out the book [[he put forward his 'mutation theory' in]].

In fact, it is an oversimplification to suggest that the author had all these possibilities open to him. In practice, the one that he chose is most likely because it is the preferred option for text in a formal register. So, although the grammar contains all these possibilities, stylistic norms tend to determine which one is chosen. All the choices are available to the language user, but statistically there are strong preferences according to the kind of text.

In another register, for example, in informal, spoken text, the push might well be in the direction of one of the other possible forms, for example, in the following utterances (from transcripts of classroom discourse by Sinclair and Coulthard, 1975: pp. 67, 71).

> (19)  Can you think of anything [[that they would be put on]]?

(20) [...] further along up the road [[you're driving on]] there are some work-men.

This time, stylistic norms push the teacher who made these utterances away from the formal options (*on which they would be put* and *on which you're driving*) towards the less formal choices. (This happens even though class-room discourse is far from being the most informal of registers.)

In fact, the most significant stylistic choice here is between the preposition occurring at the beginning and the preposition occurring at the end. The dif-ference between keeping and omitting the relative pronoun is less striking, and both occur in this discourse.

It must be borne in mind that the criteria for stylistic choices are subtle and that crude generalizations are dangerous. There may be good reasons why in specific instances the chosen form might not correspond with the spoken/written, formal/informal dichotomy suggested here. For example, in casual conversation the more formal option may be selected for humorous effect. Also, there are constructions which militate against the fronted prepo-sition option even in formal registers; hence, the well-known story that, when reprimanded for ending his written sentences with prepositions, Churchill (or some other wit) satirically replied: 'This is the kind of pedantry *up with which I will not put* ...'. There is, of course, no basis for the prescriptive view that 'fronted' prepositions are preferable in all circumstances. In fact, 'with which I will not put up' would avoid the final preposition shibboleth with less comic effect since *up* is not a preposition here, but it is a fair point.

When we speak of the omission of the relative pronoun or 'fronting' of prepositions, these are only convenient metaphors to facilitate discussion of varying but related structures. Some linguists have suggested in the past that relative structures without relative pronouns are best explained as structures resulting from so-called 'deletion transformations' operating on underlying forms which do contain nominals (see the section on Chomsky in Chapter 12); this gives a sort of precedence to the so-called full relative form. Similarly, the alternation between a preposition at the front or at the end of the clause can be described as a movement from one position to the other. Although in this book we use such terms as 'omission' and 'fronted', the terms are used loosely and metaphorically and there is no suggestion intended of any such transformational account. In Systemic Functional Grammar, the various structures discussed are seen rather as the outcome of choices open to the language user.

## 8.5  *Non-finite relative clauses*

In the previous chapter, we considered an example which we renumber here as (21). The Nominal Group *a box called a consumer unit* can be analysed as in Fig. 8.6.

| a | box | called a consumer unit |
|---|---|---|
| **Deictic** | **Thing** | **Qualifier** |
| **Premodifier** | **Head** | **Postmodifier** |

**Fig. 8.6**

(21) In modern homes the mains switch and the fuses are contained in a box called a consumer unit.

In discussing this earlier, we avoided discussing one way in which it differs from the other examples we were considering. This difference centres on the fact that the Postmodifier/Qualifier *called a consumer unit* is itself a clause, for, although it lacks the functions Subject and Finite, it does contain a Predicator (realized by the non-finite Verbal Group *called*) and a Complement (realized by the Nominal Group *a consumer unit*). This is represented in Fig. 8.7.

The term *reduced relative* is widely used for such structures, that is for non-finite clauses which have the same function as 'full' relative clauses. Note that this is not the same as a contact clause, where only the relative pronoun is omitted. Examples (22) to (26) are further illustrations of non-finite relatives. As before, the Nominal Group containing the relative clause is in italics and the relative clause is enclosed in double brackets.

(22) Hot water taps draw their water from *a pipe* [[*connected to the top of the hot water cylinder*]].
(23) *Most of the arguments* [[*presented in favour of this position*]] had little impact [. . .]
(24) *All pipes* [[*drawing water from a cold water cistern*]] should be fitted with a stop valve.
(25) Take off *the circlip* [[*holding the shaft control lever*]].
(26) [. . .] fit a new oil seal into *the clutch housing* [[*protecting the oil seal lip*]].

In these examples, then, the italicized structures have no Subject or Finite but they are clauses nevertheless: non-finite clauses. There is an obvious systematic relationship here to clauses with a relative pronoun as Subject and a

| In modern homes | the mains switch and the fuses | | | are |
|---|---|---|---|---|
| | | | | |
| **A** | **S** | | | **F** |
| contained | in a box | [[called | a consumer unit]]. | |
| | | [[ P | C | ]] |
| **P** | **A** | | | |

**Fig. 8.7**

Finite *be*. Try inserting *that is/are/was/were* at the start of each of the five relative clauses above. In some cases, you find a neat fit, and in others the result is a little clumsy; but roughly speaking there is a correspondence.

Analysed in SFPCA terms, these clauses, lacking S and F, are *moodless*, but they all have Predicators, three have Adjuncts and two have Complements. Since the missing Subject would be the relative pronoun in a corresponding full relative clause, obviously there is no relative pronoun present. Otherwise, they are just like 'full' relative clauses and, as with full relatives, they function as Postmodifiers in Nominal Groups.

## **8.6**   *Recursion revisited: multiple embedding of clauses*

In Chapter 7 we saw how prepositional phrases can repeatedly recur one within another. This is the phenomenon of *recursion* in grammar. The examples we analysed there were of Nominal Group within prepositional phrase within Nominal Group. When this recurs repeatedly, we have *multiple embedding*.

This phenomenon of repeated recursion can also happen with relative clauses, and, as with prepositional phrases, this may in principle be repeated indefinitely, though in naturally occurring text it is fairly limited, of course. Example (27) has two stages of rankshifted clause, a relative clause within a relative clause.

(27) This is [. . .] a process by which changes in expenditure lead to changes in income which lead to further changes in expenditure.

In Example (27) everything after the word *is* realizes the Complement, but this contains a rankshifted clause modifying the Head noun *process*, and this in turn contains a further rankshifted clause modifying *changes in income*. This gives us the bracketing in (27a) or, with SFPCA labels, the diagram in Fig. 8.8.

(27a) a process [[by which changes in expenditure lead to changes in income [[which lead to further changes in expenditure]] ]].

Another way in which more than one rankshifted clause can be embedded in the same clause is by embedding two or more linked clauses. The first example below, (28), contains two linked 'full' relative clauses; the second, (29), contains two linked moodless clauses ('reduced' relatives) (italics and brackets added).

(28) This presents Plato's ideal of *a man* [[*who is both wise and good in the highest degree*]] [[ *and who is totally without fear of death*]].
(29) *A radial circuit* [[*run in 2.5mm² cable*]] [[*and protected by a 20A fuse*]] can · supply an area of up to 20 square metres.

Sometimes, we find two linked relative clauses with only one relative pronoun, as in Example (30).

| This | is | a process | [[by which | changes in expenditure | lead |
|------|-----|-----------|-----------|-------------------------|------|
|  |  |  |  |  |  |
|  |  |  | [[    A | S | F/P |
| S | F | C | | | |
| to changes in income | [[which | lead | to further changes in expenditure]] ]]. | | |
|  | [[ S | F/P | A | | ]] |
|  |  | A | | | ]] |
| C continued | | | | | |

**Fig. 8.8**

(30) but *cables* [[*that run through insulation*]] [[*or run next to one another for a considerable distance*]] should be bigger.

Occasionally, we find complicated combinations of linking and embedding as in Example (31).

(31) A technological leader has to engage in expensive research and development activities which may lead nowhere, or which may lead to new inventions which have to be protected through patents [. . .]

Here we have two relative clauses linked by *or*:

(i) *which may lead nowhere*
(ii) *which may lead to new inventions which have to be protected through patents* [. . .]

Within the second clause is a further embedding:

(iii) *which have to be protected through patents*.

Clauses (i) and (ii) jointly postmodify the Head *activities*, and clause (iii) postmodifies *inventions*. The embedding here can be represented by bracketing as in (31a).

(31a) expensive research and development activities [[which may lead nowhere]], [[or which may lead to new inventions [[which have to be protected through patents]] ]]. . . .

Children's games and folk literature often exploit such characteristics of the language, pushing structures beyond normal limits. This happens in the folk poem 'This is the house that Jack built', where each successive step builds on the previous one by converting part of the previous utterance into a relative clause postmodifying a new Head:

This is the house that Jack built. (1 embedded clause)
This is the malt that lay in the house that Jack built. (2)

This is the rat that ate the malt that lay in the house that Jack built. (3)
This is the cat that killed the rat that ate the malt that lay in the house that Jack built (4)
and so on . . . and on . . . and on.

## 8.7  *Rankshifted clause as Subject or Complement*

The examples of rankshift that we have looked at so far are clauses as Postmodifiers in a Nominal Group. It is also possible for a rankshifted clause to stand in for the whole of a Nominal Group as Subject of a clause. Example (32) contains two parallel specimens.

(32) [. . .] what is beautiful is also, in some respects, ugly; what is just is, in some respects, unjust.

Before we get down to the rankshifted element, we can identify in each of the two superordinate clauses a fairly straightforward attributive clause on the pattern <X is Y> plus one or two Adjuncts:

(i) [something] is [. . .] ugly;
(ii)[something] is [. . .] unjust.

In a different text, the constituents here represented as [something] might be realized by such Nominal Groups as, for example, (i) *the picture* (ii) *this law*. This suggests that whatever fills that slot can be construed, in some sense at least, as a Nominal Group since it fulfils one of the potentials of a Nominal Group: that of realizing the Subject function. Also in each of these two parallel clauses, however, this Subject is itself a clause with a full clause structure. Thus the analysis is as in Fig. 8.9. (Double vertical lines ‖ indicate a clause boundary without rankshift.)

Once again, we have analysed the superordinate clause (represented here two lines below the text), and then, at a greater degree of delicacy, we have broken down the Subject into its own clause structure (represented as the line

| [[what | is | beautiful]] | is | also | in some respects | ugly ‖ |
|---|---|---|---|---|---|---|
| [[ S | F | C | ]] | | | |
| S | | | F | A | A | C |
| [[what | is | just ]] | is | in some respects | | unjust. |
| [[ S | F | C ]] | | | | |
| S | | | F | A | | C |

**Fig. 8.9**

immediately below the text). Apart from the additional Adjunct in the first, the two have identical structure: in both, the embedded clause (the rankshifted clause) is the Subject of the superordinate clause; in both embedded clauses, the Subject is the pronoun *what* (meaning *that which*).

Another example of a rankshifted clause as Subject is Example (33) analysed in Fig. 8.10.

(33)  That Aristotle appealed to such principles is not surprising.

The word *that* looks at first glance as if it might be the relative pronoun that we find in a sentence analysed earlier as Example (1), repeated here.

(1)  The main supply cable goes to a sealed unit *that* holds the service fuse.

However, a closer examination reveals that, whereas the word *that* in Example (1) is a crucial part of the rankshifted clause (the Subject, no less), the item *that* in the 'Aristotle' sentence (33) has no such function. Indeed, it is not part of the SFPCA structure of the clause at all, but rather has a textual function akin to that of a binding conjunction. It signals the rankshifted nature of the clause but is not a Participant and has no SFPCA

| [[That | Aristotle | appealed | to such principles]] | | is | not | surprising. |
|---|---|---|---|---|---|---|---|
| [[ | S | F/P | A | ]] | | | |
| | | | S | | F | A | C |

Fig. 8.10

function. In other words, it has no 'content'; it does not refer to any person, thing, or concept; it is not a Nominal Group or any other kind of group. Some people call this second type of *that* a *complementizer*. (It should not be confused with the SFPCA function of Complement.) When *that* is a relative pronoun, it can be paraphrased by *who, whom* or *which*; the complementizer *that* has no such correspondence. We return to structures of this kind in Chapter 10.

As well as functioning as Subject, rankshifted clauses can also function as Complement as in Example (34), analysed in Fig. 8.11.

(34)  They took what they wanted.

| They | took | [[what | they | wanted]]. |
|---|---|---|---|---|
| | | [[ C | S | F/P  ]] |
| S | F/P | C | | |

Fig. 8.11

## 8.8  Non-finite clauses as Subject or Complement

Just as rankshifted non-finite clauses can realize the Qualifier/Postmodifier functions, they also realize the Subject or Complement function, as in the following examples. Again, the rankshifted clauses are presented in double brackets.

(35)  [[Cutting plaster]] is not difficult.
(36)  You will enjoy [[meeting your fellow members]].
(37)  [[To err]] is human; [[to forgive]] divine.

An SFPCA analysis of these three gives us Fig. 8.12.

Example (37), a well-known quotation from the eighteenth-century English poet Alexander Pope, offers two examples of a minimal rankshifted clause consisting of only a Predicator. The second non-rankshifted clause *to forgive divine* is unusual in that it possesses a Subject and Complement, but no Finite or Predicator. This is possible because the presence of the preceding clause with its similar structure permits the ellipsis (omission) of the Finite in the second clause. Traditional grammarians would say that in the second clause *is* is 'understood'. In fact, it is so well understood that the line is often misquoted as: *To err is human; to forgive is divine.*

| [[Cutting | plaster]] | is not | difficult. |
|-----------|-----------|--------|------------|
| [[   P    |    C   ]] |        |            |
| S         |           | F      | C          |

| You | will | enjoy | [[meeting | your fellow members]] |
|-----|------|-------|-----------|------------------------|
|     |      |       | [[   P    | C                  ]] |
| S   | F    | P     | C                                  |

| [[To err]] | is | human; ‖ | [[to forgive]] | divine. |
|------------|----|----------|----------------|---------|
| [[  P   ]] |    |          | [[  P     ]]   |         |
| S          | F  | C ‖      | S              | C       |

**Fig. 8.12**

## 8.9  Extraposition

The utterance analysed above as Example (33), repeated here, originally occurred in a written text, a history of biological scientific discovery.

(33)  That Aristotle appealed to such principles is not surprising.

Imagine a scenario where you are engaged in high-flown philosophical chat with a friend; or, if you find that difficult to imagine, pretend that you are participating in a philosophy seminar in which a spontaneous discussion of a paper on Aristotle is taking place. It is possible that you might come up with the utterance (33) as quoted. However, it is more likely that you would say (33a):

(33a)  It isn't surprising that Aristotle appealed to such principles.

There is no significant difference in the ideational content of these two utterances, yet stylistically they differ considerably. The first typically belongs to a register at the formal end of the formality cline, whereas the second is nearer the informal end. There are also implications for Theme-Rheme and Given-New assignment (*see* Chapter 4). What is going on here syntactically?

Instead of being placed in the unmarked position for Subject, the rankshifted clause *that Aristotle appealed to such principles* is placed at the end, but, because English requires an explicit Subject in full declarative clauses, the so-called 'empty' pronoun *it* stands in, as it were, and holds the fort until the real information about the Subject comes along in the shape of the rankshifted clause. In Chapter 3, we referred to this as a 'dummy subject', on the grounds that although it functions in some sense as a Subject, it has no content and is merely a grammatical place-holder.

In this, it differs from the personal pronoun *it*, which normally co-refers with some Nominal Group in the text (providing a cohesive tie) or refers exophorically to some referent outside the text, as in Examples (38), (39), and (40) (italics added).

(38)  [. . .] there is a unity in the world, but *it* is a unity resulting from diversity.
(39)  Remove the lower suspension arm hinge pin by withdrawing *it* towards the front of the vehicle.
(40)  Is *it* a bird? Is *it* a plane?

In the first two examples, *it* refers to some item mentioned in the text, namely *a unity* and *the lower suspension arm hinge pin*, respectively. In the third, presumably, *it* refers exophorically to some object in the sky, visible to speaker and hearer.

The structure with the 'dummy' *it* in Subject position and the rankshifted clause placed later is often known as *extraposition*, on the grounds that the rankshifted clause is 'extra-posed' (literally 'placed outside'). It may also be described as *postposition* on the grounds that it is 'placed after'. As we said in Chapter 3, this structure is analysed as a discontinuous Subject starting with *it* and continuing with the rankshifted clause. Hence we have the analysis in Fig. 8.13.

Thus, Pope might have written *It is human to err; it is divine to forgive*, though, if anyone had suggested it, as a poet of some distinction, he would no doubt have rejected the idea since it would hardly have met the strict require-

| It | isn't | surprising | [[that | Aristotle | appealed | to such principles]] | |
|---|---|---|---|---|---|---|---|
| | | | [[ | S | F/P | A | ]] |
| S .. | < F | C | Subject continued | | | | |

**Fig. 8.13**

ments of his metre, and the conciseness and thematic force of the original would have been lost.

As we have already said, we must be wary of crude generalizations about register. It is true that the use of the rankshifted clause without extraposition is more typical of formal written language and the extraposed version is more typical of informal spoken language, but these are tendencies and not absolutes. It is perhaps more common to find extraposed Subject clauses in formal language than to find the non-extraposed form in casual speech. Although it seems grammatically less straightforward than its counterpart, the extraposed form is much more frequent in English and is found in a wider range of registers. In the wrong context, the structure without extraposition can easily sound stilted. The length of the Subject clause is also a factor: other things being equal, the longer and more complicated the clause, the more likely it is to be extraposed.

Non-finite rankshifted clauses can be extraposed as in Examples (41) to (43).

(41) *It* is difficult *to disentangle them.*
(42) *It* is impossible *to say how far.*
(43) *It* is important *to keep all hose clips tight and occasionally to inspect the hoses.*

Example (43) has two linked clauses in the extraposition: (i) *to keep all hose clips tight*; (ii) *and occasionally to inspect the hoses.* (*See* Chapter 9 for further discussion of such structures.)

In spite of their similar appearance, infinitival clauses of this kind should be distinguished from infinitival clauses which have the meaning 'in order to [. . .]', as in Example (44) (italics added).

(44) Follow the same procedure *to shorten an old chain.*

Clauses of this last type are analysed quite differently (*see* Chapter 9).

This does not exhaust our discussion of rankshifted clauses in Nominal Groups, but we return to the topic in Chapter 9 where we contrast certain types of rankshifted clause with dependent clauses.

## 8.10   *Other rankshifted clauses*

Some adjectives systematically permit clause embedding:

*ready* [[*to die for the cause*]]
*quick* [[*to reply*]]
*eager* [[*to help*]]
*able* [[*to concede the point*]]
*glad* [[*to oblige*]]
*happy* [[*to be of service*]]

Recall that groups with adjectives realizing Head are classed by Halliday as Nominal Groups (*see* Chapter 7).

However, rankshifted clauses do not operate only as part of or in place of Nominal Groups. Rankshifted clauses can be embedded in comparative Adverbial Groups, such as:

*more easily* [[*than anyone had imagined*]]
*faster* [[*than any of his rivals could manage*]]

and also in:

*as thoroughly* [[*as time permits*]]
*as fast* [[*as you can*]]

We also find rankshifted clauses postmodifying adverbs premodified by *too* or *so*:

*too cleverly* [[*for anyone to imitate*]]
*too hot* [[*to handle*]]
*too young* [[*to really be in love*]]
*so clever* [[*that you hate him*]]
*so sad* [[*that I cried*]]
*so soon* [[*that no one was ready*]]

Comparative adjectives and adjectives premodified by *too* and *so* may be similarly postmodified.

## Summary

In this chapter we follow up the issue of the structure of the Nominal Group (and, briefly, of other groups) by examining the phenomenon of rankshifted clauses. The function of Qualifier, which usually corresponds to the Postmodifier in Head-Modifier terms, is often realized by a prepositional phrase (*see* Chapter 7) or a rankshifted clause. A rankshifted clause is one which is used as a unit of lower rank or part of such a unit; it is also referred to as an embedded clause.

In the case of defining relative clauses, the rankshifted clause functions ideationally as Qualifier and Postmodifier within a Nominal Group, and as such can be treated as a simple constituent of the group. However, because it is a clause, it has the elements of clause structure within itself, and can be analysed as a clause in its own right. The relative pronouns (*that, who/m, which, whose, where* and *when*) may be omitted in certain circumstances to give a 'contact clause'. Also, relative clauses may be non-finite (that is, moodless, lacking Subject and Finite), in which case they may be known as 'reduced relatives'.

Multiple embedding (as well as linking) can occur in rankshifted clauses (as in prepositional phrases) and permutations of embedded prepositional phrases, relative clauses and linking may occur.

Rankshifted clauses can occur as Subject or Complement; these too can be finite or non-finite. Subject clauses can occur straightforwardly in the normal Subject position or they may be discontinuous with a dummy pronoun *it* holding the usual Subject position and the rankshifted clause 'extraposed' to a later position. The choice between these alternatives has implications for thematic meaning and there are also considerations of register.

Finally, we list some examples of rankshifted clauses embedded in Adverbial Groups.

## Further study

In this chapter, we mentioned 'The house that Jack built'. This is a great favourite not only of countless generations of children but also of introductory linguistics books. It can be used to demonstrate among other things that this potential for recursion is unlimited so long as it is 'right-branching' (the term relates to tree-diagram constituent analysis). That is to say, we can go on adding items at the end. Inserting a clause inside a clause which is inside another clause is more difficult. In Example (45) from a philosophy journal, three levels of embedding occur but only one is not right-branching: *what is communicated in an utterance*.

(45) No one disputes that there are various ways in which what is communicated in an utterance can go beyond sentence meaning.

The inserted brackets in (45a) indicate the embedding. We have numbered the pairs of brackets to show which belongs with which.

(45a) No one disputes [[₁that there are various ways [[₂in which [[₃what is communicated in an utterance]]₃ can go beyond sentence meaning.]]₂ ]]₁

Clause no. 1 is Complement of the superordinate clause, clause no. 2 is a defining relative clause postmodifying *ways*, and clause no. 3 is Subject of clause no. 2. The limits on centrally embedding can be shown by the difficulty of processing (45b), a hypothetical paraphrase of (45).

(45b) No one disputes [[₁that various ways [[₂in which [[₃what is communicated in an utterance]]₃ can go beyond sentence meaning]]₂ exist.]]₁

## Exercises

### Exercise 8.1

Identify the Qualifiers in the following examples and label them as prepositional phrase (PP), defining relative clause (rel), or 'other'.

1. a result of this discovery
2. an emphasis on re-investment
3. the problem that must be addressed
4. domestic consumption of grain
5. any routes open
6. pens in hand
7. the quest for oil
8. a nation which is self-reliant
9. the funding available
10. conditions they cannot operate in

### Exercise 8.2

Identify the relative clauses in the following examples and label them as
'full', 'contact' or 'reduced'.

1. This is an area where livestock grazing predominates.
2. Settlements linked by a network of narrow roads lack certain advantages.
3. These trucks resemble the monsters now destroying our highways.
4. The dedication they bring to the work pays dividends.
5. Accept this in the spirit in which it is intended.

### Exercise 8.3

Analyse the examples in Exercise 8.2 in terms of the clause functions
SFPCA, indicating rankshifted clauses in the usual way.

### Exercise 8.4

Analyse the following in terms of clause functions (SFPCA), indicating
rankshift:

*These are men who always serve the faction that is in power.*

### Exercise 8.5

1. Analyse the following for SFPCA, indicating rankshift.
    (a) *It is clear that there is always a difference.*
    (b) *That she had an appointment is easily verifiable.*

1(a) without extraposition of the Subject clause, and rewrite 1(b) with extraposition.

*Exercise 8.6*

1. Try to specify when you *cannot* omit the relative pronoun. One way of proceeding would be to collect a sample of sentences containing relative clauses with and without a relative pronoun, and analyse them.
2. Using a similar procedure, try to determine the grammatical conditions when a wh-relative pronoun is possible but *that*-relative is not.

## Answers

*Exercise 8.1*

1. of this discovery: PP
2. on re-investment: PP
3. that must be addressed: rel
4. of grain: PP
5. open: other
6. in hand: PP
7. for oil: PP
8. which is self-reliant: rel
9. available: other
10. they cannot operate in: rel

*Exercise 8.2*

1. where livestock grazing predominates: full.
2. linked by a network of narrow roads: reduced.
3. now destroying our highways: reduced.
4. they bring to the work: contact.
5. in which it is intended: full.

*Exercise 8.3*

1.

| This | is | an area | [[where | livestock grazing | predominates]]. |
|------|----|---------|---------|-------------------|-----------------|
|      |    |         | [[ A    | S                 | F/P          ]] |
| S    | F  | C       |         |                   |                 |

2.

| Settlements | [[linked | by a network of narrow roads]] | lack | certain advantages. |
|---|---|---|---|---|
| | [[ P | A | ]] | |
| S | | | F/P | C |

3.

| These trucks | resemble | the monsters | [[now | destroying | our highways.]] |
|---|---|---|---|---|---|
| | | | [[ A | P | C ]] |
| S | F/P | | C | | |

4.

| The dedication | [[they | bring | to the work]] | pays | dividends. |
|---|---|---|---|---|
| | [[ S | F/P | A ]] | | |
| S | | | | F/P | C |

5.

| Accept | this | in the spirit | [[in which | it | is | intended]]. |
|---|---|---|---|---|---|---|
| | | | [[ A | S | F | P ]] |
| P | C | | A | | | |

*Exercise 8.4*

| These | are | men | [[who | always | serve | the faction | [[that | is | in power]].]] |
|---|---|---|---|---|---|---|---|---|---|
| | | | | | | | [[ S | F | C ]] |
| | | [[ S | A | F/P | | C | | ]] |
| S | F | | | | C | | | | |

*Exercise 8.5*

1(a)

| It | is | clear | [[that | there | is | always | a difference]] |
|---|---|---|---|---|---|---|---|
| | | | [[ | S | F | A | C ]] |
| S | < F | C > | | S continued | | | |

1(b)

| [[That | she | had | an appointment]] | is | easily | verifiable. |
|---|---|---|---|---|---|---|
| [[ | S | F | C ]] | | | |
| S | | | | F | A | C |

2(a) That there is always a difference is clear.
2(b) It is easily verifiable that she had an appointment.

*Exercise 8.6*

1. The relative pronoun cannot be omitted:
   (i)   when it is the Subject of the relative clause;
   (ii)  in prepositional phrase relatives, when the preposition comes at the beginning  of the relative clause;
   (iii) when it is possessive *whose*;
   (iv)  when it is *where*.

   With regard to (i), the grammar permits:

   > This   is   the   man   [[*that*   she   married]].   (Relative   pronoun   as Complement.)

   OR:

   > This is the man [[^ she married]].

   and also:

   > This the man [[*that* married her]]. (Relative pronoun as Subject.)

   but NOT:

   > *This is the man [[^ married her]].

   With regard to (ii), the grammar permits:

   > the road [[^ you're driving on]]
   > the road [[on *which* you're driving]]

   but NOT:

   > *the road [[on ^ you're driving]].

   Or, to look at it from the opposite direction, if we omit the relative pronoun when it is Complement of a preposition, the preposition has to be at the end, not the beginning, of the relative clause.

   With regard to (iii) the grammar permits:

   > the woman [[whose research was so influential]]

   but NOT:

   > the woman [[^ research was so influential]]

   With regard to (iv), the grammar permits:

   > the street [[where you live]]

   but NOT:

   > the street [[^ you live]]

   Note: ^ indicates an omitted relative pronoun and * indicates an ungrammatical form.

2. *that*-relative cannot occur after a preposition.

The grammar permits:

the house which she lives in
the house in which she lives
the house that she lives in

but NOT:

*the house in that she lives.

It is possible to make a connection between the constraints on the occurrence of *that* and the omission of the relative pronoun.

# 9

# Clause complexes: expansion

## 9.1  *Ways of combining clauses*

In Chapter 8, we mentioned the folk 'poem' – or word-game –'The house that Jack built'. This plays on the recursive potential of defining relative clauses, which are rankshifted clauses functioning as Postmodifier/Qualifier in a Nominal Group. In such instances, one clause is embedded within another as part of that other's constituent structure.

There are, essentially, two further ways in which sentences can incorporate more than one clause. The first involves simply linking the clauses together on an equal footing, as in Example (1) below. The second involves binding one clause to another in a dependency relationship, where one clause is, in a manner of speaking, 'higher' than the other, as in (2).

(1) We are here 6,000 feet above the sea, and the equatorial sunshine is immensely hot and bright.

° (2) [...] the Blue Nile grows steadily wider and warmer as it advances at a slower pace into the desert [...]

Where clauses are joined together in either of these ways, we have a *clause complex*.

## 9.2  *'Equal' clauses*

When young children tell stories, they make heavy use of the conjunction *and*. This is perhaps the most basic way of combining clauses, and here too the potential is exploited in oral folk literature, where the device is used repeatedly to produce an interminable sentence.

In one such story, a cruel king with an insatiable appetite for stories offers marriage to any girl whose storytelling can make him say, 'Enough!' As is usual in such tales, the price for failure is death. The astute young woman who wins this implausible competition achieves her goal by adding identical clauses to each other:

... and a locust came and took away another grain of corn, and another locust came and took away another grain of corn, and another locust came and took away another grain of corn. . . .

Obviously, it would not take long for even the most enthusiastic listener to reach satiation point with such a story. Small wonder that the king in the story admitted defeat. In narratives composed by young children, where no humour is intended, the clauses linked together in this way are not usually identical repetitions, but the effect can be almost as monotonous if repeated too often.

Nevertheless, used with more discretion, this means of combining clauses is extremely common even in the most sophisticated writing, as shown by the first example in this chapter, Example (1) (from a popular history book), or the following text fragment (from a motor-car manual).

> (3) Lever the rear of the gearbox/transmission unit over towards the exhaust pipe and free the lefthand drive shaft from the sunwheel. Push the unit in the opposite direction and free the other drive shaft.

This text features two clause complexes. Each is in the imperative mood and consequently has no Subject. They are analysed as in Fig. 9.1. The SFPCA labels are also given. Since conjunctions do not play an integral role in the SFPCA functions, they are unlabelled here. (Double vertical lines (||) indicate a clause boundary. Triple vertical lines (|||) represent a clause complex boundary.)

Apart from the fact that the last clause has no Adjunct, these four clauses are virtually identical in structure. The author might have chosen to present them as four separate sentences, but no doubt there were good reasons for linking the two pairs in this way. In terms of the real world activity referred to here, the second proposition (*free the lefthand drive shaft from the sun-*

| |||Lever | the rear of the gearbox/transmission unit | over towards the exhaust pipe |
|---|---|---|
| |||  P | C | A |
| 1 ||||

| || and | free | the lefthand drive shaft | from the sunwheel.||| |
|---|---|---|---|
| | P | C | A    ||| |
| 2 |||||

| |||Push | the unit | in the other direction|| | and | free | the other driveshaft.||| |
|---|---|---|---|---|---|
| |||  P | C | A    || | | P | C    ||| |
| 1 |||| 2 |||

**Fig. 9.1**

*wheel*) is logically linked to the first, and the fourth has a similar logical relationship to the third. The author chose to reflect these parallel relationships in two parallel clause complexes, each containing a pair linked by *and*.

Our opening example, (1), simply links two declarative clauses with *and*. This can be represented as in (1a) or more simply as in Fig. 9.2.

(1a) ‖‖ We are here 6,000 feet above the sea, ‖ and the equatorial sunshine is
    ‖‖                **1**                   ‖                    **2**
    immensely hot and bright. ‖‖
                     ‖‖

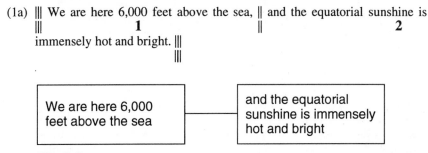

**Fig. 9.2**

The possibility of going beyond two clauses in a complex is illustrated in the examples below, taken from a telephone company's information brochure, where we have a complex of three such clauses. In the locust story and the children's narratives we mentioned, we have a number of clauses with *and* occurring before each new clause. However, most registers of English feature only one occurrence of the conjunction *and* in multiple linked clauses, and this occurs before the last in the series. In written English, the clauses are usually separated by commas, though the comma is often omitted before *and*.

(4)  Your calls will be put through quicker with your new exchange, the lines will be clearer, and there will be fewer faults.

Without indicating the SFPCA structure, we can label the clauses as in Fig. 9.3. The numerals 1, 2, 3 indicate clauses of equal status in the order in which they occur; thus, we cannot have a sequence of clauses numbered *2, 3, 1 or *3, 2, 1. The numbers have no significance other than indicating the actual order in a series of linked clauses. In the story about the locusts, of course, the numbers would continue far beyond 3.

From the same source as (4), in Example (5), analysed in Fig. 9.4, we have a complex of three imperative clauses linked by *and*.

| ‖‖ Your calls will be put through quicker with your new exchange, ‖ | |
|---|---|
| **1** | |
| the lines will be clearer, ‖ | and there will be fewer faults. ‖‖ |
| **2** | **3** |

**Fig. 9.3**

(5)  Just pick up the handset, tap in the code and enter the time you want to be con-
tacted.

| ‖ Just pick up the handset, ‖ | tap in the code ‖ |
|:---:|:---:|
| **1** | **2** |

| and enter the time [[you want to be contacted]]. ‖ |
|:---:|
| **3** |

**Fig. 9.4**

Example (5) contains a rankshifted clause embedded in the third linked
clause. Since it is embedded, it does not count as a separate element in the
clause complex, and so it does not affect our analysis of the three linked
clauses in any way except that in a more detailed analysis we could analyse
the rankshifted clause in its own terms as demonstrated in Fig. 9.5, and,
putting in all this information in one diagram, we have Fig. 9.6.

| enter | the time | [[ you | want to be contacted]]. |
|:---:|:---:|:---:|:---:|
|  |  | [[ **S** | **F/P**          ]] |
| **P** | **C** | | |

**Fig. 9.5**

| ‖ Just | pick up | the handset,‖ | tap in | the code ‖ |
|:---:|:---:|:---:|:---:|:---:|
| ‖ **A** | **P** | **C**    ‖ | **P** | **C**    ‖ |
| **1** | | | **2** | |

| and | enter | the time | [[ you | want to be contacted.]] ‖ |
|:---:|:---:|:---:|:---:|:---:|
|  |  |  | [[ **S** | **F/P**          ]] |
| | **P** | **C** | | ‖ |
| **3** | | | | |

**Fig. 9.6**

In the following short text, Example (6), from Bertrand Russell's *History
of western philosophy*, we find the repeated use of linking of paired parallels
using the conjunction *and*; then a further clause is linked to the second pair
by *but*.

(6)  The planets came out of the sun, and the sun came out of a nebula. It has lasted
some time, and will last some time longer; but sooner or later – probably in
about a million years – it will explode, destroying all the planets.

As we have said already (*see* Chapter 2), these conjunctions (*and, but*) belong to a subcategory of conjunctions called *linking conjunctions* or *linkers*. In traditional grammars, they are usually known as 'co-ordinating conjunctions'. They do not have a role in the SFPCA structure of the clause.

The semantic distinctions among *and, but, or,* and *so* can be very roughly summarized as follows: *and* is additive, indicating addition and sometimes chronological or logical sequence; *but* is adversative indicating a contrast of some kind; *or* is disjunctive, signalling alternation; *so* is consequential, indicating a cause-effect type of relation. In fact, the semantics of these words can be very subtle and shades of meaning can often be distinguished only in context.

The phenomenon of such linking is called *parataxis*, and clauses linked in this way are said to have a *paratactic* relation to each other. The term derives from two Greek words: *para* meaning 'by the side of' and *taxis* meaning 'arrangement'. (Compare *paramedic*, a term used to refer to someone who works alongside a doctor; *syntax* meaning literally 'arrangement with', which is the way grammatical forms combine together to make grammatical structures.) Clauses in a paratactic complex are numbered **1, 2,** etc. as they occur.

## 9.3   *Dependent clauses*

We have just looked at the way that clause complexes can be formed by linking two clauses of equal status in a paratactic relation. The second way in which a clause complex can be formed is to combine the clauses in such a way that one is dependent on another. This is known as *hypotaxis*, and the clauses are said to have a *hypotactic* relation. Etymologically, this derives from the Greek *hypo* meaning 'below' plus *taxis* (arrangement); hence: 'arrangement below'. (Compare: *hypodermic* 'below the skin', which is from *hypo* + *derma* 'skin'.) The rationale for this term is that one clause is attached to the other but with a lower status, hence it is, as it were, arranged below. A more usual term for this is *dependency*, and we shall normally use the term *dependent clause* to label a clause which is bound to another in a hypotactic relationship. The clause to which it is bound is called the *dominant clause*.

The example we gave of a dependent clause at the beginning of this chapter involved the conjunction *as*. The example is repeated here for convenience.

(2) [. . .] the Blue Nile grows steadily wider and warmer as it advances at a slower pace into the desert [. . .]

Here the second clause *as it advances at a slower pace into the desert* is bound in a hypotactic relation to the first clause *the Blue Nile grows steadily wider and warmer*. The conjunction *as* signals this relationship. We have already said that *as* and other words that belong in the same class form the subclass of conjunctions known as *binding conjunctions* or *binders* (traditionally, 'subordinating conjunctions'). A complete list of these would be very long, but it would include such items as: *when, while, until, before, after, if, unless, since, because, where, whereas, so that*. This is not to say, of course, that some of these words (or rather phonologically and graphologically identical forms) cannot also show up in different word classes or realize different functions.

In the previous section, we indicated that clauses in a paratactic (equal) relation can be labelled with the numerals **1, 2**, etc. Hypotactic (dependent) relations are conventionally labelled using the Greek alphabet symbols: α Alpha; β Beta; γ Gamma; δ Delta, ε Epsilon, etc. The use of the Greek alphabet avoids the confusion that would arise from using the symbols A, B, C, etc., which are already in use as grammatical labels; for example, A has already been taken as an abbreviation for Adjunct and C is used for Complement.

So we can analyse Example (2) as below or as in Fig. 9.7.

||| The Blue Nile grows steadily wider and warmer || as it advances at a
                              α                                              β
slower pace into the desert. |||

| The Blue Nile grows steadily wider and warmer |
| as it advances at a slower pace into the desert. |

**Fig. 9.7**

In Fig. 9.8, the SFPCA labels are added.

| ||| The Blue Nile | grows | steadily | wider and warmer||| |
|---|---|---|---|
| ||| S | F/P | A | C    || |
| α |||||
| as it advances | at a slower pace | into the desert.||| |
| S | F/P | A | A    ||| |
| β |||||

**Fig. 9.8**

### 9.3.1 Sequencing of clauses: Theme and Rheme revisited

One striking way in which hypotactic clause relations differ from paratactic ones is that the sequence can vary. In paratactic clauses, as we have already said, the sequence **1**, **2**, etc., cannot be altered. Or to put it another way, if we change around the sequence of the clauses, then the numbers will reflect the new sequence. In one of the clause complexes quoted earlier, we had the sequence:

||| The planets came out of the sun, || and the sun came out of a nebula. |||
|||         **1**         ||         **2**         |||

In this complex, we hear first about the more recent event in pre-history, and then about an event preceding it. The effect of this is that we perceive pre-history from our present standpoint, seeing first the event which is closer to us in time and secondly the event which is further back in time. Suppose that Russell had decided to put this the other way round, as he might well have done to achieve a somewhat different effect, placing the events in their chronological order. The clauses in first and second place would be different in content, but in our analysis the first would still be numbered **1** and the second **2**.

||| The sun came out of the nebula, || and the planets came out of a sun. |||
|||         **1**         ||         **2**         |||

This is self-evident in view of what the numbers signify, namely the sequence, the order of occurrence of the clauses. (The numbering has nothing to do with the sequence of the real-time events being recounted.)

However, the labels α, β, and so on, used to label clauses in a hypotactic relationship of dependency, do not say anything about sequence. They comment rather on the hierarchical relationship whereby one clause depends on – 'hangs from' – another. Thus if we change round the order of the clauses, they retain the same labels, as in (2a); the dependency relation is expressed more literally in Fig. 9.9, the diagram being read from left to right but the dependency indicated by the level on the page.

(2a) ||| as it advances at a slower pace into the desert, || the Blue Nile grows
                         β                                                    α
steadily wider and warmer. |||

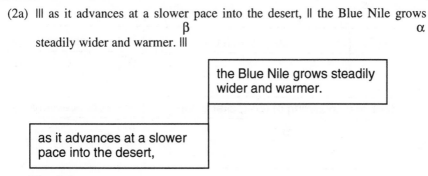

**Fig. 9.9**

A corollary of this is the fact that whereas the linking conjunction (*and*, *but*, *or*, *so*) never occurs at the beginning of the complex which it links, the binding conjunction (*as*, *because*, *when*, and so on) *can* occur at the beginning of the complex which it binds.

The decision to put the dependent clause before or after the clause on which it depends (the *dominant* clause) is not an arbitrary one. There are significantly different meanings attached to such choices, notably those identified with the functions of Theme and Rheme discussed in Chapters 4 and 5. As we indicated there, the functions of Theme and Rheme are most significant *within* the clause, as reflected by the sequencing of S, F, P, C, and A. Clearly, however, placing a clause at the beginning of a clause complex suggests a thematic role for that clause as a whole in relation to the other clause(s) within the complex.

> The thematically *unmarked* sequence is: dominant clause followed by dependent clause: α, β.
> The thematically *marked* sequence is dependent clause followed by dominant clause: β, α.

So far we have been discussing a hypothetical alternative to an actual unmarked utterance, but let us now consider some authentic examples of thematically marked clause complexes.

We begin with an example from our motor-vehicle manual.

> (7) Unless wear or damage is apparent, further dismantling of the rocker shaft is unnecessary.

This example has the sequence β, α, that is dependent clause followed by dominant clause. Example (7) can be analysed as in Fig. 9.10, giving the clause complex labels and the SFPCA labels.

The fact of making the dependent clause the starting point has meaning for the message conveyed. Both clause complexes express a contingency, constraining the proposition expressed in the dominant clause. By placing the condition first in Example (7), the author signals that this is the 'peg' on which the clause complex hangs. The same is true of the time clause in Example (8).

| ||| Unless | wear or damage | is | apparent, | || |
|---|---|---|---|---|
| ||| | **S** | **F** | **C** | || |
| β | | | | |
| further dismantling of the rocker shaft | | is | unnecessary. ||| |
| **S** | | **F** | **C** | ||| |
| α | | | | |

**Fig. 9.10**

(8) When the gap is correct, the feeler blade should just fall by its own weight.

The starting point (the Theme) is *when the gap is correct*; the Rheme is the dominant clause *the feeler blade should just fall by its own weight.* Of course each clause has its own internal thematic organization. So the analysis for Theme and Rheme in these two complexes can be shown as in Fig. 9.11.

The Themes of the first clause in both complexes are Multiple Themes and so they could be more delicately analysed, as in Fig. 9.12.

| Unless wear or damage | is apparent, |
|---|---|
| **Theme** | **Rheme** |
| **THEME** ||
| further dismantling of the rocker shaft | is unnecessary. |
| **Theme** | **Rheme** |
| **RHEME** ||

| When the gap | is correct, |
|---|---|
| **Theme** | **Rheme** |
| **THEME** ||
| the feeler blade | should just fall by its own weight. |
| **Theme** | **Rheme** |
| **RHEME** ||

**Fig. 9.11**

| Unless | wear or damage |
|---|---|
| When | the gap |
| **Textual Theme** | **Topical Theme** |

**Fig. 9.12**

Although dependent clauses of this type usually begin with a binder (*when, if, unless, because,* and so on), they are not always signalled in this way. Consider Example (9).

(9) Should the crankshaft sprocket teeth be worn, remove the sprocket with a suitable extractor.

An alternative to this, without any striking change of meaning, would have been (9a).

(9a)  If the crankshaft sprocket teeth are worn, remove the sprocket with a suitable extractor.

In the authentic example, (9), instead of using the binding conjunction *if* to signal a condition, the author has exploited the less frequently used possibility of Subject-Finite inversion with *should*.

Sometimes we find the binder *if* in the dependent clause used in connection with *then* in the dominant clause. In such cases, *if* goes with the dependent clause and *then* with the dominant clause. This can happen only when the dependent clause precedes the dominant as in Example (10).

(10)  If an argument is valid, then it is consistent.

This example comes from a textbook on formal logic, which is a field that exploits the *if . . . then* combination a great deal since it is a basic formula in logic. However, we can find frequent examples of it in fields other than logic and in genres other than the textbook. In Example (11), we find *then* following a dependent (condition) clause which, instead of using *if*, uses Subject-Finite inversion as in Example (9). This suggests that *then* is tied to the condition-consequence relation rather than to the actual word *if*.

(11)  Should the tests prove the pump is functioning correctly, then obviously other causes for fuel starvation must be sought.

*Then*, used to express this consequence relation, seems to be semantically unnecessary since its function is only to 'underline' a semantic relation between the two clauses that is already explicit in the use of *if* or in the inversion with *should*. Of course, there may well be cases where such 'underlining' serves a useful textual purpose (*see* Chapter 5 on Cohesion). Note that *then* can be used in this way only when the clause expressing the consequence (the dominant clause) follows the clause expressing the condition (the dependent clause).

## 9.3.2   Non-finite dependent clauses

All the examples of hypotaxis that we have so far considered have involved finite clauses. However, dependent clauses are frequently non-finite, as in the following examples. The dependent clauses are in italics.

(12)  Remove the fan and the water pump pulley and the drive belt *after slackening off the generator securing bolt and strap bolt*.
(13)  Refill the cooling system *as previously described in this chapter*.
(14)  *Hearing these words*, even an amateur mathematician would trot out Laplace's equation.
(15)  *Looking down from the top*, one sees far below a narrow gorge filled with water.

In Examples (12) and (13), the dominant clause precedes the non-finite dependent clause; in (14) and (15), they are the opposite way round. In (12) and (13) there are binders (*after* and *as*, respectively) to signal the dependency relation, but (14) and (15) do not have such an item. The Predicators in (12), (14) and (15) are present participles (V-ing forms) and in (13) the Predicator is a past participle (passive). Paraphrasing with finite clauses, we might recast the examples as:

(12a) Remove the fan and the water pump pulley and the drive belt *after you have slackened off the generator securing bolt and strap bolt.*

(13a) Refill the cooling system *as the process was previously described in this chapter.*

(14a) *If* (or *When*) *he/she heard these words,* even an amateur mathematician would trot out Laplace's equation.

(15a) *When one looks down from the top,* one sees far below a narrow gorge filled with water.

There are obvious strong correspondences between the authentic non-finite versions and the constructed finite ones, but they are not entirely straightforward, and so it would be rash to argue that they carry exactly the same meaning. Example (13a) involves some rather clumsy readjustment; the choice of *when* and *if* is in doubt in (14a) and perhaps (15a), and so on. Even so, there are strong resemblances. Sometimes, however, there is no obvious corresponding finite clause, as in Example (16).

(16) *Using a micrometer,* measure the dimension across two splines on the final drive pinion.

Non-finite clauses in a clause complex with a finite clause are always dependent. Earlier, *so* was mentioned as a linking conjunction (for example, *I have started so I'll continue,* where the two clauses are in a paratactic relation). However, in (17) we have a different *so,* an adverb functioning as Adjunct with a meaning similar to *thus* or *thereby.* The two clauses are in a hypotactic relation, with the first clause dominant and the second dependent.

(17) Electric light simulates daylight, *so inducing the fowl to lay more frequently.*

Present and past participles are not the only Predicators to appear in non-finite dependent clauses. Infinitives are also common, as in (18), (19) and (20).

(18) *To remove the skin,* cut off the tail and scrape towards the head.

(19) An RCD can be fitted as a separate unit between the meter and main switch *to protect the whole house.*

(20) [...] the laws of perspective were first studied by the geometer Agatharcus *in order to paint scenery for the plays of Aeschylus.*

The examples we have considered in this chapter so far all have a similar function: they expand on the proposition in the dominant clause, indicating some contingency relating to that proposition: of condition, time, purpose, means, manner, and so on. For example, the infinitive clauses in Examples (18), (19) and (20) all express purpose. In fact, the functions of these dependent clauses have much in common with those of Adjuncts within the clause, and in traditional grammar they are called 'adverb clauses' and subclassified as adverb clauses of time, manner, condition, purpose, and others.

We shall label this class of dependent clauses *expansion clauses*. The expansion function cuts across the paratactic/hypotactic dimension so that both hypotactic and paratactic clauses can realize that function. The counterpart to the expanding function is that of *projection*, which is dealt with in Chapter 10. First we take a look at a somewhat different dependent clause, also with an expanding function: the non-defining relative.

### 9.3.3   Non-defining relative clauses

In Chapter 7, we discussed the defining relative clause (also known as the restrictive relative clause), demonstrating that this is a form of rankshifted clause functioning as Qualifier/Postmodifier in a Nominal Group. This function involves the limiting of the scope of reference of the Head. Thus, when we read the example from Chapter 7,

Any circuit that is to be worked on must be dead,

we understand that the predication 'must be dead' applies not to just 'any circuit' but only to any 'that is to be worked on'. The defining relative clause is part and parcel of the Nominal Group and it restricts the scope of the Head.

*Non-defining relative clauses* (also known as 'non-restrictive' relative clauses) are less intimately bound up with the item that they relate to, and are analysed not as rankshifted clauses but as dependent clauses.

(21) [...] he then measured the shadow of the pyramid, *which was of course equal to its height.*

(22) This general rejection was mainly due to Hipparchus, *who flourished from 161 to 126* BC.

(23) There is even a slight note of derision from Fanny Burney, *who also met Bruce at this time.*

The relative clauses italicized in (21), (22) and (23) are non-defining: they do not pinpoint their antecedents in the way that defining relatives do, their function is rather to provide additional information about the antecedent. Their function is not to restrict the scope of reference of a Head, but, almost parenthetically, to comment further. Such a clause is grammatically dependent on the dominant clause, but it is not an integral part of it. We could roughly paraphrase Example (21) by saying:

(21a) he then measured the shadow of the pyramid, *and it was of course equal to its height.*

However, we could not paraphrase the defining clause example by saying:

Any circuit must be dead, and it is to be worked on.

However, non-defining relatives are analysed not as paratactic but as hypotactic structures. They are not integrated into the clause that contains the antecedent in the way that rankshifted clauses are, but they are dependent. Example (21) is analysed as in Fig. 9.13.

| ||| he | then | measured | the shadow of the pyramid, || |
|---|---|---|---|
| ||| S | A | F/P | C                                    || |
| α |||||

| which | was | of course | equal to its height. ||| |
|---|---|---|---|
| S | F | A | C                                    ||| |
| β |||||

**Fig. 9.13**

Along with this difference in meaning between defining and non-defining clauses, there are some additional implications for the grammar, as well as for intonation (in the spoken mode) and for punctuation (in the written).

In the construction of defining relative clauses, speakers of English usually have the option of using either wh-pronouns or *that*. In non-defining clauses, the relative pronoun is always – or nearly always – a wh-pronoun. Also, the frequent simple omission of the relative pronoun that occurs with defining clauses (in contact clauses such as: *the book ^ you lent me*) is not paralleled in non-defining clauses. However, 'reduced' non-defining relatives do exist (that is, moodless, non-finite relative clauses) as in Example (24).

(24)   The citadel, *built by Saladin in the twelfth century*, was a fine complex of dun-coloured battlements.

There is a striking difference in the intonation of defining and non-defining clauses that is reflected in the practice of setting apart non-defining clauses with commas. Of course, punctuation is not always practised consistently enough for this to be a sure way of distinguishing the two clause types, but it is the norm in careful writing, and can often avoid potential ambiguity. Without the commas, and out of context, we would probably read the relative in (24) as a defining clause, inferring a distinction between this citadel built by Saladin and other citadels that were built by other people. In fact, when we look at Text 9A, we can see that this has to be a non-defining clause.

The citadel is mentioned twice in this text fragment; the first time it is '*a* citadel'; the second time it is '*the* citadel'. We already know by the time of the second mention which citadel is being referred to here. There is therefore no need for a defining clause. For the purposes of this fragment of discourse, there is only one citadel. The fact that it was built by Saladin in the twelfth

Cairo, on the other hand, was a flourishing place [. . .]. It lay a little distance from the right bank of the river under the cover of the Mokattam Hills, and was ringed by high walls and dominated by a citadel.

The skyline, seen from a distance, had romantic aspects: the domes and minarets of 300 mosques rose from the smoke of cooking fires, and the palm trees and cultivated fields along the river bank gave the place a placid and rather rural air. The citadel, built by Saladin in the twelfth century, was a fine complex of dun-coloured battlements, and in the desert beyond, on the opposite side of the river, one descried the pyramids.

**Text 9A**    (Moorehead, *The Blue Nile*,[1] p. 73).

century is an expansion, a further piece of information that the author chooses to express as a non-finite dependent clause, a non-defining relative. He might have expressed it in a separate sentence or in a 'full' finite dependent clause (*which was built by Saladin in the twelfth century*), but, without more drastic changes, he could not have expressed it as a rankshifted clause modifying *citadel*.

There is a moral here. Although, for the purpose of exposition in this book, we frequently deal with isolated examples torn from their setting, we do not wish to suggest that sentences are constructed without regard to the sentences around them. We can say a great deal about the structure of clauses by looking at clauses in isolation, but language is produced and understood not as individual clauses but as text. What happens in any clause is determined by the rest of the text in which it occurs. We have made this point already, but it is important to bear it in mind, and we feel justified in repeating it from time to time.

There is another difference in the work done by defining and non-defining relative clauses. A non-defining clause may have as its antecedent not just a Nominal Group or its Head, but an entire clause or clause complex. To look at it in another way, non-defining relatives sometimes express a comment on an entire proposition or set of propositions. This is exemplified in (25) and (26).

(25) (He then told me) [. . .] he would postpone his remunerations till then, *to which I agreed.*

(26) (He thinks that if A is greater than B and less than C), then A is at once great and small, *which seems to him a contradiction.*

In (25) the antecedent of the relative pronoun (*which*) is the clause *he would postpone his remunerations till then*. As with defining relatives, the relative pronoun itself in a non-defining clause may be Subject, Complement or Adjunct, or, as in this example, part of an Adjunct. Here the relative pronoun is part of the prepositional phrase *to which*, realizing the function Adjunct.

In (26), the antecedent of the relative pronoun (*which*) is the clause *then A is at once great and small*. This antecedent is itself part of a hypotactic clause complex with the *if*-clause in a dependent relation to the *then*-clause, which is in turn part of a larger complex. (Clause complexes with this degree of complexity are discussed in more detail in Section 9.4 and in Chapter 10.)

You will recall that *proper noun* is the label given to nouns which refer to the individual names of people, places, institutions, and so on; for example, Hipparchus, Fanny Burney, Tokyo, Gautama, Upper Volta. Obviously, when a relative pronoun has a proper noun as its antecedent, the relative clause is likely to be a non-defining relative. The reason for this is that a proper noun defines its referent by virtue of the fact that it uniquely names it. Of course, there may be more than one person called Fanny Burney, or city called Tokyo, but that is not a factor that is taken into account when we use the name *Fanny Burney* or *Tokyo*; we speak as though only one existed. For example:

Oenopides, *who was slightly later than Anaxagoras*
Aristarchus of Samos, *who lived approximately from 310 to 230* BC
Cicero, *in whose time there was probably no Latin translation*
Einstein's General Theory of Relativity, *from which the conception of force in the Newtonian sense has been banished.*

In the above examples, the assumption is that there is only one Oenopides, one Aristarchus of Samos, one Cicero and one Einstein's General Theory of Relativity. The relative clause is an expansion of the dominant clause; it is non-defining.

The exception to this is where an item which is normally a proper noun is treated as a common noun, as in the following example.

(27)  This was the Maria *whom he had toasted at the source of the Little Abbai.*

Here, the author treats *Maria* as though it were a common noun. There is a determiner (*the*) before it (not usual with people's names in English), and the clause which follows is a defining relative; it tells us which Maria he is talking about. Here the assumption is that there are many Marias – or at least more than one – and some modification is needed to pin down the reference; hence the rankshifted clause. *Maria* in this example is not a unique sign for a unique individual but stands rather for any one of the class of individuals called Maria, just as the sign *woman* potentially stands for any of the class of adult female humans. The Modifier *whom he had toasted at the source of the Little Abbai* serves to make the expression refer more precisely. In the same way, some nostalgic native of Birmingham might speak of *the Birmingham where I grew up*, opposing this by implication to *the Birmingham of today* or, conceivably, to some other city or cities called Birmingham. (Incidentally, you may be relieved to know that *toasted* in Example (27) refers to the custom of drinking to the health of someone and not to basic culinary techniques.)

In this particular example, (27), far from being an optional expansion, the

defining relative clause is the main focus of information. The clause in which it is embedded has an identifying function (*see* Chapter 6). The sentence which comes before it in the original text is:

> The real reason, however, was that he had discovered, like so many soldiers returning from the wars, that his girl had abandoned him for another man.

Therefore, the pronoun *This* in the sample sentence (27) co-refers with *his girl*. The Deictic as Head word *this* (referring to his girl) functions as Identifier and *the Maria whom he had toasted at the source of the Little Abbai* is the Identified. We can only be sure of these grammatical facts, however, if we have read another section of the narrative (nine pages earlier), which runs as in Text 9B and describes the behaviour of the Scottish explorer, Bruce, at what he thought was the source of the Nile. Here again is evidence of the fact that grammatical choices emerge from factors outside the clause itself, often at considerable distance in the text.

> There was still another toast. "Now, friend," Bruce said, "[. . .], here is to – Maria!" [. . .] We are to hear more of this lady later, on Bruce's return to Europe.

**Text 9B**    (Moorehead, *The Blue Nile*,[1] p. 34).

## 9.4    *More complicated complexes*

Real text in English can – and usually does – contain very complicated grammatical structures. Most of the examples we have looked at in this chapter are relatively straightforward cases of complexes of two clauses, either in a paratactic or a hypotactic relation. These are authentic samples of text, except where otherwise indicated, but it is easy to find more difficult samples. Example (28), analysed in Fig. 9.14, contains two hypotactic clauses, one dependent on the other. We thus have a clause complex of the pattern α, β, γ.

(28) Phenoxy compounds can also be sprayed over a newly planted field to kill young weed seedlings as their shoots appear.

| ||| Phenoxy compounds can also be sprayed over a newly planted field || | |
|---|---|
| α | |
| to kill young weed seedlings  || | as their shoots appear.||| |
| β | γ |

**Fig. 9.14**

Example (29), from a description of pest control in Africa, involves a combination of paratactic and hypotactic relations.

(29)  At first the scheme was threatened by considerable tsetse reincursion, but
this has now been remedied, mainly by using insecticide sprays within the
consolidation barrier, clearing more bush and hunting game which had now
re-entered the cleared land.

This clause complex falls initially into two paratactically related chunks
linked by *but*. We label these **1** and **2**. Clause **1** is a simple clause, but **2**
contains a hypotactic expansion of the dominant clause. We therefore label
the dominant clause $\alpha$, and since it is already **2**, it is labelled **2$\alpha$**. The rest of
the sentence, being in a hypotactic relation to **2$\alpha$**, is labelled **2$\beta$**. This in turn
consists of three (non-finite) clauses in a paratactic relation to each other;
we number them **1, 2, 3**, but as they are all part of **2$\beta$**, they are respectively
**2$\beta$1**, **2$\beta$2** and **2$\beta$3**. There is also a rankshifted clause, which does not affect
the clause complex relations. This analysis can be summed up as in Fig.
9.15.

| ‖ At first the scheme was threatened by considerable tsetse reincursion, ‖ | | |
|---|---|---|
| **1** | | |
| but this has now been remedied, ‖ | mainly by using insecticide sprays within | |
| **2$\alpha$** | **2$\beta$1** | |
| the consolidation barrier, ‖ | clearing more bush ‖ | and hunting game |
| **2$\beta$1** *continued.* | **2$\beta$2** | **2$\beta$3** |
| [[which had now re-entered the cleared land]] ‖. | | |
| **2$\beta$3** *continued* | | |

**Fig. 9.15**

Sometimes, as in Example (30), we find clause complexes within
rankshifted clauses.

(30)  His thesis is that the actual outbreak of war is almost inevitable, provided
certain broad sociopolitical, economic and technical patterns are present.

This sentence realizes a Relational Process in the form *X is Y*. So one stratum is a simple **S, F, C** structure. However, the Complement is realized by an
embedding in the form of a hypotactic clause complex. This is illustrated in
Fig. 9.16, which also includes SFPCA labels. The second line in the figure
gives the SFPCA labels for the rankshifted clauses, the third line gives the
clause labels and the fourth line the SFPCA labels for the clause as a whole.
The items *that* and *provided*, being binders, have no SFPCA function.

| His thesis | is | [[ ‖ | that | the actual outbreak of war | is | almost inevitable, ‖ |
|---|---|---|---|---|---|---|
| | | [[ ‖ | | S | F | C ‖ |

| | | α | | | | |
|---|---|---|---|---|---|---|
| S | F | C | | | | |

| provided | certain broad sociopolitical, economic and technical patterns | are | present.‖ ]] |
|---|---|---|---|
| | S | F | C ‖ ]] |

| β |
|---|
| · *C continued* |

**Fig. 9.16**

## Summary

In this chapter, we have focused on various methods of combining clauses together in English by means of the clause complex. Clause complexes differ crucially from rankshifted (that is, embedded) clauses because in a clause complex the clauses are not 'demoted' to function at some lower rank. Clause complexes may involve *expansion* or *projection*: in this chapter we have considered only expansion.

Clause complex relationships are of two kinds: (i) Paratactic, that is equal in status; and (ii) Hypotactic, that is involving a dependency relation. Paratactic relations are labelled according to the sequence in which the clauses occur: **1, 2,** etc. Hypotactic relations are labelled according to their hierarchical relationship of dependency, regardless of the order in which they occur. Greek alphabetic symbols (α, β, γ, δ, ε) are conventionally used to show 'descending' dependency. Thus β is dependent on α, γ on β, δ on γ, and so on. A clause which has another depending on it is called the dominant clause; a clause which depends on another is called the dependent clause. Dependent clauses are not rankshifted.

Non-defining relative clauses are one kind of dependent expansion. A non-defining relative may have as its antecedent a Nominal Group or an entire clause or clause complex. Non-defining relatives are distinct from defining relatives, which are rankshifted.

In many texts, there is a complex interplay of parataxis, hypotaxis, and embedding. Any instance of one of these phenomena may occur inside another instance of the same phenomenon or inside an instance of one of the others.

## Further study

A possible alternative analysis to Halliday's treatment of hypotactic expansions as dependent clauses is to analyse them as rankshifted clauses functioning as Adjunct. This view is taken by Fawcett, among others (for example Fawcett, 1974). On this analysis, Example (2), from the opening of this chapter, would be analysed as a single clause with an embedded (i.e., rankshifted) clause as Adjunct rather than as a clause complex with an α, β relation. Thus, for Fawcett, *as it advances at a slower pace into the desert* is an Adjunct, though it is also a clause (rankshifted) with its own structure: S, F, P, A, A. *See also* Downing and Locke (1992: pp. 60–61), who present both analyses but express a strong preference for the dependent clause analysis.

## Exercises

### Exercise 9.1

The following examples are all paratactic clause complexes, consisting of two or more clauses. Indicate each clause boundary with a double vertical line, and number the clauses.

1. Loewi got out of bed, went to his lab, and did the experiment.
2. An oil vapour re-intake system is fitted and oil pressure lubrication is provided by a gear driven pump.
3. Remove the starter shield and disconnect the starter electrical leads.
4. Fire lives the death of air, and air lives the death of fire; water lives the death of earth, earth that of water.
5. The engine is mounted ahead of the front axle line and the combined gearbox/differential is situated immediately to the rear of the engine.

### Exercise 9.2

Each of the following is a hypotactic clause complex containing one dominant and one dependent clause. Label the clauses α or β.

1. When we read of horses, the reference is usually to war-horses.
2. For instance, the vagus nerves slow down the rate of the heartbeat while the accelerator nerves increase it.
3. Though today there are no more than about 400 of these magnificent trees, the cedars of Lebanon were once famous all over the ancient world.
4. Reference to the cedar is made many times in the Bible, in which it is always mentioned as the symbol of power and beauty.
5. If you win tonight, you're not likely to see me again.
6. This bearing cannot be changed as the bearing inner track ring is bonded to the final drive pinion.
7. Extract the bearings from the differential using a bearing extractor.
8. Using a suitable drift, punch out the rollpin in the control shaft end fitting.
9. Fit the synchro spring onto the first-speed gear so that it covers the three notches in the hub.
10. But now I kept my own head while Nixon lost his.

*Exercise 9.3*

(a) Identify the following clause complexes as Paratactic or Hypotactic.
(b) Indicate clause boundaries and label the paratactic clauses **1**, **2**, etc. and the Hypotactic clauses α, β, etc.

1. Subsequently released, he escaped to England.
2. As Brenner tells the story, there was one inviolable rule in their office.
3. Secure the clamp plate to the cylinder block and connect the LT and HT leads to coil and plugs.
4. The high-tension (HT) cables should be kept clean by wiping them periodically with a petrol soaked cloth.
5. Depression in the manifold actuates the vacuum unit, the vacuum applied varying with each load.
6. When a new synchro is being fitted, mark both parts in relation to one another.
7. A plug cleaning machine is preferable but a wire brush is a good alternative.
8. Using a suitable drift, punch out the rollpin in the control shaft end fitting.
9. When people disagree about it, one, at least, is making an intellectual error.
10. Reference has been made above to the construction of silt traps, but the effectiveness of such methods is limited.

*Exercise 9.4*

Indicate the clause and clause complex boundaries and label the clauses in Text 9C. Indicate rankshifted clauses with double square brackets.

The more scientific systems of 'New World' commercial pastoralists keep the animals scattered, so ensuring more uniform grazing and reducing the danger of producing bare patches completely devoid of vegetation. A country with much experience of semi-arid livestock farming is Australia, where wide areas of grazing land do not receive more than 250 mm of rainfall a year. It has been found that cattle withstand such arid conditions better than sheep. Interior Australia is still a land of pioneer settlement, and as the better-watered areas become fully settled and developed, land-hungry farmers will inevitably be forced into the so-called 'desert' country. Hitherto the carrying capacity of the outback has remained rather low, averaging 1–4 animals per square kilometre [. . .]

**Text 9C**    (Lowry, *World population and food supply*,[2] p. 60).

*Exercise 9.5*

Analyse the following examples, indicating SFPCA and clause complex labels.

1. $\overset{1}{||}$ Japan has its own great cities, $||$ and it has evolved its own elaborate systems $\overset{2}{||}$ [[to control urban congestion.]] $||$
2. $||$ Shimura is superb in the central role, $||$ and not the least of Kurosawa's achievements is his triumphant avoidance of happy-ending uplift.
3. $|$ Yuko sings quietly to herself $|$ as she watches the water. $|$
4. $||$ One of the few films [[that never fails]] is this one, $||$ which is a Japanese classic. $\underset{\beta}{}$ $\underset{\alpha}{}$
5. Saddled with a slavish, boring laundry job, Kikuchi barely leaves his apartment.

## Answers

*Exercise 9.1*

1. $|||$ Loewi got out of bed, $||$ went to his lab, $||$ and did the experiment. $|||$
   $|||$       1      $||$    2     $||$       3      $|||$

2. $|||$ An oil vapour re-intake system is fitted $||$ and oil pressure lubrication is
   $|||$              1               $||$                2
   provided by a gear driven pump. $|||$
                       $|||$

3. $|||$ Remove the starter shield $||$ and disconnect the starter electrical leads. $|||$
   $|||$       1        $||$          2           $|||$

4. $|||$ Fire lives the death of air, $||$ and air lives the death of fire; $||$ water lives the
   $|||$      1.1         $||$        1.2        $||$       2.1
   death of earth, $||$ earth that of water. $|||$
            $||$     2.2      $|||$
   (OR possibly 1, 2, 3, 4.)

5. $|||$ The engine is mounted ahead of the front axle line $||$ and the combined
   $|||$                1                   $||$
   gearbox/differential is situated immediately to the rear of the engine. $|||$
                2                       $|||$

*Exercise 9.2*

1. $|||$ When we read of horses, $||$ the reference is usually to war-horses. $|||$
   $|||$         $\beta$         $||$           $\alpha$          $|||$

2. $|||$ For instance, the vagus nerves slow down the rate of the heartbeat $||$
   $|||$                    $\alpha$                   $||$

while the accelerator nerves increase it. |||
        β                |||

3. ||| Though today there are no more than about 400 of these magnificent
   |||                             β
trees, || the cedars of Lebanon were once famous all over the ancient world. |||
   ||                           α                 |||

4. ||| Reference to the cedar is made many times in the Bible, || in which it is
   |||                      α                        ||
always mentioned as the symbol of power and beauty. |||
             β                        |||

5. ||| If you win tonight, || you're not likely to see me again. |||
   |||     β      ||            α         |||

6. ||| This bearing cannot be changed || as the bearing inner track ring is
   |||           α           ||                      β
bonded to the final drive pinion. |||
               |||

7. ||| Extract the bearings from the differential || using a bearing extractor. |||
   |||            α              ||      β          |||

8. ||| Using a suitable drift, || punch out the rollpin in the control shaft end
   |||     β          ||                  α
fitting. |||
    |||

9 ||| Fit the synchro spring onto the first-speed gear || so that it covers the
  |||                 α                 ||             β
three notches in the hub. |||
             |||

10. ||| But now I kept my own head || while Nixon lost his. |||
   |||          α           ||    β     |||

*Exercise 9.3*

1. Hypotactic
   ||| Subsequently released, || he escaped to England.|||
   |||         β           ||       α       |||

2. Hypotactic
   ||| As Brenner tells the story, || there was one inviolable rule in their office. |||
   |||           β           ||           α          |||

3. Paratactic
||| Secure the clamp plate to the cylinder block || and connect the LT and
|||                  1                                    ||
HT leads to coil and plugs. |||
   2                            |||

4. Hypotactic
||| The high-tension (HT) cables should be kept clean || by wiping them
|||                       α                           ||
periodically with a petrol soaked cloth. |||
      β                           |||

5. Hypotactic
||| Depression in the manifold actuates the vacuum unit, || the vacuum
|||                       α                        ||
applied varying with each load. |||
     β                   |||

6. Hypotactic
||| When a new synchro is being fitted, || mark both parts in relation to one
|||             β                 ||                  α
another. |||
     |||

7. Paratactic
||| A plug cleaning machine is preferable || but a wire brush is a good
|||                  1                  ||                2
alternative. |||
      |||

8. Hypotactic
||| Using a suitable drift, || punch out the rollpin in the control shaft end
|||            β          ||                     α
fitting. |||
    |||

9. Hypotactic
||| When people disagree about it, || one, at least, is making an intellectual
|||              β             ||                 α
error. |||
   |||

10. Paratactic
||| Reference has been made above to the construction of silt traps, || but
|||                          1                              ||
the effectiveness of such methods is limited. |||
                2                      |||

*Exercise 9.4*

| ||| The more scientific systems of 'New World' commercial pastoralists keep |
|---|
| |||                                      α |
| the animals scattered, || so ensuring more uniform grazing || and reducing the |
| ||                       β1                  ||           β2 |
| danger of [[producing bare patches completely devoid of vegetation.]] ||| |
| *β2 continued*                                                      ||| |
| A country with much experience of semi-arid livestock farming is Australia, || |
| α                                                               || |
| where wide areas of grazing land do not receive more than 250 mm of rainfall |
| β |
| a year. ||| It has been found [[that cattle withstand such arid conditions better |
| ||| |
| than sheep]]. ||| Interior Australia is still a land of pioneer settlement, || and |
| |||                            1                                    || |
| as the better-watered areas become fully settled and developed, || land- |
| 2β                                                      || |
| hungry farmers will inevitably be forced into the so-called 'desert' country.||| |
| 2α                                                            ||| |
| ||| Hitherto the carrying capacity of the outback has remained rather low, || |
| |||                              α                                    || |
| averaging 1–4 animals per square kilometre. ||| |
| β                           ||| |

*Exercise 9.5*

1.

| ||| Japan | has | its great cities || | and | it | has | evolved |
|---|---|---|---|---|---|---|
| ||| S | F | C          || | S | F | P |
| 1 | 2α |

| its own elaborate system|| | to control | urban congestion. ||| |
|---|---|---|
| C                      || | P | C                  ||| |
| | 2β |

2.

| ||| Shimura | is | superb | in the central role || | and | not the least of Kurosawa's achievements |
|---|---|---|---|---|---|
| ||| S | F | C | A ‖ | | S |
| 1 | | | | | 2 |

| is | his triumphant avoidance of happy-ending uplift. ||| |
|---|---|
| F | C ||| |
| 2 continued | |

3.

| ||| Yuko | sings | quietly | to herself || |
|---|---|---|---|
| ||| S | F/P | A | A ‖ |
| α | | | |

| as | she | watches | the water||| |
|---|---|---|---|
| | S | F/P | C ||| |
| β | | | |

4.

| ||| One of the few films | [[that | never | fails]] | is | this one,|| |
|---|---|---|---|---|---|
| | | [[ S | A | F/P]] | | |
| ||| | S | | | F | C ‖ |
| α | | | | | |

| which | is | a Japanese classic.||| |
|---|---|---|
| S | F | C ||| |
| β | | |

5.

| ||| Saddled | with a slavish boring laundry job, ‖ |
|---|---|
| ||| P | A ‖ |
| β | |

| Kikuchi | barely | leaves | his apartment. ||| |
|---|---|---|---|
| S | A | F/P | C ||| |
| α | | | |

# Notes

1. Moorehead, Alan 1969 (originally published 1962): *The Blue Nile* (NEL Four Square Edition. London: Hamish Hamilton.
2. Lowry, J.H. 1970: *World population and food supply*. London: Edward Arnold.

# 10

# Clause complexes: projection

## 10.1 Projection clauses

This chapter follows on from the previous one in looking at clause complexes, but, instead of the expansion function, it is projection that is considered. In Chapter 6, we discussed the functions Sayer, Quoted and Reported in Verbal Processes. Here we look at the same kind of utterances from a different point of view, namely their logical organization: the paratactic and hypotactic combination of projecting and projected clauses.

## 10.2 Paratactic projection clauses

As we have seen, when we are dealing with direct speech, where the actual words – or what purport to be the actual words – of a speaker are presented verbatim, there is usually a clause conveying something like 'X says' and a clause or a number of clauses that represent the words spoken (not necessarily in that order). In looking at the clause as representation (the ideational function), we may label these as Sayer and Quoted, respectively. Considered in terms of clause complex structure, the relation between these clauses can be described as paratactic. The notation for this, then, is **1** and **2**, just as it is for paratactically linked expansions; see Example (1).

(1) ||| He said, || 'Get in there, Hunt.' |||
   |||  **1**   ||      **2**       |||

If the order of Sayer and Quoted is reversed, of course, it is still the first clause that is numbered **1** and the second that is numbered **2**; see Example (2).

(2) ||| 'That's all we need,' || he said.|||
   |||      **1**       ||  **2**  |||

Representations of thought may take exactly the same form as direct speech and in such cases are analysed in the same way.

(3) ||| I thought, || 'This is the end of the road for me.' |||
   |||   1   ||             2              |||

In Text 6A, there are a number of instances of quoting; these are mostly ellip-tical structures simulating spontaneous speech. We list them here, numbered for convenience.

(4) 'This all?' I asked Thaler.
(5) 'Nick said there were fifty of you.'
(6) 'Fifty of us to stand off that crummy force!' he sneered.
(7) A uniformed copper held the gate open, muttering nervously: 'Hurry it up, boys, please.'
(8) 'See you later,' the gambler whispered.

All these except (5) are paratactic. In (7) the clause that contains Sayer and the quoting verb comes before the clause that realizes the Quoted function, and in (4), (6) and (8) it is the other way round. Labelling these is very straightforward, then. No matter what the function, the clause that comes first is numbered 1 and the clause that comes second is 2. Example (7) is a little more complicated than the others, and we shall return to it shortly. So the analysis of the remaining clauses is as in Fig. 10.1.

| ||| 'This all?' || | I asked Thaler. ||| |
|---|---|
| ||| 'Fifty of us to stand off that crummy force!' || | he sneered.||| |
| ||| 'See you later,' || | the gambler whispered.||| |
| **1** | **2** |

**Fig. 10.1**

In novels, memoirs, biographies and other written narrative texts, direct speech (Quoted) is sometimes presented without the Sayer function being made explicit, as we see in Example (9).

(9) He lowered his voice. 'That is a price you must pay.'

Clearly, the identity of Sayer here is deducible from the co-text. The author of this narrative has chosen to present the information about Sayer and man-ner of saying in a separate sentence. Therefore, since the Quoted is presented as an isolated clause, this is not an example of a clause complex. An approx-imate paraphrase is (9a), which *is* a clause complex.

(9a) In a lower voice, he said, 'That is a price you must pay.'

Example (5) is a more awkward case: it is a Quoted without a Sayer, but it is complicated by the fact that the quotation is itself made up of a clause com-plex, in the form of a projection containing both Sayer and Reported func-tions. This will be discussed later.

Sometimes the clause that contains the Sayer interrupts the clause that realizes the Quoted as in (10) and (11).

(10) 'War,' he says, 'is the father of all and the king of all.'
(11) 'Apparently,' wrote Trembley to Réaumur, 'these gentlemen have some cherished system [. . .]'

The clause *he says* interrupts the Quoted (*War is the father of all and the king of all*), but, because the Quoted starts first, it is numbered 1, and *he says* is numbered 2. Similarly, in (11) the number 1 clause (*Apparently these gentlemen have some cherished system*) is interrupted by the number 2 clause *wrote Trembley to Réaumur*.

To indicate that the number 1 clause is discontinuous, interrupted by, rather than followed by, number 2, we use the notation: 1 <<2>>. Thus the analysis in terms of clause complex structure is as follows:

||| 'War,' <<he says,>> 'is the father of all and the king of all.' |||
|||    1    <<   2   >>                                          |||
||| 'Apparently,' << wrote Trembley to Réaumur, >> 'these gentlemen have
|||      1          <<              2            >>
some cherished system.' |||
          |||

The inversion of the reporting verb and Subject/Sayer illustrated in the first example (*wrote Trembley*) is largely restricted to formal, planned texts, usually published writing. Note that inversion cannot readily take place (in a declarative clause) where the quoting expression precedes the entire Quoted; we would not normally write:

Wrote Trembley to Réaumur, 'Apparently these gentlemen [. . .]'

It is not unprecedented, however. Poe wrote *Quoth the raven: 'Nevermore!'*; and *Time* magazine has indulged in similar structures. In modern English, as we have said earlier, inversion of Subject/Sayer and quoting verb is a stylistic option more likely to occur with a Nominal Group with noun as Head than with a personal pronoun such as *he* or *she*. In (10) *says he* would be virtually ruled out in most varieties of modern English except for humorous effect.

## 10.3  *Hypotactic projection clauses*

In Chapter 6, we discussed reported (indirect) speech (including thought and writing) in terms of the functions Sayer and Reported. Looked at from the perspective of the clause complex, these differ from direct speech structures in that the relationship between the two key clauses is hypotactic, that is, there is a relation of dependency. The clause containing the Sayer and the reporting verb is the dominant clause and the Reported element is the dependent clause. Thus Example (12) breaks down into two clauses: the dominant clause *he says* and the dependent clause *that the general ignorance on this subject is disgraceful.*

(12) He says that the general ignorance on this subject is disgraceful.

Thus, using α, β notation, we could represent the analysis of this clause complex as follows:

||| He says || that the general ignorance on this subject is disgraceful. |||
|||   α   ||              β                                           |||

When we were discussing the direct speech examples above, we postponed discussion of Example (5), repeated here.

(5) 'Nick said there were fifty of you.'

This appears in quotation marks as Quoted, but it is not an example of a paratactic clause complex, because there is no clause explicitly giving the Sayer and Verbal Process verb of the Quoted. However, the Quoted element itself is a clause complex, a hypotactic one analysed as follows:

||| Nick said || there were fifty of you.|||
|||   α    ||       β          |||

Like speech, thought can be projected in direct (paratactic) or reported (hypotactic) form.

(13) Haeckel thought that the *Origin* had one grave defect.

Example (13) similarly breaks down into two clauses: *Haeckel thought*, which is the dominant clause, and *that the Origin had one grave defect*, which is the dependent clause, hence the labelling given below:

||| Haeckel thought || that the *Origin* had one grave defect. |||
|||    α       ||        β                          |||

In reported speech (including thought and writing) the projected element, the speech (or thought or writing), is grammatically integrated with the reporting clause (such as *he says*) with the result that the choice of tense, pronouns, and other Deictic elements such as adverbs of time and place, in the reported clause may be influenced by the general orientation of the reporting clause. This does not happen with direct speech. If Haeckel's thought were to be expressed as direct speech, the verb could be in the present tense, as in (13a).

(13a) Haeckel thought, 'The *Origin* has one grave defect.'

Conversely, the direct speech of Example (11) might be expressed in reported speech as (11a), where both tense and determiner are realigned to the fact that, from the point of view of the reporter, the situation described is in the past and the gentlemen are, as it were, further away.

(11) 'Apparently,' wrote Trembley to Réaumur, 'these gentlemen have some cherished system [. . .]'

(11a)  Trembley informed Réaumur that those gentlemen apparently had some cherished system.

In Example (14), the verb in the dependent clause has to be in the present tense to express this particular proposition because the projecting verb is also in the present: *he says* rather than *he said*. If the author had written *he said*, there would have been the option of a present tense verb (14a) or past tense verb (14b) in the reported clause. The reason for this choice being open is that the statement is a general truth, which can be seen in relation either to the time when it was spoken (past) or, since it is still applicable, to the time at which it is reported (present).

(14)   He says that the general ignorance on this subject is disgraceful.
(14a)  He said that the general ignorance on this subject is disgraceful.
(14b)  He said that the general ignorance on this subject was disgraceful.

It would be an oversimplification to suggest that reported speech always represents what was actually said in this precise one-to-one manner. It may be only an approximation to what was actually said, but the point is that it is coded as if it corresponded in the way we have outlined. Example (14) would be an acceptable account of an utterance like (14c).

(14c) The general ignorance about this is a disgrace.

Unlike direct speech, reported speech does not purport to be a precise reproduction of the words used.

The most frequent signal of a hypotactic projection (that is, a dependent reported speech clause) is the presence of the word *that*. However, *that* realizes several functions. To put it another way, there is more than one *that* in English. In Chapter 8 we discussed *that* as a relative pronoun, an alternative to *who* or *which*. *That* can also be a determiner, the singular form of *those*; hence *those gentlemen: that gentleman*. The word *that* which introduces a dependent projecting clause is yet another *that*, and belongs to a different word class, namely the class of binding conjunctions (or binders). This is arguably the same *that* that we find introducing *fact*-type rankshifted clauses (for example, *the fact that heat is transferred*) though a dependent clause is not, of course, the same as an embedded clause.

*That* differs from the other binding conjunctions (*although, since, because, when*, and so on) in at least one way. Although binders cannot normally be omitted from finite dependent clauses, *that* is an exception. It is often optional, and so we frequently hear or read sentences like (15) and (16).

(15)  She said she hadn't known anything about my being called to Personville by her employer.
(16)  He didn't know his father was in it as deep as anybody else.

Where the projection is a reported interrogative, with a verb such as *ask*, *enquire* or *wonder*, the binding conjunction is likely to be *if* or *whether*; or some other wh-word may be involved: *who, which, where, how, why* or *what*.

These items, unlike *that*, cannot be omitted. To wonder if or whether something is the case is to ask oneself a question. For example, (17), using *if*, is a projection of an either-or question (17a); and (18) is a projection of a wh-question involving *why*, (18a).

(17)  I wondered if he meant pick him up or pick him off.
(17a) Does he mean pick him up or pick him off?
(18)  May I ask why I am being questioned in this manner?
(18a) Why am I being questioned in this manner?

Notice that the inversion of Subject and Finite which characteristically occurs in direct questions does not occur in the reported (indirect) version. In fact, Example (18) has a direct question with an indirect question dependent on it. There is Subject-Finite inversion in the first: *May I*, but not in the second: *I am*.

Mental processes involving verbs like *believe, hope, pretend, wish*, and *wonder* can project; and so can verbal processes involving verbs like *argue, claim, declare, explain, insist, promise, vow*.


## 10.4  *Non-finite projections*

Like expansion clauses (*see* Chapter 9), projection clauses may be finite or non-finite. Reported commands and requests are particularly strong candidates for realization as non-finite dependent clauses, and so are promises, as in (19) and (20).

(19)  Ron told you to check the regulations.
(20)  I promised to do that.

The verb *ask* can be used to project not only questions but also requests. Of course, one politeness strategy for eliciting what Halliday refers to as 'goods and services' is to use the interrogative so that instead of using the imperative, as in Example (21), we may prefer the less threatening interrogative, as in (21a).

(21)  Give me some water.
(21a) Will you give me some water?

Hence, it is not surprising that we frequently find indirect requests projected by *ask*.

(22)  She asked me to give her some water.

Again, the hypotactic projection is not necessarily a one-to-one transposition of the actual wording of the original. Example (22) could be a report of (21) or (21a) or a number of other wordings.

In structures of this kind *ask* is almost synonymous with *request*. Although finite clauses with *that* can express such projected requests, as in Example

(23), they are rare in most registers of modern English.

(23)  She asked that I should give her some water.

All these non-finite projections are analysed along the same lines as hypotactic projected finite clauses, so the reporting clause (containing the Sayer) is dominant and the reported clause is dependent. The analysis is represented in Fig. 10.2.

| ||| Ron told you || | to check the regulations. ||| |
|---|---|
| ||| I promised || | to do that. ||| |
| ||| She asked me || | to give her some water. ||| |
| α | β |

**Fig. 10.2**

## 10.5   *Dependent versus embedded projections*

Many of the verbs that can introduce projections have noun counterparts which are also associated with projections. In Figure 10.3 the set of verbs in the left hand column is paralleled by the set of nouns in the right-hand column. There are spaces where no counterpart exists, however. There is no obvious linguistic reason why these particular words are lacking, but it is a widely acknowledged fact that all languages have lexical gaps.

Though fairly long, Fig. 10.3 is by no means a complete list of relevant items. The gaps in the noun column can be filled with gerunds (*holding, saying, swearing, imagining*) but these exist for all lexical verbs and are not straightforward lexical nouns like the words given in the table. Obviously, there is a nominal equivalent of the verb *imagine* in the form *imagination*, but this does not occur with embedded *that*-clauses as the other nouns in the list do.

All the verbs and nouns in the table can occur with projection clauses introduced by the word *that*. Some of them can also occur with to-infinitive clauses. There is a grammatical difference between the projections with verbs and with nouns, however, in that the clauses projected by the verbs are dependent clauses, whereas those which occur with the nouns are embedded; that is, the projections take the form of rankshifted clauses occurring as Postmodifiers of the Head nouns in question. Examples follow.

(24)  Servetus had thrown off the idea that the blood is circulated through the lungs.
(25)  He demonstrated his argument that there are three innate emotions.
(26)  Du Bois-Reymond himself drew the conclusion that there was no real difference between organic and inorganic nature.

| VERB | NOUN |
|------|------|
| assert | assertion |
| argue | argument |
| claim | claim |
| confess | confession |
| declare | declaration |
| deny | denial |
| hold | — |
| insist | insistence |
| proclaim | proclamation |
| promise | promise |
| say | — |
| state | statement |
| swear | — |
| tell | (tale?) |
| vow | vow |
| assume | assumption |
| believe | belief |
| conclude | conclusion |
| desire | desire |
| hope | hope |
| hypothesize | hypothesis |
| — | idea |
| imagine | — |
| know | knowledge |
| speculate | speculation |
| suppose | supposition |
| theorize | theory |
| think | thought |
| — | view |
| wish | wish |

**Fig. 10.3**

Using a projecting verb instead of a noun, we can construct a parallel structure for (26) in (26a).

(26a) Du Bois-Reymond himself concluded that there was no real difference
between organic and inorganic nature.

The crucial difference between (26) and (26a) is that, whereas (26) contains a noun *conclusion* with a projection as Postmodifier, (26a) contains a verb *conclude* with a projection as a dependent clause. The diagrammatic analysis in Fig. 10.4 highlights the difference, namely that the *that*-clause in one is a rankshifted clause embedded as part of a Nominal Group, and the *that*-clause in the other is a dependent clause.

| Du Bois-Reymond himself drew the conclusion [[that there was no real difference]]. | | | | | | |
|---|---|---|---|---|---|---|
| | | [[ | \| S \| F \| | C | ]] |
| S | \| F/P \| | | C | | |

| \|\|\| Du Bois-Reymond himself concluded \|\| that there was no real difference. \|\|\| | | | | | | |
|---|---|---|---|---|---|---|
| \|\|\| | S | \| F/P \|\| | \| S \| F \| | C | \|\|\| |
| | α | \|\| | β | | |

**Fig. 10.4**

## 10.6   *More complicated examples*

Most of the examples considered so far have involved only two clauses, either paratactically or hypotactically related. However, clause complexes are frequently more complicated than this, and we find dependent clauses within dependent clauses, hypotactic within paratactic, or vice versa. Earlier in this chapter we promised to return to Example (7), repeated here.

(7) A uniformed copper held the gate open, muttering nervously: 'Hurry it up, boys, please.'

In this clause complex, we have a paratactic projection as part of a dependent expansion clause. The second half of the clause complex:

*muttering nervously: 'Hurry it up, boys, please.'*

is in a hypotactic (expansion) relationship with the first clause:

*A uniformed copper held the gate open,*

We therefore label the first clause α and the rest β. The β part, however, consists of two clauses in a paratactic relation, and so we label these two clauses **1** and **2**. Since **1** and **2** together make up the dependent (β) to the dominant (α) of the first clause, we call them β1 and β2. This information can be expressed as in Figure 10.5.

A further example of a paratactic complex forming the dependent clause within a hypotactic complex is (27), but this time only projections are involved.

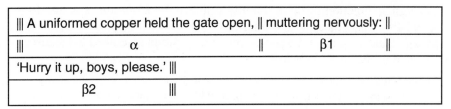

**Fig. 10.5**

(27) Wallace thought that perhaps the earth's orbit had formerly been less eccentric, and that this might have made a difference.

This may be analysed as in Fig. 10.6.

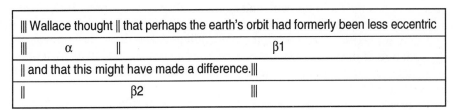

**Fig. 10.6**

Sometimes we find a hypotactic complex (α, β) inside a paratactic complex (**1, 2**), as in Example (28); the projection here also includes an embedded clause.

(28) ||| He said, || 'I think || it's time [[I went back to the factory]].|||
    |||   1   || 2α   ||          2β              |||

Sometimes there is an even more complicated hierarchical relationship in a clause complex. In Example (29), we have three clauses in a hypotactic sequence dependent on another projection as the second element in a paratactic clause complex.

(29) ||| Nixon said, || 'Krogh told me || he didn't believe || I ordered the break-in.' |||
    |||    1    ||    2α    ||    2β    ||     2γ      |||

In (29), *I ordered the break-in* is dependent on *he didn't believe*, which in turn is dependent on *Krogh told me*; hence the labels α, β, γ. All of this, however, is in a paratactic relation to *Nixon said*; hence the labels **1** and **2**.

Example (30) has a paratactic clause complex within a hypotactic clause complex.

(30) ||| She reported || Starr saying to her, || 'It will never work.' |||
    |||    α    ||    β1    ||    β2    |||

In Example (31), we have a clause complex within an embedded clause. *To maintain that everything could be demonstrated* is an instance of extraposition with *it* functioning as a dummy Subject. *To maintain* is a non-finite Verbal Process projecting the final clause *that everything could be demonstrated*. Thus we have a dependent projection within an embedded clause, as indicated in the analysis below:

(31) It was of the essence of his system, ethically as well as metaphysically,
[[ ||| to maintain || that everything could be demonstrated.||| ]].
[[ |||     α    ||           β                     ||| ]]

Authentic texts sometimes throw up examples of much greater complexity, a sample of which is to be found in Example (32).

(32) A second approach is to assume that in some fashion the cells 'know' where they are situated within a developing organism and behave accordingly.

The dependency relationships are entirely within the rankshifted clause complex, which is the Complement, and so the totality is in a sense a free-standing clause with the structure **S, F, C**.

The complexity arises within the embedding and so does not impinge on the structure of the whole, but the embedding can be analysed in its own right as a clause complex, each clause in the complex being analysable in its turn in terms of SFPCA.

To break this down, let us look at the complex in subsections, as in Fig. 10.7. When we put all these labels together and add SFPCA labels, we come up with Fig. 10.8. Within the rankshifted clause, the dependency relations are as follows: *to assume*, although non-finite, is the projecting clause (the dominant or α-clause), and all that follows it is the hypotactic projection from that α-clause. Thus all the rest is labelled β (that is the first symbol in the string

| to assume | that in some fashion the cells know where they are situated within a developing organism and behave accordingly. |
|---|---|
| α | β |

| in some fashion the cells know where they are situated within a developing organism | and behave accordingly |
|---|---|
| 1 | 2 |

| the cells know | where they are situated within a developing organism |
|---|---|
| α | β |

**Fig. 10.7**

on the third and seventh line of Fig. 10.8). However, the β section is a paratactic complex of two parts linked by *and*; hence we add the labels **1** and **2**. The first member of this paratactic pair is itself a hypotactic projection complex consisting of a projecting, dominant clause (*in some fashion the cells know*) and a projected, dependent clause (*where they are situated within a developing organism*), so we label these respectively α and β, the third symbol in the string.

| A second approach | is | [[ ||| to assume || | that | in some fashion | the cells | know || |
|---|---|---|---|---|---|---|
| | | [[ ||| **P** || | | **A** | **S** | **F/P** || |
| | | α | | β1α | | |
| **S** | | **F** | | **C** | | |
| where | they | are | situated | within a developing organism || | and | behave | accordingly ||| ]] |
| | **S** | **F** | **P** | **A** | || | **F/P** | **A** ||| ]] |
| | | β1β | | | | β2 | |
| | | | | *C continued* | | | |

**Fig. 10.8**

## 10.7  *Ambiguous structures*

A potential for ambiguity arises when it is not clear whether a structure is, for example, an expansion or a projection, as in the invented Example (33).

> (33)  He promised to placate the generals.

Where this string of words could be roughly paraphrased as (33a), the clause *to placate the generals* is an expansion; where it can be roughly paraphrased as (33b), it is a projection. Example (33c) has only one possible reading; it must be an expansion and not a projection. In speech, the two different readings of (33) are distinguished by different intonation. The labelling of the clauses as α, β is not affected by this distinction between expansion and projection, of course, since both involve dependency.

> (33a)  He made a promise in order to placate the generals.
> (33b)  He made a promise that he would placate the generals.
> (33c)  To placate the generals, he promised.

Sometimes, as in Example (34), something similar happens when the clause follows certain nouns.

> (34)  He made a promise to placate the generals.

There is possible confusion between a *to-infinitive* clause (i) as a dependent expansion clause and (ii) as a rankshifted clause, Postmodifier of a Head. In the first reading, *to placate the generals* means *in order to placate the gener-als*; in the second, *to placate the generals* is what he promised.

## *Summary*

In this chapter we complete our treatment of paratactic and hypotactic clause complexes by considering the function of Projection.

Paratactic projection clauses are typically 'direct speech' (including ver-batim speech, thought or writing). Projecting and projected clauses may occur in any order or projecting clauses may interrupt projected clauses. Paratactic clauses are labelled **1, 2**, and so on, in sequential order of occur-rence, regardless of whether the projecting clause or the projected clause comes first.

Hypotactic projection clauses are typically 'reported speech' (or thought or writing). Hypotactically related clauses are labelled α, β, and so on to indi-cate grammatical dependency, regardless of the order in which the clauses occur. However, in hypotactic projections, projecting (dominant) clauses typically precede projected (dependent) clauses.

Hypotactic projections may be realized by finite clauses or non-finite clauses. The latter often occur as indirect questions and commands when the projecting process is realized by verbs such as *tell, order, ask, wonder* (though these verbs can also occur with finite projection clauses). When the projecting process is realized as a noun (for example, *statement, assertion, insistence*), the clause which realizes the projection is embedded as Postmodifier of that noun; that is, as a rankshifted clause within the Nominal Group. As such, it does not count as a clause in a clause complex.

In the latter part of the chapter, some more complicated examples and potential ambiguities are presented.

## *Further study*

### Clause complex versus group complex

In this grammar, structures with verbs like *want* followed by a to-infinitive are on the boundary between projected dependent clauses and verbal com-plexes.

As mentioned in Chapter 2, examples of Verbal Group complexes are the italicized items in (35), (36) and (37).

(35)  They *seem to enjoy* it.
(36)  The exporters *had started to find* other routes.
(37)  Just *keep working*.

These are structures where one verb is triggered by the other so that the first verb almost resembles an auxiliary though it is not one of the closed set of auxiliary verbs, which are forms of *be*, *have* and the modals. Thus, two (or more) Verbal Groups are combined to make up a group complex within a single clause.

Verbs such as *want, wish, expect, hope* obviously resemble these in their potential for combining with to-infinitives, but they also resemble Mental Process projecting verbs such as *think* and *believe*. When they combine with *that*-clauses (as *wish, expect,* and *hope* readily do), we do have clear cases of hypotactic projection with the *that*-clause as a dependent, as in Example (38).

(38) I hope that you can follow all this.

However, when they combine with to-infinitive structures, as in (39) and (40), the analysis is more debatable.

(39) I hope to follow all this.
(40) I want them to follow all this.

In Chapter 7 of *Introduction to Functional Grammar*, Halliday (1994) points out that these structures can be analysed as verb complexes in a single clause or as hypotactic projections in two clauses. He expresses a preference for treating instances like (39) as the former and instances like (40) as the latter, but concedes that the decision is not at all clear-cut. On the two-clause analysis (40) would be analysed as follows:

||| I want || them to follow all this. |||
||| α || β || |||

One drawback of this analysis is that the pronoun in the second clause must be construed as the Subject, yet it is clearly in the objective form. In a verb complex analysis *them* would be construed as simultaneously Object Complement of *want* and Subject of *to follow*, which is messy but seems to capture something of what is going on here.

## Nominalization

Halliday (1994) and Halliday and Martin (1993) discuss nominalization in an illuminating manner as 'grammatical metaphor'.

## *Exercises*

*Exercise 10.1*

Identify the italicized dependent clauses in the following as Expansions or Projections.

1. *If there are*, they can be made the basis both for rules of private conduct and for a theory of politics.
2. He can prove *that his ideal republic is good.*
3. *When adjusting the gap*, never bend the centre electrode but always the outer one.
4. Driesch conceded *that the environment exerted some effect on development.*
5. Remove the steering wheel *as described in Chapter 9.*
6. Unscrew the switch securing screw *to expose the locking fork.*
7. *Having by now been a week or more in Egypt*, the French had heard many stories of the magnificence and the ferocity of the Mamelukes
8. Bonaparte seems to have hoped almost to the end *that Josephine would come with him.*
9. By what mechanism could he have hoped, even in principle, *to predict the future with certainty on the basis of knowledge of the present?*
10. Vito Volterra was an outstanding Italian mathematician of the first part of this century, *whose work strongly influenced the development of modern calculus.*

*Exercise 10.2*

From the italicized clauses below, distinguish between rankshifted and dependent clauses.

1. It was the Press *that was responsible for instigating the unrest.*
2. Of course, we cannot say *that the Press is to blame for all the trouble.*
3. He gave an assurance *that policemen would be available at all polling stations.*
4. And that's when I realized *that talking to those people was futile.*
5. The idea *that the brain was in constant activity* was thought absurd.
6. Nobody is asking you *to do any of these things.*
7. Mr Haskell said *that both factories had been closed.*
8. It was an obvious guess *that a special cell-division must occur.*
9. In short, the hypothesis is *that every time series of price change data has Bachelier's independence, stationarity and normality properties.*
10. The stationarity hypothesis says *that regardless of when we start taking observations, i.e., the initial time t\*, the time series of price changes obeys the same probability law.*

*Exercise 10.3*

Indicate clause boundaries and label hypotactic complexes as α, β, and paratactic complexes as **1, 2**.

1. His company's bid stated that sales in the first year would be about £2bn.
2. 'It must be my lucky day,' he says.

*I objected that [banning the Post] would create all kinds of repercussion and [blow up into a public relations mess [[ that would spoil the wedding ]]*

3. Nixon said he hadn't read the speech yet.
4. He concedes the effect was a touch farcical.
5. I said, 'She *may* see him.'
6. He replied: 'I am not concerned with the intention of the law.'
7. 'What happened to your hotels?' I asked.
8. I asked him whether he had ever felt threatened.
9. He added, startlingly: 'We have regular meetings.'
10. In the Rivonia trial, a number of the defendants admitted openly that they resorted to violence.

*Exercise 10.4*

Label the following examples in the same way as the previous exercise. These are more complex. Indicate rankshifted clauses with double square brackets.

1. 'Any news about when we're getting out of here?' said Jack.
2. David Rigg explains: 'As you poise your pen over the piece of paper, you think of your girlfriend's number.'
3. I suppose uncle had told the family that he would take care of everything.
4. ' But you said you'd have a real holiday,' said Paul, 'and now you work.'
5. I objected that banning the *Post* would create all kinds of repercussions and blow up into a public relations mess that would spoil the wedding.
6. This time the manager asked the secretary to tell us of the decision that we were fired.
7. Weir said, 'Get out before another one blows.'
8. Bachelier thought it was reasonable to assume that the Central Limit Theorem of probability theory would apply to these price fluctuations.
9. In particular, he envisioned not only that the machine's scanning head would be capable of reading symbols from the tape, but also that the head could be in any of a finite number of internal 'states'.
10. This is similar to the situation you might face after a call from your banker telling you that the royalty cheque you received from your publisher just bounced.

*Exercise 10.5*

Analyse the following clause complex and add SFPCA labels.

/ Seated in Sawiyeto's second house, / we were asked [if we wanted coffee]] and we accepted. /

*Exercise 10.6*

Consider the dialogue in Text 10A.

'You mean you're going to tell me you knew me when you braced me yesterday?' I asked. 'And you're going to tell me Bush hadn't told you to bet on him? And you didn't until afterwards? And you knew about his record because you used to be a bull? And you thought if you could get me to put it to him you could clean up a little dough playing him?'

**Text 10A**    (Hammett, *Red harvest*,[1] p. 85). Note: obsolete American slang: *brace* – face up to; *bull* – policeman; *dough* – money.

1. What impression do you think the narrator (the I-character) is trying to give?
2. How does he achieve this?
3. What is striking about the clauses in the first paragraph?
4. How many clauses are there in the first sentence: 'You mean ... asked.'
5. What is the relation of *you knew me* to *you're going to tell me*?
6. What is the relation of *when you braced me yesterday* to *you knew me*?
7. Indicate clause boundaries and label the clauses in the clause complex:

   *And you're going to tell me Bush hadn't told you to bet on him.*


**Answers**

*Exercise 10.1*

1. Expansion.    2. Projection.    3. Expansion.    4. Projection.
5. Expansion.    6. Expansion.    7. Expansion.    8. Projection.
9. Projection.    10 Expansion.


*Exercise 10.2*

1. Rankshifted.    2. Dependent.    3. Rankshifted.    4. Dependent.
5. Rankshifted.    6. Dependent.    7. Dependent.    8. Rankshifted.
9. Rankshifted.    10. Dependent.


*Exercise 10.3*

1. ||| His company's bid stated || that sales in the first year would be about £2bn. |||
   |||              α                ||                       β                          |||

2. ||| 'It must be my lucky day,' || he says. |||
   |||              1                ||    2    |||

3. ||| Nixon said || he hadn't read the speech yet. |||
   |||      α       ||              β                  |||

4. ||| He concedes || the effect was a touch farcical. |||
   |||      α        ||              β                    |||

5. ||| I said, || 'She *may* see him.' |||
    |||   1   ||      2      |||

6. ||| He replied: || 'I am not concerned with the intention of the law.' |||
    |||    1    ||           2           |||

7. ||| 'What happened to your hotels?' || I asked. |||
    |||         1         ||   2   |||

8. ||| I asked him || whether he had ever felt threatened.|||
    |||    $\alpha$    ||       $\beta$       |||

9. ||| He added, startlingly: || 'We have regular meetings.' |||
    |||       .1       ||      2      |||

10. ||| In the Rivonia trial, a number of the defendants admitted openly ||
     |||                        $\alpha$                  ||
     that they resorted to violence. |||
            $\beta$       |||

## *Exercise 10.4*

1. ||| 'Any news about [[when we're getting out of here]]?'|| said Jack. |||
    |||                    1                 ||   2   |||

2. ||| David Rigg explains: || 'As you poise your pen over the piece of paper, ||
    |||      1      ||           2$\beta$           ||
    you think of your girlfriend's number.' |||
           2$\alpha$          |||

3. ||| I suppose || uncle had told the family || that he would take care of
    |||    $\alpha$    ||      $\beta$      ||      $\gamma$     
    everything. |||
        |||

4. |||'But you said || you'd have a real holiday,' || said Paul, || 'and now you work.' |||
    |||   1$\alpha$   ||      1$\beta$      ||   2   ||    3    |||

5. ||| I objected || that [[banning the *Post*]] would create all kinds of repercussions ||
    |||    $\alpha$    ||                 $\beta$1              ||
    and blow up into a public relations mess [[that would spoil the wedding]].|||
                     $\beta$2           |||

6. ||| This time the manager asked the secretary || to tell us of the decision [[that
    |||                 $\alpha$                 ||        $\beta$       
    we were fired]]. |||
        |||

7. ||| Weir said, || 'Get out || before another one blows.' |||
    |||   1   ||   2$\alpha$   ||      2$\beta$      |||

8.

| ‖ Bachelier thought ‖ | it was reasonable | [[to assume ‖ | that the Central |
|---|---|---|---|
| | | [[      α | β |
| α | | β | |

| Limit Theorem of probability theory would apply to these price fluctuations ‖ ]]. |
|---|
| *embedded clause β continued* |
| *superordinate clause β continued* |

9.

| ‖‖ In particular, he envisioned ‖ | not only that the machine's scanning head |
|---|---|
| α | β1 |

| would be capable of [[reading symbols from the tape]] ‖ |
|---|
| *β1 continued* |

| but also that the head could be in any of a finite number of internal 'states'. ‖‖ |
|---|
| β2 |

10. ‖‖ This is similar to the situation [[you might face after a call from your banker
[[telling you ‖ that the royalty cheque [[you received from your pub-
[[    α        ‖                                                    β
lisher]] just bounced. ‖‖ ]]
                                    ]]

Note: in 10 the projection is entirely within the embedded clause.

*Exercise 10.5*

| ‖‖ Seated | in Sawiyeto's second house,‖ | we | were | asked‖ |
|---|---|---|---|---|
| ‖‖   P | A | S | F | P    ‖ |
| β | | α1α | | |

| if | we | wanted | coffee‖ | and | we | accepted. ‖‖ |
|---|---|---|---|---|---|---|
| | S | F/P | C   ‖ | | S | F/P    ‖‖ |
| α1β | | | | α2 | | |

*Exercise 10.6*

1. Open-ended question. One answer is that he is trying to create an impression of knowing a great deal about the situation, to show that he is one step
ahead of the other speaker. (Out of context, it may appear that he is
expressing incredulity.)
2. By predicting what the other character was going to say. (A more techni-

cal answer would be the same as the answer to 3.)
3. Lots of hypotactic projections; projections within projections. Lots of sen-
   tence-initial *and*.
4. Five.
5. Hypotactic projection.
6. Hypotactic expansion.
7. ||| And you're going to tell me || Bush hadn't told you || to bet on him?' |||
     |||         α        ||      β     ||   γ    |||

## Note

1.  Hammett, Dashiel 1975 (originally published by Cassell & Co. 1950): *Red
    harvest*. London: Pan Books.

# 11

# Applications of Functional Analysis

## 11.1   *Explanations and theories*

Perhaps the main message of this book is that language is worth studying for its own sake. In the same way that scientists have sought for many hundreds of years to understand the nature of the universe, the secret of living things and the functions of the human body, grammarians and other linguists have struggled to understand more about how human language is structured and to explain how communication takes place. Some people, however, not only find this objective daunting but they fear that the analysis of language, even a functional analysis, may subtract from the richness and beauty of language.

The philosopher Daniel C. Dennett (1991: p. 454) writes about explanations in the following way:

> When we learn that the only difference between gold and silver is the number of subatomic particles in their atoms, we may feel cheated or angry – those physicists have explained something away: the goldness is gone from the gold; they've left out the very silveriness of silver that we appreciate. And when they explain the way reflection and absorption of electromagnetic radiation accounts for colors and color vision, they seem to neglect the very thing that matters most. But of course there has to be some 'leaving out' – otherwise we wouldn't have begun to explain. Leaving out something is not a feature of failed explanations, but of successful explanations.

In the previous chapters of this book, we have introduced methods of analysis that can be used to give insight into how the English language is structured. Each method of analysis can be seen as a hypothesis about *part of* the structure of English. We can see, for example, that the analysis of clause as exchange (by splitting it into its SFPCA components) is making the claim that clauses are constructed of up to five kinds of constituents, each having its own distinct characteristics. Similarly, the analysis of clause as message (into Theme-Rheme and Given-New) makes the claim that information is structured by the ordering of two sets of parallel elements selected on the basis of the speaker's and hearer's shared understanding and on the textual constraints that govern the speaker's choice of starting point for the clause. These hypotheses, along with all the other claims about language summarized in this book, make up together a linguistic theory, a theory that incorporates the idea mentioned in Chapter 1 of this book that a language is a set of systems.

In this chapter we address some major questions. How can we test the truth of individual hypotheses and the validity of the theory? What use is the theory to the nonlinguist who may nevertheless have an interest in language and the use of language: the teacher, the writer, the politician, the translator, the literary critic, the therapist, and so on? If a functional theory of language has any validity, it should, we believe, render insights into the way language works in social interaction.

Halliday (1994: p. xxix) described a theory as 'a means of action'. By this he means that we should be able to use a theory, and the hypotheses related to it, as the basis for a very wide range of tasks, not only our grand aim of understanding the nature and functions of language, but also more practical tasks like helping people to learn foreign languages, improving our writing skills, or training interpreters. Halliday, in fact, lists twenty-one distinct applications of functional linguistics and concedes that there are more.

The years since 1985 have seen a rapid expansion of functional linguistic applications, particularly in text analysis, and much of the research in this area is presently feeding into spoken language development and the teaching of language use at the levels of school and university.

## 11.2 *Writing in science and technology*

One area of interest for applied linguists is the way in which scientific and technical ideas are expressed in English. Many people, both native speakers and non-native speakers find the language of scientific thought extremely difficult to access, and some educators believe that the language of science acts as a barrier to learning in the field, effectively stopping some children from achieving success in science. There are also many adults, with no technical training or background, working in business, journalism or the arts, who have, in recent years, needed to learn computational techniques and have had to struggle with instruction manuals that are extremely difficult to understand. Internationally, scientists whose first language is not English often need to read textbooks or research articles published in English, and many themselves wish to publish in English. Such practical problems of teaching and learning in relation to science have led to a number of investigations into the nature of scientific writing.

Halliday and Martin (1993) address the problem from two points of view: the identification of the particular characteristics of scientific prose and the issues involved in educating children to use and understand language appropriate to specific contexts. In both these tasks, they use aspects of functional grammar to analyse and describe the language and to explain how it developed (from an historical perspective) in the way it did.

Among the specific grammatical features of scientific writing discussed by Halliday and Martin is the nominalization of *processes* (*see* Chapter 6), and we discuss this further as an example of the type of approach that has proved enlightening.

Nominalization allows a process, more obviously realized as a verb, to be realized as a noun and hence to become a participant in a further process. Some examples of this type of nominalized process (though not necessarily scientific ones) can be seen in Fig. 11.1.

| Verb | Noun |
|------|------|
| accelerate | acceleration |
| compare | comparison |
| describe | description |
| distil | distillation |
| indicate | indication |
| terminate | termination |

**Fig. 11.1**   Nominalized processes

If we use a verb to express a process, it is necessary to give the verb a Subject, and in the case of some verbs, like *describe* for example, a Complement as well. This entails expressing the participants in the process. However, if we nominalize the process, we can exclude the participants relating to that process, as we can see from the following invented examples, numbered (1) and (2).

(1)  Moorehead described the journeys of Bruce.
(2)  The description is incomplete.

With the use of the verb in (1), it was necessary to include a reference to the person who wrote the description (Moorehead in this case) and also a reference to *what* he described (the journeys of Bruce), whereas in (2), where the process is nominalized, neither of these participants is required.

Example (3), explaining the term *pollination*, comes from an agricultural textbook by O. Akinsanmi.

(3)  Pollination is the physical transfer of pollen grains from the anther to the stigma. There are two types of pollination: self-pollination and cross-pollination. Self-pollination takes place when the pollen grains are transferred from the anther to the stigma of a flower on the same plane. Cross-pollination occurs when the pollen grains are transferred from the anther of a flower of one plant to the stigma of a flower of a different plant of the same species.

Here the Agent of the process of pollination is not mentioned as a participant in the process. The text refers to the *physical transfer of pollen grains* but does not explain how this transfer takes place or what causes it. The writer in the passage above presents the transfer as an abstract process in such a way as to cover all cases. A few sentences further on in the same text, however, we find (4), a clause where the writer of the text chooses to introduce, as New information, precise details about the animate and inaminate things which undertake the work of pollination.

(4) The common agents of pollination are insects, birds, wind and animals, especially man.

The writer makes the assumption that the reader 'understands' that there must be agents of pollination and so feels able to put *the common agents of pollination* in Theme position. He can then present his New information (*are insects, birds, wind and animals*) in Rheme position.

The tendency to use Nominal Groups rather than verbal processes has a number of major effects on scientific text. Firstly, it is a means whereby all reference to people can be omitted, and scientific knowledge can be presented as though it has some external objective reality quite apart from the people who are engaged in observing or researching it. This facilitates the expression of general 'truths' and 'claims' about the nature of the world. Secondly, it gives the writer a wide choice of elements for Theme position in the clause. Not only can a process easily become the starting point in the clause (which can be useful for textual cohesion as we saw in Chapter 5), but it allows agents – or even further processes – to be left to the end of the clause (in Rheme position) where they carry more communicative dynamism. Thirdly, it allows the process to become the *Head of a Nominal Group* and, as such, available for modification, or *Classifier in a Nominal Group*. Examples can be seen in Fig. 11.2.

| Nominal as Head | Nominal as Classifier |
|---|---|
| oil gallery *lubrication* | *lubrication* process |
| muscular *contraction* | *contraction* rate |
| root *penetration* | *weld penetration* zone |
| sheet metal *fabrication* | *fabrication* engineering |
| technical *information* | *information* technology |

**Fig. 11.2**   Nominalized processes in Nominal Groups

Furthermore, the nominalization of processes enables the writer to concisely display relationships (like *cause, result, reason, comparison* and *dependency*) between processes, as in the following examples, the first of which is quoted by Halliday (Halliday and Martin, 1993: p. 87).

(5) The rate of crack growth *depends on* the chemical environment.

(6) Evaporation *causes* cooling.

(7) The multiplication of fractions *is easier than* addition or subtraction.

Halliday (Halliday and Martin, 1993: pp. 86–93) refers to verbs like *cause*, *depend on*, *result in*, as expressing 'internal relations' between different parts of the clause. 'Cooling', in (6), is an example of the gerund form of a process and is representative of an alternative form of nominalization in English.

Nominalization and other grammatical characteristics of scientific texts are discussed by Martin (Halliday and Martin, 1993), who shows, in some detail, both how important they are for the expression of scientific knowledge and also how schoolchildren need to be oriented into the use of appropriate scientific language at an early age. In a perceptive critique of misguided syllabus documents for primary education (in an Australian context but equally applicable in many countries), Martin (p. 172) makes the following observations (slightly abridged here):

> People sometimes complain that science uses too much technical language which they refer to pejoratively as 'jargon'. They complain because the jargon excludes: it makes science hard to understand. This is a problem. Jargon is often used where it is not needed. . . . However, the simple fact is that no scientist could do his or her job without technical discourse. Not only is it compact and therefore efficient, but most importantly it codes a different perspective on reality, a perspective accumulated over centuries of scientific enquiry. It constructs the world in a different way. Science could not be science without deploying technical discourse as a fundamental tool. It is thus very worrying when syllabus documents discourage teachers from using technical language with students, especially in the early years.

Martin is not, of course, denying that it is perfectly possible to have popularizations of science, writing designed to explain scientific research to non-scientists. School textbooks (which are a main concern of Martin's discussion) are a type of popularization of scientific information, but efficient textbooks gradually introduce the important technical language for expressing scientific concepts and functions (like *classification*, *definition*, *analysis*, and *explanation*) so that the student is oriented into scientific discourse and empowered to take on roles in scientific discourse (see also Martin, 1989).

On the issue of accessibility to knowledge, there have been a number of studies of the differences between the discourse of research articles published in specialist journals and the discourse of popular versions directed at non-scientists, written for popular books, newspapers or magazines.

Using the tools of thematic analysis and the description of processes, mood and modality, Francis and Kramer-Dahl (1991) contrast the writing of two neuroscientists, one (Kertesz) who writes in the traditional 'dry and factual' style of a professional case report and the one (Sacks) who consciously breaks away from the 'objective', restrained style and replaces it with an apparently more subjective, popular and less 'scientific' style, closer to narrative and biography. Starting from the three metafunctions, ideational, interpersonal and textual, Francis and Kramer-Dahl are able to show how Sacks incorporates science into his storytelling and how he is making a serious attempt to 'bridge the gap between distant and near experience, between scientific and everyday knowledge and between specialized and everyday audiences'.

Other studies also contrast the language of writing published in serious science journals with that of the more popular versions of scientific research found in magazines such as the *New Scientist* and *Newsweek*. Bloor and Nwogu (1991: pp. 369–84) show how the patterns of thematic progression (explained in Chapter 5) differ in two types of medical text. Although the Constant Theme Pattern and the Linear Theme pattern occur frequently in both genres, journalists who write popular versions of medical research seem to prefer the Linear Theme pattern whereas the scientists, who write research articles proper, use more examples of the Constant Theme pattern. They also report that Themes in popular versions are normally realized by names of scientists acting as Agents in the clause rather than by nominal processes, which are more often found in serious research articles. They comment as follows:

> It is a truism of register analysis that scientific prose is by convention impersonal, and the received rationale for this is that it is the 'science' that matters rather than the individuals who engage in it. To a large extent this is the correct explanation. Although no one who has experience of the academic world can believe that individual scientists genuinely wish to play down their own role in the enterprise, they do wish to give the impression of doing so, thereby conforming to the expectations of the scientific peer group.

The study of thematic progression in texts has also been used to compare the work of native speakers writing in English with that of non-native speakers. In a study of the way in which Finnish scientists write in English, Ventola and Mauranen (1991) analyse patterns of thematic progression and find that the native speaker texts show more variation in thematic patterns than the Finnish writers' texts. The Finnish writers used, almost exclusively, either a Linear Theme or a Constant Theme Pattern whereas the native speakers used all available patterns. The study also found that the Finnish writers, on the whole, used less lexical cohesion between Themes, fewer cohesive conjunctions and overused a very limited number of 'favourite' connectors, such as *however, thus, therefore,* and *also*.

A rather different application of functional grammar to academic writing has concerned the use of different verbal processes in research articles. So-called *reporting verbs* commonly function as sources of projection, as in the following examples:

Keyseling *pointed out* that ...
McGin *explains that* ...
Nagel *claims* that ...

These are generally known as *reporting verbs* since they are used to introduce the ideas and views of cited authors whose work is being reported. Their use in research articles has attracted some attention, usually with the objective of preparing teaching materials for overseas learners of English for academic purposes.

Using a functional model, Thompson and Ye Yiyun (1991) investigate the reporting verbs used in the introductions to one hundred research articles from a variety of fields. They propose a three-part classification of reporting verbs as follows.

> *Textual.* Verbs referring to processes in which the verbal expression is an obligatory component. For example: *state, write, challenge, point out, deny.*
> *Mental.* Verbs referring primarily to mental processes. For example: *believe, think, consider, prefer.*
> *Research.* Verbs referring primarily to the mental or physical processes that are part of research work. For example: *measure, calculate, quantify, obtain, find.*

(Within a pure Hallidayan analysis, processes in what is termed here the 'research' group would be mainly classified as *material processes*.)

They also consider the stance (or attitude) of the author being cited to the reported information and the stance of the writer as revealed in the reporting verbs chosen.

Thomas and Hawes (1994) have followed up this study with a detailed analysis of the reporting verbs in medical journal articles and have identified the patterns of choice available in terms of a network. They name their major categories: (1) Real-world Activity Verbs, such as *observe, find* and *categorize*; (2) Cognition Verbs, such as *think, believe* and *consider*; and (3) Discourse Activity Verbs, such as *state, suggest,* and *report*.

## 11.3    *Valued texts*

The question of how to speak or write more effectively is one that has been of interest to educators and critics for hundreds of years. Most teachers and literary critics have something to say on the subject, and innumerable books and leaflets have been written setting out advice on public speaking and on how to write everything from school essays to business letters. Although classical rhetoric considered the relationship between language and communicative effects in some detail, most educational approaches in recent times (at least for English) have focused on matters such as preparation and planning and how to approach the topic without overt discussion of language. For public speaking and lecturing, we find advice on tone of voice and volume, and for writing, on correct layout and the mechanics of spelling and punctuation, but lexicogrammar is largely neglected, except for pointing out common stylistic 'errors' or infelicities.

Most people would agree that language users differ in their ability to communicate effectively. There is an intuitive concept of 'valued text', which is to say instances of speaking or writing that are considered 'better' in some ways than others. Yet it is very difficult sometimes to explain precisely why one speaker or writer seems better than another. We tend to use vague descriptive terms such as 'clearer', 'more interesting', 'easier to understand', but novices often find that advice given in such terms is not of much practical use. The teacher puts 'write more clearly' or 'confusing' at the end of a student's essay, but the student is none the wiser about *how* to write more clearly, and the teacher might also be hard put to specify the differences between the clear writer's text and the poor writer's text.

In recent research in applied linguistics, some of the techniques of functional grammar are being used to discover the precise features of valued texts, and there is clearly a lot of scope for further work in this area, not only for educational purposes but also for business, journalism, politics and other fields where effective communication is important.

Martin (Halliday and Martin, 1993: pp. 211–13) uses Theme analysis to show the differences between the writing of an eight-year-old and the more sophisticated writing style of a sixteen-year-old on the same topic. The older writer uses much lengthier themes (for example, *the atmosphere at the dawn service*) than the younger writer, who favoured Themes like *I*, *some* and *there*.

Methods of linguistic analysis give us the tools for investigating the characteristics of valued text, and a number of research studies have identified measurable characteristics of such texts or compared successful with less successful communication.

Berry (1989) uses the analysis of Theme to investigate children's ability to write appropriately in the specific genre of a guidebook for tourists. The task of writing a town guide was set as a writing competition for schoolchildren. Some children clearly captured a suitable style for a tourist guide (*Grantham is 108 miles north of London*; *On Saturday, there is a market near the centre of the town*), especially in their selection of third person Topical Themes, whereas others used a less appropriate style with first and second person pronoun Themes referring to the writer and the supposed readers, such as *I think Grantham is a nice place to visit*; *You can pay some money to get into Belvoir castle*. Berry shows how the more successful writers were able to control their thematic choices more consistently than the less successful writers.

Following on from Berry's study, McCarthy and Carter (1994) show how an advertisement for time-share holidays utilizes contrastive thematic structure within the same text. The persuasive section of the text is written in an interactional, informal style, with the use of personal pronouns (*we* and *you*) in Theme position (*You could be enjoying a five star holiday*; *All we ask is that you spend two hours of your time attending a Barratt sales presentation* ...). The 'small print' section of the text, where the restrictions and regulations are listed, displays a more formal style with a different selection of Themes. (*To qualify you must be over 21*; *Present owners are not eligible*; *All flight arrangements are made by ...*). McCarthy and Carter claim that the latter type of writing can 'distance the reader from the text' and discourage 'any sustained reading of this section', which may be to the advantage of the advertiser: successful advertisements sell more products. Linguistic research into the language of advertising is not new. As long ago as 1966, Leech used a functional model to describe the language of advertising. Such work is, of course, of interest to copywriters, but studies like those of McCarthy and Carter also provide a strong argument for raising the linguistic awareness of consumers, since, as McCarthy and Carter appreciate, readers who are aware of linguistic tricks are better equipped to read critically and hence better able to evaluate persuasive texts properly.

Turning to spoken English, Tyler (1994) is interested in the effect of hypotactic and paratactic structures on the comprehensibility of lectures. Previous research has shown that native speakers of English use more hypotactic structures than paratactic structures in planned spoken discourse (*see* Chapters 9 and 10 for an explanation of hypotactic and paratactic structures). Moreover, in spite of a popular view that simple sentences are easier to understand than clause complexes, Tyler claims that there is little evidence for the idea that anyone finds it easier to understand less complex structures. In fact, Anderson and Davison (1988), who consider a wide body of research in this area, conclude that complex clause structures can facilitate text comprehensibility.

Tyler analyses botany lectures given by two similarly qualified teaching assistants, a native speaker and a non-native speaker of English, in an American university. The non-native speaker had a good level of grammar and pronunciation, as indicated by previous tests. Both lectures were given in English and both followed a prepared plan, provided by the supervising professor. Yet, in spite of these similarities, several independent adjudicators, all native speakers, perceived the non-native speaker's discourse as being more difficult to understand. The same results were obtained when written transcripts of the lectures were read by five native speakers of English (who were not informed of the language background of the presenters): the consistent judgement was that the native speaker's discourse was easier to follow. The subsequent linguistic analysis found that the native speaker used twice as many hypotactic structures in his presentation as the non-native speaker. In particular, the frequency of relative clauses is well over twice as high in the native-speaker text.

Tyler argues that a quantitative analysis is only part of the story. If we examine the texts qualitatively we can observe that the function of the hypotaxis is to signal the speaker's intended logical and prominence relations. The non-native speaker's discourse is predominantly a string of unconnected independent clauses, whereas the native-speaker signals the clause relations and 'peaks of prominence' in the message. This study does not, of course, show that all native speaker lectures would give evidence of sophisticated dependencies or that non-native speakers would necessarily lack the appropriate skills to signal peaks of prominence. It does, however, suggest that there are significant grammatical features of valued texts that can be learned by speakers or writers who wish to improve their communication skills, and it establishes beyond doubt that simplistic linguistic analysis, based only on grammatical 'error', is little help in the evaluation of the success of communication. For such purposes we need a rich linguistic system, such as that provided by a functional lexicogrammar.

## 11.4    *English language teaching*

A major field of application of functional linguistics is in language teaching, and much of the work reported above into scientific writing and valued texts can help the language teacher to understand more about their students' developmental needs by seeing how effective communication works in English. Hopkins and Dudley-Evans (1988: p. 113) stress the importance of teachers understanding the features of the genres that their students need to master so that they are able 'to convey to learners the features of a particular text that make it a good text – in the sense that it performs the function for which it was intended and that it is acceptable by the community within which it was produced.'

Halliday himself has been personally involved in applying his insights to teaching ever since the early days of systemic functional linguistics when he was a co-author with McIntosh and Strevens of the influential work *The linguistic sciences and language teaching*, first published in 1964. This work provided guidance for a whole generation of teachers, textbook writers and teacher trainers both for the general principles on syllabus design and also for the detailed discussion of the phonology and intonation of English and for the introduction to the concepts of register and language for specific purposes.

Over the years, probably the most widespread Hallidayan influence on language teaching has been the work on cohesion. Nowadays work on cohesion is often related to specific genres, but from the date of the publication (1976) of *Cohesion in English* by Halliday and Hasan it attracted the attention of teachers of English as a foreign language, who realized that here was an aspect of English that had been seriously neglected. A glance at textbooks written before that time reveals that most cohesive devices were not taught at all in any systematic way, and certain aspects of the grammar, particularly the nature of ellipsis and substitution in English, had previously been misrepresented in pedagogic grammars.

Nowadays, all general course books and most reading and writing courses incorporate work designed to help learners grasp the cohesive devices of written English. A relatively early example, published only four years after *Cohesion in English*, is found in *Reading and thinking in English*, a course prepared by a team of teachers in Colombia under the direction of John Moore. Nuttall (1985), in her important book for teachers on the development of reading skills, emphasizes the importance of readers' mastery of cohesive devices. She comments:

> Pronoun reference, elliptical sentences and so on are often so straightforward that their potential difficulty is overlooked, and it is only when he (*sic*) encounters problems that the student will think them worth attending to. The problems that arise concern the signification of sentences: the reader who does not know what a pronoun refers to, or who cannot supply the full version of an elliptical sentence, will not be able to establish its signification.

Nuttall's book provides a detailed account (1985: Chapter 7) of how to apply Halliday's and Hasan's description of cohesion in English to the teaching of reading, and much of what is covered would be of equal use in the teaching of writing. Although aimed at the foreign language learner, many of the suggested teaching techniques can also be used beneficially with native speakers.

Whereas cohesion has for many years been a standard element in the English language teaching syllabus, with great benefit to the learner, it is only in more recent years that other aspects of the textual functions of discourse, Theme and Rheme and Given and New, which affect the structure of the clause, have attracted the attention of applied linguists, and very little of their research has yet found its way into the classroom.

In one study, Bloor and Bloor (1992) identified three types of stylistic infelicity in written academic texts caused by unusual use of the Theme-Rheme and Given-New dimension of the grammar. They found that inexperienced writers do not always have sufficient command of the grammatical devices that can be used to control the position of Given and New information in the clause. Since there can be no recourse to intonation and stress in written English, they suggest that more attention needs to be given in teaching to this aspect of the grammar. A sophisticated writer in an academic context needs a good control of the grammar of thematic equatives, predicated theme, and the various exponents of textual theme (*see* Chapters 5 and 6) as well as an understanding of the distribution of Given and New information. This control is, of course, often intuitive, but there is no doubt that some writers, particularly those working in a foreign language, can be helped to improve their style by teachers who can raise their awareness of such issues.

Some recent grammar books and language course books have begun to incorporate work on information structure and focus. Willis's *Students' grammar* (1991) has a unit entitled 'Changing the focus of a sentence' which provides practice exercises in manipulating the word order of sentences to allow for different Given and New information. Breiger and Sweeney (1994), in a book designed to teach the language of Business English, approach the subject from a functional point of view, and incorporate explanations of the use of grammatical forms in ways which are sensitive to functional theory. It is, for example, one of the few pedagogic grammars that explains (p. 50) that one of the uses of the passive voice is to allow the speaker to 'put the information to be emphasized at the end of a clause'. The more usual alternative explanation is also given ('to avoid mentioning the doer' or *agent*) and issues of formality and text type are also discussed, but it is interesting to find information focus (in reality an important use of the passive) being paid some attention in a textbook. There is a great deal of scope for developing this type of work especially in support of advanced writing skills and spoken rhetoric.

In many other respects functional grammar has been particularly useful in the development of course design in English for Specific Purposes and English for Academic Purposes. Munby's work (1978) on the design of communicative syllabuses, which calls for close attention to appropriate language use in course design for adult learners, is based on the assumption that 'language varies as its function varies; it differs in different situations' (Halliday *et al.*, 1964). In fact, much of the descriptive research using a Hallidayan model has been driven by the needs of language course designers who find that not enough is known about typical linguistic behaviour in specific social contexts.

In a particularly useful piece of genre analysis, Ventola (1983; 1987) investigated the structure and language of goal-directed verbal exchanges in a shop, post office and travel agency. Similarly, Swales (1984; 1990; and elsewhere) is influenced by functional models in his development of *genre analysis* as an aid to the teaching of language skills for specific communicative events. He develops a methodology for analysing rhetorical *moves* in written texts (specifically the introductions to research articles) and identifying the significant linguistic expressions related to each move.

A major interest of genre analysts has continued to be writing in an academic context, particularly research articles published in academic journals. Such work has involved the use of both lexical and grammatical analysis, and a particularly interesting and fruitful line of enquiry has been concerned with features of modality. Stubbs (1986), while providing a fascinating overview of work on modality at the time of writing, made a strong case for continued analytical field work into the use of modal forms and 'vague language'. Since his paper was published, a great deal of work has been done on vague language (for example Channell, 1994) and the use of hedging in academic journal articles.

Surprisingly, when researchers writing in English make knowledge claims based on their research evidence, they rarely make bald confident statements, but they usually modify their propositions by the use of modal verbs such as *may*, modal adjuncts such as *possibly* or lexical items that decrease the force of a proposition such as *indicate* or *appear*. Thus, we find, for instance, *This would appear to be in conflict with* ... rather than *This is in conflict with* ... and *These results may have relevance to* ... rather than *These results have relevance to* ... and (in an example from Myers' 1989 data) *These results suggest that U1 RNP is essential for the splicing of mRNA precursors* ... rather than *These results show that*. ...

Myers (1990; and elsewhere) has argued that hedging of this type in scientific articles does not, as some have argued, indicate a lack of commitment to the proposition on behalf of the writer(s) – indeed it is clear in most cases that the writers are fully committed to the value of their claims – but rather that hedging is used to mitigate what might otherwise be considered a face-threatening activity, something that could cause offence to fellow researchers, after the earlier work of Brown and Levinson (1987) on politeness in spoken English. Myers sums up his own view in the following (suitably hedged) claim: 'The hedging of claims is so common that a sentence that looks like a claim but has no hedging is probably not a statement of new knowledge.'

Myers' work on hedging in scientific articles has been followed up with work on economics articles (Dudley-Evans, 1993; Pindi and Bloor, 1987; Bloor and Bloor, 1993) where a rather more complex picture emerges. Hedging is equally common in economics, particularly hedging of major claims on theoretical issues in economics, but a variety of types of claim can be observed, some of which are not hedged. It has also been noted that hedging of claims may be more common in English than in some other languages (Bloor and Bloor, 1991), which has implications both for translation of research articles and for writers whose first language is not English but who are seeking to publish in English language journals.

Hyland (1994) not only provides a useful overview of many studies of hedging not discussed here but also surveys the teaching of such aspects of modality in textbooks on English for academic purposes. He finds that this area of the language is widely neglected even in the teaching of writing with only a patchy coverage of a limited range of items. This is a very important finding, which may well extend to other aspects of the language. Hyland supports Dudley-Evans' view that: 'Materials writers need detailed analyses of the rhetorical and linguistic organization of the tasks (that need to be taught) if they are not to be over-reliant on their own intuition.'

It is precisely because of such detailed analysis that genre and register studies have proved useful in many educational projects. In Australia, for example, the Department of Education, Queensland, undertook a project entitled *Literacy for further studies*, the aim of which was to find ways of developing highly skilled teachers to support students' need for complex literary skills in tertiary education. Basic genres were identified as those which students needed to master (for example, the *factual and persuasive expository essay* and *reports*, such as *laboratory reports*) and teachers were trained to understand the complexity of demands on the learners through the application of systemic functional linguistics to analysing the longer texts typical of tertiary study. The results of the analysis were then used in curriculum development and course planning. Similar work is described in Drury and Webb (1994).

## 11.5    *Language and power*

Since language is a human social phenomenon it develops and changes as people use it for social purposes. Much of our understanding of reality (our models of the world and the way in which we represent the world) is dependent on language. Usually we take this for granted and imagine that we can talk and write about the world in a completely objective way, using language as a tool that is separate from our experience, but, if we stand back, and look at the language that we use or the language that is used around us, we can see how the words and grammar picture reality in certain ways that at the same time reflect our attitudes and influence our future perception of the world. Halliday (1990) illustrates this with the way in which modern societies use the word *grow* with favourable connotations even when writing about activities that may not be good for the planet in any real long-term ways. Starting from the association of *growth* with such ideas as the *growing child* or the *growth of food and plants*, we now talk about *economic growth, industrial growth, growth in air transport*, and so on, and, regardless of reality, the idea that 'growth is good' permeates the language. He quotes from the Sydney Morning Herald, 12 March 1990, to the effect that the annual market forecast of an airplane manufacturing company 'says airline traffic to, from and within the Pacific area *will lead the growth* with rates unmatched anywhere else in the world' and adds that 'the rationale for *a more optimistic outlook* includes prolonged air travel expansion *driven by continued growth* in discretionary incomes' (our italics). This relates to a very common, but questionable, idea of Western culture that 'more is better' and 'bigger is better' discussed by Lakoff and Johnson (1980).

The example of *growth* is a good illustration of how a particular ideology can become set into the form of the language (in this case the lexical item 'grow') and where what might appear to be a standard – even objective – form is in fact coloured by a stock of opinions and attitudes.

A similar case, this time involving the grammatical use of possessive pronouns, concerns the use of the word *my* or *our* in conjunction with nominals representing things that, in fact, cannot be owned in any real sense, as for example in well-attested examples like *our language, my country, my home town, my wife/husband*. It seems likely that the use of possessives in this way can colour people's attitudes to the world and, as well as encouraging traditional loyalty and care, can also encourage possessiveness, nationalism and other negative emotions. If we think of a national group, for example, as belonging to 'us', we may seek to exclude others from having any right to live in that community. This is the type of situation that can lead to the so-called 'ethnic cleansing', where people from one community, who may not actually be the sole owners of the land they live on, assert a privileged position with respect to land or property and force other people (the 'not-us') to leave on pain of death. In this way, political or national power can be reflected in the language and the language in turn can reinforce such power. Similarly, if we talk about the language we learn as infants as 'our' mother tongue or 'our' language, we are encouraged towards an affinity to that language which may discourage us from a desire to engage in interaction in other languages (which may be seen as 'belonging' to foreigners). It seems that some Central African languages, used in regions where most people tend to be multilingual, moving from one small language group to another, do not have the linguistic possibility of using possessive adjectives with the word *language* or of using a possessive pronoun to stand in place of the word *language*. Although speakers can talk about the language of such and such a village or such and such a region, the language is considered to be available to those who use it whether they are native speakers or not, and the notion that a language can be the 'property' of any group is considered nonsense.

Andersen (1988), who used linguistic approaches to look at political issues and at power and success in the academic world, believed that, although our experiences are largely shaped by the discourses of the societies in which we grow up, we can use our consciousness to re-articulate our experience. He wrote:

> Language can help us to become aware of the unconscious pressures that operate on the ways we think and behave. These pressures are not all related to deep and distant experiences lost in our infancies, but also to immediate social expectations that we should act out certain roles, behave and talk in certain ways. We can become more aware of these pressures and so make ourselves less liable to be influenced by them.

The exertion of power by individuals with certain social roles in particular social situations is often revealed in the form of the language, as is the corollary, lack of power. This has been studied, for example, in the context of the traditional classroom, where teachers, who have responsibility for both discipline and learning, dominate the interaction. Reynolds (1990) provides examples from classroom discourse which show how the teacher controls turns at speaking: (a) by naming the pupil they want to speak; (b) by preventing certain pupils from answering questions (calling on 'someone else'); (c) by taking turns themselves by interrupting a pupil's turn; and (d) by control of the topic. He points out that there are cases in his data where pupils challenge the teacher's power by commenting or initiating questions, and he shows how the teacher adapts his language, by making it more forceful, to reassert control. In such cases the teacher specifically names the addressee directly and uses imperatives:

> *Don't try'n be clever, Faisal.*
> *Explain yourself, Faisal.*
> *Answer the question, please, Faisal.*

Reynolds, following other writers, suggests that language becomes more assertive when power is most threatened and the speaker feels under pressure.

The examples we have so far looked at involve lexical choice, grammatical metaphor and grammatical form in an interactive context. Fairclough (1989) comments on the range of linguistic features that he has noted in his investigations into the exercise of power relations in discourse, and adds that he hopes his readers who do not have a background in language analysis will appreciate how 'a close analysis of texts ... can contribute to our understanding of power relations and ideological processes in discourse.'

While stressing that *description* is only one stage in critical discourse analysis (the others are *interpretation* and *explanation*), he specifies the type of descriptive linguistic analysis that is appropriate for critical investigations into language use and suggests ten questions concerning vocabulary, grammar and textual features that we can ask about the features of a text. The questions concern the choice of words, grammatical form and text structure in terms of their experiential values (*how is the speaker/writer's experience of the world represented?*), relational values (*how are social relationships between interactants expressed?*) and expressive values (*how are the speaker/writer's attitudes to the topic expressed and social identities revealed?*). As lack of space here prevents a more detailed consideration, we list Fairclough's grammar questions below.

1. What experiential values do grammatical features have?
   What types of *process* and *participant* dominate?
   Is agency unclear?
   Are processes what they seem?
   Are *nominalizations* used?
   Are sentences active or passive?
   Are sentences positive or negative?
2. What relational values do grammatical features have?
   What *modes* (*declarative, interrogative, imperative*) are used?
   Are there important features of *relational modality*?
   Are the pronouns *we* and *you* used, and if so, how?
3. What expressive values do grammatical features have?
   Are there important features of *expressive modality*?
4. How are simple sentences linked together?
   What logical connectors are used?
   Are complex sentences characterized by *co-ordination* or *subordination*?
   What means are used for referring inside and outside the text?

None of these questions will seem strange to readers of this book, who, if they have worked though Chapters 1 to 10, should now have a basis in the skills necessary for this type of applied analysis.

Fairclough makes a further important point which could apply equally well to all types of text and discourse analysis:

> The set of formal features we find in a specific text can be regarded as particular choices among the options available. [...] In order to interpret the features which are actually present in the text, it is generally necessary to take account of what other choices might have been made, i.e. of the system of options in the discourse types which actual features come from. Consequently, in analysing texts, one's

focus is constantly alternating between what is 'there' in the text and the discourse type(s) which the text is drawing on.

Theoretically, this is precisely so. In actual analysis, language is so complex and the options available to the speaker/writer of any clause are so many that it is too ambitious to expect the analyst to consider all optional systems at a paradigmatic level. Nevertheless, there are often clear alternatives available that are relevant to the significance of the message. Fairclough gives the example of the difference between the potential newspaper headlines (where the first agentless passive allows the writer to avoid the mention of the aggressor entirely):

Libya attacked.
Libya attacked by Reagan.
Reagan attacks Libya.

Whichever headline is chosen here, the writer (the journalist in this case) is reporting the event and taking some responsibility for the truth of the report. The information is presented as 'news' and the fact that the news has been selectively represented by the news reporter or editor is not always evident to the reader.

In a similar way, Reynolds' discussion of the way in which the teacher used imperatives when taking control in the classroom (see above) shows that he is aware that the teacher could have used interrogatives (*Would you mind explaining yourself, Faisal?*) or declaratives (*I'd like you to explain that*) to different effect.


## *Summary*

In this chapter we have looked at just a few of the ways in which the functional analysis of English has been used to help us understand human communication in social contexts. This type of applied research can, we have claimed, help us in many ways: to use language more effectively, to develop language teaching syllabuses, to resist linguistic pressures and to recognize when people are using language to exploit or oppress others. The fact that a Hallidayan model has been found to be an effective tool for practical analysis in such a wide variety of research can act to some extent as a justification for the model. This chapter began with a discussion of justification of linguistic theory and the nature of applications and continued with a survey of just a few of the applications of functional grammar that have proved productive: writing in Science and Technology, the features of valued texts, studies of the grammatical variation between professional and popular scientific texts, and the use of Theme analysis and clause analysis (hypotaxis and parataxis) in distinguishing successful from less successful communication. The chapter also discussed applications of functional analysis to the teaching of English, including cohesion, genre and register analysis and specific points of sentence grammar, such as the expression of modality. Finally, it looked at some of the work on language and power relations in social settings.

## Further study

Like the work of Fairclough discussed above, much of the current work on Discourse Analysis is conducted within the general framework of functional approaches to language study. A good general introduction is McCarthy (1991), which includes practice activities incorporating many of the textual and grammatical features covered in this book and has a chapter on 'Discourse analysis and grammar'.

McCarthy and Carter (1994) also cover many aspects of the links between grammar and discourse, demonstrating very clearly how, in order to understand and explain the features of discourse, we need a grammar that is able to handle functional issues at the ideational, interpersonal and textual level. Carter has been closely involved in relating the study of grammar in discourse directly to the teaching of language awareness and language use in schools (Carter, 1990a) and has made proposals for innovations in grammar teaching (for example Carter, 1990b).

For further interesting work on scientific discourse, not precisely within a Hallidayan framework but with many identifiable links, you cannot do better than to read *Writing biology*, the work of Myers (1990). This discusses the construction of scientific knowledge through writing. As Myers explains, his title is not *Writing ABOUT biology* because that would imply that biology is there before the writing takes place. He argues instead that 'writing produces biology'. This book also contains an interesting discussion of the relationship between science and ideology which relates to the work in this chapter on language and power.

The relationship of language to social issues and processes has long been of primary concern to Halliday (see Halliday, 1978; 1993) and also to Kress, who uses a Hallidayan framework for, among other things, showing how newly formed social groups develop new classification systems through language (for example Kress, 1989; Kress and Hodge, 1979).

The study of how language varies depending upon who is using it and for what purposes it is being used has also inspired a new area of study, known as 'forensic linguistics'. This uses descriptive linguistic techniques to identify features in recorded or written texts which indicate who was responsible for speaking or writing the words. This is important both in identifying criminals (to verify, for example, whether or not a certain person may have written a particular message or made a certain telephone call) and in discovering whether or not evidence could have been fabricated. Cases involving such work are reported in the journal *Forensic Linguistics*, edited by Coulthard and French.

Another major area of application which has not been discussed in this chapter is that of literary studies. Butler (1985) reviews several interesting applications to poetry, short stories and the novel. Short (1988) and Toolan (1992) contain a number of relevant chapters, and the journal of the Poetics and Linguistics Association, *Language and Literature*, edited by Short, regularly publishes articles which utilize aspects of functional grammar in literary analysis.

Various journals publish research on text and discourse analysis from time to time. Likely to be of interest to readers of this book are articles in *English for Specific Purposes* (Pergamon), *The Review of ELT* (Modern English Publications and the British Council), *Discourse and Society* (Sage), *Text* (de Gruyter Inc.), and *Applied Linguistics* (Oxford University Press).

# 12

# Historical perspectives

## 12.1 *Origins*

Given enough background knowledge and determination, we can trace most
ideas back to earlier ones, or can at least see that they have their origins in
some notion that was present in earlier work. This volume is primarily concerned with one particular approach to the study of language, that of
Halliday. In many respects this is unique, but it has its origins in the work of
earlier scholars. It is informative to consider what these are, and it may also
be of interest to see how it differs from some other approaches.

## 12.2 *Before the twentieth century*

There is a long history of ideas about language. Perhaps it might be more
accurate to say that there are numerous histories, with various traditions in
different cultures (Western, Middle Eastern and Far Eastern) and different
preoccupations and purposes. These histories are complex and not always
distinct from each other.

For example, the main line of Western thought about grammar can be
traced back to the Ancient Greeks from about the fourth century BC, a tradition which arguably reached its peak with the grammar of Dionysius Thrax
in about 100 BC, though it has continued up to the present with modifications
– first by the Romans, adapting Greek models to Latin, later by others.
Although modern grammars may differ from traditional grammar in very significant ways, they all owe something to this tradition. Among the many
valuable concepts that we inherit from the ancients are the word classes (or
parts of speech); and also the notion of *active* and *passive voice*; *tense*; *subject* and *object*; *gender, person, number* and *subject-verb agreement*, to name
but a few.

The Western classical tradition, however, has been greatly affected at various times in history by contact with other traditions, notably those of the
Arab world and of India. With the exception of Hebrew, investigated primarily in connection with Biblical studies, non-European languages were

relatively neglected in the West for centuries, but in the Middle Ages Arab culture and scholarship had spread widely and was well established in Spain as well as the Middle East and North Africa so that Islamic philosophy and linguistic studies made a major contribution to medieval thought. The complexity of the relationship can be seen in the fact that the Arab grammarians had themselves long been aware of Classical Greek ideas. Similarly, Jewish scholars working with Hebrew had a symbiotic relationship of ideas with Arab and European grammarians.

The influence of Indian traditions was at least as important, though less reciprocal. At the end of the eighteenth century, largely as an indirect result of British imperialism, there was an expansion of European interest in Asian languages. Beginning with the work of a British colonial officer, Sir William Jones, startlingly new information became available about the relationship of many Indian and European languages; in addition, an impressive Indian tradition of linguistic analysis, more sophisticated in many respects than the classical European tradition, was revealed to European scholars, and some were quick to profit from it. For over a hundred years after Jones, linguistic research was dominated by a concern with tracing the historical connections between languages, particularly those in the Indo-European family, and accounting for the changes that languages undergo as time passes. Research into regional dialects played a part in this, as it does today.

Meanwhile, traditional grammar dominated the education system. A quaint, beautifully illustrated booklet for children called *The infant's grammar or a picnic party of the parts of speech* (Harris, 1824, republished 1977) introduces (in verse) the parts of speech personified as people attending a party. A sample fragment gives the tone.

And these actors the VERBS, when they'd room to DISPLAY
Both WRESTLED, and TUMBLED and GAMBOLLED away.

The value of this as an educational tool is open to doubt, but its very existence, clearly targeted at young children, says something about the status of grammatical studies in the early nineteenth century.

Although modern linguistics differs significantly from traditional approaches, the insights of earlier times underpin much modern thought, including Halliday's, and provide a core of terms and concepts, which is crucial to the grammatical analysis of most modern schools of linguistics.

In the words of J. R. Firth (1957: p. 216):

The great languages of the older civilizations were well served by grammarians whose eminence has not been levelled or overlaid by the thousands of grammars of modern languages [. . .]. What modern linguist would wish to find serious fault with the grammatical outlines of Panini for Sanskrit, of Dionysius for Greek, of Donatus and Priscian for Latin, or of Sibawayhi and Al Khalil for Arabic?

There seems to be a suggestion in Firth's words that, good as they were for their original purpose, traditional grammars are inadequate for the task of describing other languages, and this is a widespread view. However, it would be wrong to suggest that the centuries of applying traditional grammar to languages other than Sanskrit, Classical Greek, Latin and Classical Arabic were entirely wasted effort. It would also be wrong to think that there is one monolithic traditional grammar, unchanged since ancient times. In fact, there has been debate and reformulation of ideas about grammar throughout history. However, there is a recognizable commonality of ideas and approaches sufficient to justify this broad label.

## 12.3   *De Saussure*

Discussion of the development of modern linguistics often starts with the Swiss scholar, Ferdinand de Saussure (1857–1913), whose *Course in general linguistics* was put together by his students and colleagues and published in 1916, three years after his death. De Saussure (translated by Baskin, 1959) set out what he considered to be the principles of a science of linguistics, and many of these remain central to modern approaches. Though few, if any, linguists accept all his views, they at least take account of them and usually have recourse to some of his terminology. Although his fame in his lifetime rested on his historical comparative work, including his doctoral thesis completed at the unusually early age of twenty-one, one of de Saussure's contributions was the redirection of linguistic studies away from historical concerns to the 'synchronic' analysis of contemporary language. Others had already suggested a need for less historically oriented studies, but his comments distinguishing linguistic descriptions as either diachronic (through historical time) or synchronic (at a particular point in time) provide a historical marker for this shift of emphasis. Not all linguists accept this dichotomy, and Halliday has expressed reservations about it.

De Saussure argued that a language in general could never be fully explained, but that it can be perceived on the one hand as *langue*, which is the collectively inherited set of *signs*, the language system; and, on the other, as *parole*, which can be roughly glossed as the individual's use of the system. (For de Saussure a *sign* is a combination of a concept and its representation.) He argued that *langue*, and not *parole*, is the proper object of linguistic enquiry. Half a century later Chomsky took a similar line in his positing of *competence* and *performance* (or later *I-language* and *E-language*). In answer to a direct question on this point, Halliday (1978) rejects the need for the dichotomy, citing his mentor, Firth; but he adds that whether you need to make such suppositions depends to some extent on why you are looking at the language. Halliday does not find it useful for his purposes.

Another key contribution to linguistic thinking, and one that plays a significant part in Systemic Functional Grammar is the Saussurian distinction between *syntagmatic* and *paradigmatic* dimensions. De Saussure observed that linguistic items are significant only in relation to other linguistic items in the system. Using a spatial metaphor, he says that language is systematically organized along two axes: horizontal and vertical.

The horizontal (*syntagmatic*) axis is typified by the fact that, in any utterance, words follow each other in prescribed sequences; in the sequence *if I rewrite this chapter*, each word has a syntagmatic relation to every other word: *if+I+rewrite+this+chapter*. In compound words such as *rewrite*, the two morphemes (*re-* and *write*) relate syntagmatically. We could say that *re-* is significant in English because (among many other things) it combines with *write*; that the significance of *this* is in part its potential for co-occurring with *chapter*, and so on. Phenomena such as Subject-Finite agreement and word order are syntagmatic. Likewise, sounds relate to each other sequentially: for example, /i/ and /f/ combine syntagmatically to make up /if/.

However, items are also significant because they relate to other items on the *paradigmatic* axis. Part of the significance of *write* is that it contrasts with *read*. When we say *write*, we choose not to say *read*. The same can be said of *write* with regard to *inscribe*, or *scribble*, or for that matter any other verb. The relation is a paradigmatic one in that the items are in a sense alternatives within sets. The relation between *write, writes, wrote, written* and *writing* is thus also paradigmatic, as is the relation between *written, bitten, spoken, taken* and *broken*. In the sound system, the paradigmatic significance of the phoneme /i/ is that it is not /o/ or some other sound; so /i/ and /o/ are paradigmatically related, and, by extension, /if/ has a paradigmatic relation to /of/.

Therefore the /i/ and /f/ in /if/ exemplify paradigmatic and syntagmatic relations, since /i/ relates syntagmatically with /f/ because they combine in a sequence, and /i/ also relates paradigmatically with /f/ by virtue of being a distinct sound in the English sound system. Syntagmatic relations, then, realize the items' potential for combination in a string; paradigmatic relations are the alternations between items. In Systemic Functional Grammar, syntagmatic and paradigmatic relations are sometimes discussed as *chain* and *choice*, but the terms syntagmatic and paradigmatic are more frequently used in more recent publications; a *system* is a set of paradigmatic choices; a *structure* is a syntagmatic phenomenon, a chain of elements, in which each element is the result of some paradigmatic choice.

De Saussure saw linguistics as merely part of a larger discipline, at that time non-existent, which he called *semiology*, 'a science that studies the life of signs within society' (1959: p. 16). In addition to linguistics, he mentions such systems of signs as 'writing, the alphabet of deaf mutes, symbolic rites, polite formulas, military signals, etc.' (1959: p. 16). In the second half of the twentieth century, de Saussure's thinking has perhaps been as noticeable in the field of semiotics as in linguistics itself. European philosophers and semioticians such as Roland Barthes and Umberto Eco, whose essays have included studies of such social phenomena as wrestling, striptease and blue jeans, might be regarded as de Saussure's intellectual grandchildren, but the influence on linguistics has also been profound. One collection of Halliday's work is titled *Language as Social Semiotic*, and the introduction begins with a detailed reference to de Saussure, albeit to distance Halliday somewhat from his views: 'This certainly encompasses the view that language is a social fact, though probably not in the Saussurian sense.' (Halliday, 1978: p. 1).

## 12.4   *Some American linguists*

The foundations of American linguistics were laid by the German emigré, Franz Boas (1858–1942), an anthropologist, and Edward Sapir (1884–1939), who was also born in Germany. Under Boas' influence, Sapir turned away from orthodox European historical linguistic studies (philology) to examine the languages of Native Americans (or North American Indians, as they used to be called). The work of Boas and Sapir led to new ways of describing the grammatical structure of languages, rejecting the classical model which had evolved from Ancient Greek grammar.

Sapir (1921: p. 8) gave a definition of language that clearly places him in an empiricist tradition that sees language as a social – and arbitrary – communication system:

> Language is a purely human and non-instinctive method of communicating ideas, emotions, and desires by means of voluntarily produced symbols.

This statement occurs as part of the introduction to Sapir's classic work, *Language* (1921), a chapter subtitled 'Language Defined'. In this, Sapir (1921: p. 4) contrasts language with the human capacity for walking, 'an inherent biological function of man'.

> Not so language. It is, of course, true that in a certain sense the individual is predestined to talk, but that is due entirely to the circumstance that he is born not merely in nature, but in the lap of a society that is certain, reasonably certain, to lead him to its traditions.

Probably the most prestigious figure in the first half of twentieth-century American linguistics, however, was Leonard Bloomfield (1887–1949), who also began as a philologist and had studied in Germany. Bloomfield established the basis for structural analysis which dominated American linguistic scholarship for nearly thirty years. He set out to make linguistics an autonomous subject and a scientific one, and the type of analysis which he developed, usually called American Structuralism, had a major effect on language teaching in providing the linguistic basis for pattern practice drills and other aspects of the so-called 'audio-lingual approach', dominant in the 1950s and 1960s. Bloomfieldian linguistics was strong in the areas of phonology (pronunciation) and morphology (word-formation) and made some inroads into syntax (sentence structure) but it had little to say about semantics (meaning). Many modern linguists see this last as its major weakness, together with Bloomfield's espousal of behaviourist psychology, which argued that language is merely a set of acquired habits.

The dominance of Bloomfieldian linguistics lasted in America until the late 1950s, when it was ousted by Noam Chomsky. Chomsky (born 1928) was himself a product of American Structuralist training, and his linguistics reflects that fact, not least in its relative downgrading of meaning, but it also represents a significant departure from Bloomfield's (or Sapir's) approaches, especially in its psychological and philosophical orientation. In the first fifteen years or so of Chomsky's reign, his most significant contributions seemed to be in two technical notions in the field of syntax: (i) deep and surface structure; and (ii) the mechanism of the transformation (which gave rise to the name Transformational (Generative) Grammar). Both these apparently central notions gradually faded from view as the case for them became less tenable under the pressure of further research, and they now appear vestigially, if at all. Chomsky's overwhelming dominance in America and beyond was well established by the mid-1960s and, in spite of challenges, this situation still largely prevails at the time of writing.

It is interesting to compare Chomsky with Halliday: they are linguists of the same generation but Chomsky's position is in many ways the antithesis of Halliday's.

One of Chomsky's preoccupations is with the universals of language; hence the model's later preferred name of Universal Grammar. Unlike Halliday, and most of the people mentioned above, Chomsky has no interest in the social aspect of language, but views language as essentially a biologically determined phenomenon: something with which we are endowed by our genetic structure as humans. Comments by Chomsky about the nature of human language contrast markedly with the quotations from Sapir (above). Halliday's views are closer to Sapir's on this score since, for both, language is primarily a social phenomenon.

Furthermore, Chomsky has a view of language comparable to de Saussure's dichotomy of langue and parole, regarding actual manifestations of language as E-language (external), which is only a very rough, 'degenerate' representation of I-language (internal). Formerly, he discussed this aspect of the theory under the labels *performance* and *competence*. For Chomsky, the goal of linguistics is to explain the human grammatical faculty by focusing on I-language. As we have seen, Halliday rejects such dualistic claims; in his comment on de Saussure's langue and parole, he concedes that some degree of abstraction is necessary but says that it should be kept to a minimum.

Chomsky's concept of I-language leads to a process of *idealization*, discussing abstract forms rather than authentic samples of language in use. The linguistic data which Chomskyans examine are not texts, or even fragmentary utterances actually produced in communication, but examples thought up by the linguist to check the plausibility of the grammar that is proposed. Chomsky is interested in models of mental grammars; Halliday is interested in languages and communication.

Halliday's views are incompatible with Chomsky's on other issues, too, notably the Chomskyan claim that the grammatical structure of a sentence (its syntax) is autonomous with regard to meaning (semantics): that is to say that the rules of syntactic structure operate without reference to semantics. For Chomsky semantics merely interprets the syntactic structures. For Halliday, meaning is at the heart of everything in language.

Mention must be made of the American sociolinguist Dell Hymes, who responded to Chomsky's preoccupation with grammatical competence by positing the construct *communicative competence*, of which grammatical competence was only one component. This has been a highly influential notion, though very diversely interpreted – not to say abused – over the years. Hymes' slogan was: 'There are rules of use without which the rules of grammar would be useless' (Hymes, 1972: p. 277). We might expect this approach to be in line with Halliday's, but Halliday objects to Hymes' acceptance of the Chomskyan dichotomy of competence and performance and opts to 'reject the distinction altogether on the grounds that we cannot operate with this degree and this *kind* of idealization' (Halliday, 1978: p. 38). From occasional comments, Halliday appears to be more sympathetic to the work of another great American sociolinguist, William Labov (born 1927), whose research produced major insights into the role of situational factors in systematic dialectal variation and historical change.

The category 'American' as applied to linguists is to some extent unhelpful. There are important American contributors to Systemic Functional Grammar working in the USA: Peter Fries (mentioned elsewhere), and Jay Lemke, for example. Limitations of space preclude discussion of major modern American scholars whose interests are more akin to Halliday's than some we have considered: Bolinger, Chafe, Grimes, Lamb, Longacre and Pike spring to mind. There is one historical figure, however, who cannot be omitted: Benjamin Lee Whorf.

## 12.5 *Whorf*

Sapir's name is often linked with that of Whorf (1897–1941), a remarkable figure in the history of linguistics. Whorf was a fire-insurance inspector, a graduate in chemical engineering and an amateur linguist, who contributed what has since become one of the most debated theories of the language field: the Whorfian (or Sapir-Whorf) Hypothesis.

To simplify somewhat, Whorf places great emphasis on the role of language in culture by arguing that a society's perception of reality is determined by the language of that society. Thus, a person who speaks one language will experience a different world from a person who speaks a fundamentally different type of language. Whorf based his opinion on his extensive knowledge of the Native American language, Hopi, which, he claimed, interprets – or creates – the world in a different way from the languages which he called collectively 'Standard Average European' (SAE). Outside Whorf's work, often-cited examples of this phenomenon are: (i) the large range of expressions for different kinds of snow in Inuit ('Eskimo') languages, where SAE has very few (*snow, sleet, slush*); and (ii) the way different languages split up the colour spectrum at different points, so that the speakers of one language may describe two objects as, say, *red* and *orange* (English) where those who speak another will describe them with the same term, say, *kai* (Amharic) – or, even within SAE languages, one describes two objects as *brown* (English) where another distinguishes them as *brun* and *marron* (French). These are fairly trivial examples in the scales of Whorf's hypothesis, however.

According to Whorf, the Hopi's perception of time (among other things) is fundamentally different from that of the speaker of SAE because the Hopi language and SAE languages have fundamentally different ways of dealing with time. Indeed, Whorf (1956: pp. 57–8; originally written about 1936) goes so far as to claim that the Hopi language has:

> no words, grammatical forms, constructions or expressions that refer directly to what we call 'time', or to past, present, or future, or to enduring or lasting, or to motion as kinematic rather than dynamic [. . .] Hence the Hopi language contains no reference to time, either explicit or implicit.

Thus, Whorf argues, there is no reason to suppose that the Hopi has any conception of time as flowing from past through present into future or of time as separable from a static space, perceptions which Europeans and Euro-Americans (speakers of SAE) often take to be universal, even indisputable, facts of physical reality.

This does not mean, however, that the Hopi has a defective or less subtle perception of the world than the SAE speaker (Whorf, 1956: p. 58):

> The Hopi language is capable of accounting for, and describing correctly, in a pragmatic or operational sense, all observable phenomena of the universe.

Where SAE languages separate phenomena in terms of time (expressed linguistically as tense and aspect), Hopi makes distinctions on such bases as objective reality versus subjective experience (though the terms *subjective* and *objective* are themselves SAE concepts and may not be perceived in the same way by the Hopi).

What one culture may perceive as a *thing* another may perceive as an *event* (Whorf, 1956: p. 63):

> Hopi with its preference for verbs, as contrasted with our own liking for nouns, perpetually turns our propositions about things into propositions about events.

Furthermore, far from suggesting that SAE languages or world view are superior, Whorf claims that the Hopi language is better attuned to Hopi life than are the SAE languages to SAE life, and '[. . .] the Hopi language gets along perfectly without tenses for its verbs' (Whorf, 1956: p. 64)

The opinion that European and Euro-American thinking may not have a monopoly of truth with regard to the physical nature of the world, or that so-called 'primitive' societies may have some insights that are lacking in more 'civilized' societies, has acquired considerable popular currency in recent years, but at the time of Whorf's writing (mostly in the 1930s), it was a startling idea to many Americans and Europeans (notwithstanding the 'noble savage' concepts of the Romantic movement, more than a century earlier). The relativistic approach to the nature of the world, the debate about whether there is an objective reality independent of our perceptions, is a hardy perennial in philosophy, as is the debate about the extent to which we are products of society or of nature, but Whorf's work puts these ideas in a new light.

There are, of course, disputes about the validity of the Sapir-Whorf hypothesis (other people's label; not theirs); Boas (1964; originally written 1911) himself had expressed views diametrically opposed to it:

> It does not seem likely, therefore, that there is any direct relation between the culture of a tribe and the language they speak, except in so far as the form of the language will be moulded by the state of the culture, but not in so far as a certain state of culture is conditioned by morphological traits of the language.

There are also debates about what Whorf actually meant, and whether Sapir agreed with Whorf, and so on, but we shall not pursue this further here. Suffice it to say that, of all the American approaches discussed here, Whorf's is the one that can be seen to be closest to the thinking of Michael Halliday.

Modern preoccupations with the centrality of metaphor in language (Lakoff and Johnson 1980; Lakoff 1987) directly relate to the Whorfian hypothesis, and tie in with Halliday's innovative notion of *grammatical metaphor*.

## 12.6 *Prague School*

In the 1920s a group of linguists, mainly Czech and Russian, and centred on Prague and Vienna, formed the Linguistic Circle of Prague and published a series of scholarly papers. Some of their thinking can be attributed to Saussurean principles. Major members included the Russians Trubetskoy and Jakobson and the Czech Mathesius. With World War II, the circle broke up and some members were obliged to leave for other countries, but the tradition has survived and still flourishes in the Czech and Slovak republics. This approach is known as Prague School Linguistics and has more recently been associated with such figures as Jan Firbas at Masaryk University and František Daneš at Prague.

The prestige of the Prague School has perhaps been most identified with their insights into phonology, but, for the purposes of this volume, that is not their most interesting contribution. Unlike some of the Americans discussed here, the Prague linguists were not content simply to describe grammatical structures but were interested in finding functional explanations for them. The example of Theme and Rheme as conceived by the Prague School may suffice for our purposes here (*see* Chapters 4 and 5). Like the Prague School's grammar, Halliday's has also come to be called Functional Grammar, and like theirs, it places considerable emphasis on the investigation of thematic organization, though, as we have seen in this volume, Halliday usefully separates the concept of Theme/Rheme from the related concept of Given/New.

Prague School linguists were greatly influenced by the German psychologist Bühler ('arguably the greatest psycholinguist and psychologically oriented language theorist of the first half of the twentieth century', according to Innis, 1987: p. 125). His model of three functions of language (*expressive*, *conative*, and *referential*) can be seen as a forerunner of Halliday's three metafunctions: Ideational, Interpersonal and Textual, which differ significantly from Bühler's, but are probably in part inspired by them. Halliday gives a concise explanation of the similarities and differences (Halliday, 1978: p. 48).

## 12.7   *Firth and Malinowski*

When influences on Halliday are discussed, the two names most frequently cited are Firth and Malinowski.

Bronislaw Malinowski was an anthropologist of Polish origin whose professional career was mainly in Britain. He was a colleague of J.R. Firth's at London University, where he was Professor of Anthropology from 1927. Malinowski's best known work was carried out in the Trobriand Islands in the South Pacific, now part of Papua New Guinea. Malinowski argued that language was primarily a form of action. He based this view on his observations of the Trobriand islanders' fishing expeditions where verbal exchanges were a crucial part of getting the work done. At first, he thought that this 'doing' aspect of language was largely restricted to what he then called 'primitive' languages, but later he dropped the notion of 'primitive language' and extended this functional view to all forms of language, including Western scientific discourse.

Malinowski coined the term *context of situation*, a notion which was to play a large part in Firth's thinking and, later, in Halliday's. The claim made here was that, in order to understand an utterance, we need to know not only the literal meanings of the words, in the form of their approximate equivalents in another language, for example, but also all the complex of social detail in which the utterance occurs. Indeed, meaning in language is its meaning in the events where it is used, taking into account such factors as the people engaged in the discourse and the social context in which they are functioning with all the broader presuppositions of the society, the nature of the task in hand, and so on.

J.R. Firth became the first person to hold a chair of general linguistics in a British University when he was appointed professor at the School of Oriental and African Studies, London University, in 1944. Firth had studied Oriental, especially Indian, languages. (It is interesting to note that Halliday, too, specialized in Oriental languages early in his career, in his case Chinese.) Firth had been Professor of English at the University of the Punjab before returning to teach phonetics at University College London in 1928. He did not publish a great deal, and his influence has been felt mainly through the work of his successors, most notably Halliday. Perhaps it is in the field of phonetics and phonology that Firth's direct contribution to current practice is most apparent, particularly in work on *prosody* (intonation, tempo and stress), which can be found in the publications of Halliday and others such as Brazil *et al.* (1980) and Davies (1994).

One very important concept of Firth's that has played a large part in the work of Halliday is the *system*, a paradigmatic set of choices (*see* earlier chapters). Firth argues that the grammar of a language is polysystemic, a system of systems. Halliday (1972) defines a system as follows:

> We define a system as a set of options together with an entry condition, such that if the entry condition is satisfied one option from the set must be selected.

In Halliday's systemic grammar, Firth's somewhat sketchy suggestions about system are developed more rigorously into elaborate networks representing the choices available to speakers of the language.

Where Firth differed most significantly from de Saussure was in his refusal to perceive the proper topic of investigation for a linguist as *la langue*, the system of language signs divorced from actual use. In 1950, he endorsed the criticism of de Saussure's approach as 'static mechanical structuralism'. He added (Firth, 1957: p. 181; originally written 1950):

> For my own part and for a number of my colleagues, I venture to think linguistics is a group of related techniques for the handling of language events [...] In the most general terms, we study language as part of the social process.

As already indicated, this characteristic contrast of approach is even more marked between Halliday and Chomsky, for, unlike de Saussure, Chomsky entirely excludes social factors from his analysis, focusing exclusively on individual mental processes, which he perceives as being biologically determined.

Firth stressed the role of the individual as a member of society; hence the important interaction between *nature* and *nurture* (Firth, 1957: p. 185):

> You weave *nurture* into *nature*, and you do this with the most powerful magic – speech.
> In order to live, the young human has to be progressively incorporated into a social organization, and the main condition of the incorporation is sharing the local magic – that is, the language.

In works such as *Explorations in the functions of language* (1973) and *Learning how to mean* (1975), Halliday takes such general observations as a starting point for an extensive theory of child language development based on detailed observation of his own son's language.

## 12.8   *Two other contemporary approaches*

In the past twenty years or so, there has been a proliferation of models of grammar, of which we will briefly mention two.

An alternative grammar which calls itself Functional Grammar (FG), was originated by Simon Dik (1978) and seems to have a following mainly among linguists in Belgium and the Netherlands. It shares some of the concerns of Halliday's linguistics and claims to be more 'explicit' (Siewierska, 1991: p. 3):

> FG shares with other functionally oriented models all the major theoretical assumptions of the functional paradigm; chief among them is the priority of the communicative over the cognitive function of language, with the accompanying socio-cultural as opposed to psychological bias.

Word Grammar is the brainchild of Richard Hudson, who started out some years ago as a Systemic-Functional linguist but has gradually moved away from the Hallidayan approach, via a semi-systemic model known as daughter-dependency grammar, to his latest model (for example Hudson, 1984; 1990). It is radically different from both Chomskyan or Hallidayan linguistics. However, it resembles Chomsky in being cognitive and mentalistic, though it is unlike Chomsky in placing linguistic knowledge in a more general hierarchy of knowledge, and it resembles Halliday in its concern to integrate sociolinguistic information in the grammar, though it does so in ways far removed from Halliday's. As the name suggests, Word Grammar focuses on the word rather than the phrase or group as the essential syntactic unit. The key grammatical relation is that of dependency. For example, Subject and Object are perceived as dependent on the verb; the role of Subject or Object is identified uniquely with what Halliday, and many others, would call the Head word and not with the Nominal Group or phrase, which is only a derivative notion in Hudson's grammar. Like Halliday, Hudson is interested in the application of his grammar to text, to computers and to teaching. He is also a persuasive popularizer of linguistic ideas (for example Hudson, 1992a).

## 12.9   *Corpus linguistics*

Advances in computer technology have facilitated great progress in *corpus linguistics*, which involves the computational analysis of vast collections of textual data. A forceful advocate for this approach is John Sinclair, who established the Cobuild corpus at Birmingham University. Sinclair is a former colleague of Halliday's. With Malcolm Coulthard, he developed the seminal discourse analysis model on Hallidayan principles ('All the terms used – structure, system, rank, level, delicacy, realization, marked, unmarked – are Halliday's. Sinclair and Coulthard, 1975: p. 24). Halliday is closely involved in the Cobuild project and has used it explicitly in his own research (for example Halliday and James, 1993).

At the time of writing, the Cobuild project has produced, among other publications, a major dictionary and spin-offs as well as the Cobuild Grammar and a pedagogic student's grammar (Willis, 1991), and further publications are in train. The main grammar research project carried out by Gill Francis and Susan Hunston makes use of Halliday's model.

Corpus linguistics is not a model of language like Halliday's, Bloomfield's or Chomsky's, but rather a means for analysis. It has the capacity for providing powerful challenges to common assumptions about linguistic phenomena, enabling the analyst to discuss such issues as frequency of occurrence and patterns of collocation (i.e., co-occurrence) of items whose relationship is not transparent to intuition.

Nor is corpus linguistics an entirely modern development. Traditional grammarians such as the great Danish scholar Otto Jespersen (1860–1943) used literary sources to produce descriptive grammars. Jespersen's massive work *A modern English grammar on historical principles* (1909–1949) is still a valuable source of information about English usage. The American structuralists also advocated the use of corpora, and C. C. Fries (eminent father of the Systemic Functional linguist Peter Fries) recorded telephone conversations as a basis for his iconoclastic model of English grammar (Fries, 1952). In fact, Chomsky's refusal to use a corpus might be viewed as an eccentric departure from normal practice in twentieth-century linguistics. The computer has revolutionized corpus studies, first in terms of the sheer quantity of material that can be stored and second in the techniques for analysis.

One of the best known products of computer-stored corpus work is the descriptive reference grammar of Quirk and colleagues (Quirk *et al.*, 1972; Quirk *et al.*, 1985) and its various spin-offs. In terms of the grammatical model, this is eclectic. It is easy to identify Hallidayan characteristics but there are also influences of other approaches: in the preface to the 1972 edition, Quirk mentions transformational grammar as one such influence, though it is not very evident. The Quirk description is the outcome of a major research project, the Survey of English Usage, which set up the London-Lund corpus.

Other notable corpora are the Brown University corpus of American English, the oldest of this type and scale, and the Lancaster-Oslo-Bergen (LOB) corpus of British English established by Geoffrey Leech and Jan Svartvik. Corpora of various sizes and significance continue to be established.

As far as grammar is concerned, it seems so far that, besides providing a major tool for implementing and testing existing grammatical models, corpus linguistics throws up interesting facts about the language rather than suggesting major theoretical shifts in areas such as grammatical categories. One claim of profound theoretical significance, however, is Sinclair's argument that linguistic choices are much more tightly constrained (by lexical considerations) than has previously been suggested. These are still relatively early days, and is not hard to imagine that computers will help linguists to still more revolutionary perceptions.

## **12.10**    *Hallidayan reference grammars*

Throughout this volume we have used the term *grammar* mostly in an abstract sense referring to the principles on which language, or more particularly a specific language, is organized. Or we have used it to refer to a model, or account, of this, as in *Halliday's grammar*. In this section we use it in a sense that is perhaps more frequent outside academic circles, namely for a book describing the grammar of a language. In this context, we have already mentioned the reference grammars of Jespersen and Quirk *et al.*, the latter showing many features found in Halliday's work but not committed to this or any other orientation.

Reference grammars which are wholeheartedly Hallidayan do exist though on a smaller scale than the colossal works of Jespersen or the Quirk team. An early one was Scott et al. (1968), *English grammar*; this was the work of a group of scholars at the University of Auckland. Four years later Sinclair's *A course in spoken English: grammar* was published (Sinclair, 1972), and 1980 saw the publication of David Young's *The structure of English clauses*. By far the most comprehensive and detailed Systemic Functional reference grammar to date is Downing and Locke (1992), *A university course in English grammar*.

All these works combine the task of description (as in Jespersen or Quirk *et al.*) with an explanation of the model and exercises in its application. Thus they combine the features of a reference grammar with the expository qualities of a book such as Halliday's *Introduction to functional grammar* (1994) or, to take a less exalted example, the present volume. Also, Downing and Locke present their volume as a pedagogic grammar for non-native speakers.

There are some differences of terminological and conceptual detail between these books and Halliday (1994); in the case of the earlier ones this is mainly because the model has evolved since they were published, and in the case of Downing and Locke it is presumably as a principled decision. However, the differences are relatively small, and it is to be expected – and desired – that there will be some differences of opinion even in the best run schools of linguistics.

## *Summary*

In this chapter, we have attempted a very brief survey of the linguistics background to the subject matter of this volume. Such brevity incurs drastic selectivity and a lack of depth; however, the intention is not to give a full picture but only to raise a few of the basic issues and demonstrate some affinities and oppositions.

The relation of de Saussure to Halliday is somewhat ambivalent, and, of major modern schools of thought, both Bloomfield and Chomsky are strikingly different in their goals and methods. A significant influence on the Hallidayan approach to language study was Whorf, who believed that the language of a community has a causal relation to the way in which that community perceives reality. Another important source is the Prague School's 'functional' account of language, particularly the concept of Theme and Rheme, considerably modified by Halliday. More immediate input is provided by Firth and Malinowski with their emphasis on the importance of context of situation and language as action. Halliday's model of linguistics, at least at the outset, has been seen as essentially a detailed and rigorous development of Firth's less well-worked-out proposals, but it has far excelled Firth's work.

Computer-based corpus linguistics is perceived as fully compatible with Halliday's grammar, enhancing and reinforcing it rather than undermining it. We concluded with a brief mention of reference grammars which use the Halliday model.

## *Further study*

Robins (1967) gives an excellent chronologically organized summary of the history of Western linguistics from the ancient Greeks to the twentieth century.

Readers with a good knowledge of French would do well to consult de Saussure in the original 1916 version as edited by Bally and Sechehaye in collaboration with Reidlinger. Probably the best-known English translation is by Wade Baskin (de Saussure, 1959). Compared with many more recent linguistics publications, it is not difficult to read.

Also quite intellectually accessible is Bloomfield's substantial volume *Language* (1934), a fairly detailed but lucid account of the American structuralist view of language and linguistics. Sapir's *Language* (1921) is also very readable. A selection of Whorf's original work was published in a volume edited and introduced by Carroll (Whorf, 1956).

Lyons' *Chomsky* (1991) offers a useful overview. There are numerous introductory texts such as Ouhalla (1994), Radford (1988) and Borsley (1991), which compares Chomsky's grammar with Generalized Phrase Structure Grammar and its later variant, Head-driven Phrase Structure Grammar.

Brief comparative studies of twentieth-century schools of linguistics can be found in Lepschy (1982) and Sampson (1980). Unfortunately, in their discussion of Prague School and Firth/Halliday (referred to by Sampson as the London School), both focus on phonology to the exclusion of other aspects of analysis. The Lepschy volume is in any case very cursory in its treatment and is eccentric in classing Halliday as a structural linguist. Hudson (1992b) gives an enlightening overview of ten contemporary syntactic theories, including Halliday's and his own.

Harris (ed., 1988) has chapters on Malinowski (by Jan Szymura) and Firth (by Nigel Love). A collection of Firth's papers was made in 1957. These are mostly on phonology and phonetics, and the chapters most relevant to the present book are Chapter 15 and Chapter 16. See also Firth (1964). Gunther Kress's (1976) introduction to his selection of Halliday's papers has a penetrating discussion of the roles of Firth and Malinowski and also Whorf in the development of Halliday's thinking. The first chapter of Butler's scholarly critique of systemic linguistics (1985) also gives a very succinct account of Firth in relation to Halliday.

Berry's classic introduction (1975) has a section which answers the question 'In what ways is systemic linguistics different from other schools of linguistics?' Berry also gives a clear account of networks, and Butler (1985) offers some challenging critical comments on the theoretical implications of this and other aspects of the model. For a highly advanced treatment of networks see various publications by Robin Fawcett (for example Fawcett, 1987).

Sinclair (1991) is an excellent short introduction to computational corpus linguistics. See also the edited collection by Sinclair *et al.* (1993).

# Glossary

**Adjunct (A)** A function at the rank of clause (the others being *Subject, Finite, Predicator, Complement*). A grammatically optional element with a wide range of positions in the clause. Subclasses: **Circumstantial** (telling when, where, how, who with, etc.); **Conjunctive** (signalling how the parts of a text relate to each other); **Modal** (indicating the speaker/writer's degree of commitment to or viewpoint on what he/she is saying). Realized in various ways, most typically by Adverbial Group or prepositional phrase.

**Adverbial Group** A group with adverb as Head and as Modifiers where these are present. Typically realizes Adjunct.

**article** A word class, subclass of *determiner*. Can be more delicately classed as **definite article:** *the*; **indefinite article:** *a/an*.

**auxiliary (verb)** One of a closed set of verbs whose meaning is largely grammatical (contrast *lexical verbs*). Combines with lexical verb in Verbal Group. Sometimes used to mean non-finite auxiliary.

**Circumstance** One of a set of three ideational functions in the clause as representation, the others being *Process* and *Participant*. Expresses the circumstances, conditions, constraints, accompaniments, etc., of the Process. Conflates with Adjunct.

**Circumstantial Adjunct** *See* Adjunct.

**Classifier** One of a set of experiential functions in the Nominal Group (the others being *Deictic, Numerative, Epithet, Thing* and *Qualifier*). Its function is to subclassify the Thing. Typically conflates with Modifier. Typically realized by a noun, participle or adjective. Examples (in italics): *bird* cage; *mineral* deposits; *supporting* beam.

**clause** The highest rank in the rank scale (unless we allow *sentence*), immediately above the rank of *group*. Analysable into the following functions: *SFPCA*; *Process and Participant*; *Theme and Rheme*; *Given and New*.

**clause complex** A combination of two or more clauses by linking or binding, i.e., by *parataxis* or *hypotaxis*.

**cline** A continuum of categories with fuzzy boundaries.

**closed set** A set of (lexico-grammatical) items that cannot readily be added to (e.g., personal pronouns, auxiliary verbs).

**cohesion** The quality of being bound together as a text. Cohesive resources are reference, conjunction, ellipsis, substitution and lexis.

**collocation** The statistical tendency for a pair of lexical items to co-occur in text within some specified degree of proximity; in current corpus linguistics this is usually within a distance of four or five words each way from the word being measured.

**Complement (C)** A function at the rank of clause (the others being Subject, Finite, Predicator, Adjunct). Typically follows Predicator in an unmarked declarative clause but there are many exceptions to this. Subclasses include: Direct Object Complement (C$^{do}$), Indirect Object Complement (C$^{io}$), Intensive Complement (C$^{int}$). Typically realized by Nominal Group. The Nominal Group in a prepositional phrase is sometimes described as Complement of the Preposition(al Group).

**conflate** When a single element or structure realizes two or more functions, these functions are said to conflate (or be conflated); e.g., in *The boat has left a stormy land*, the functions of Actor, Subject and Theme conflate and are realized by the Nominal Group *the boat*.

**Conjunctive Adjunct** *See* Adjunct.

**contact clause** A finite relative clause with relative pronoun omitted.

**copular verb** A grammatical verb (as opposed to lexical verb) which signals relation, typically relating Subject and an Intensive Complement. Examples: *be, seem*.

**declarative** An option in the Mood system, contrasting with *interrogative* and, indirectly, with *imperative*. A declarative clause is characterized by the sequence **S, F**. Stereotypically identified with the speech act functions *statement, assertion*, but there is no one-to-one relationship.

**defining relative clause** Also restrictive relative clause. A rankshifted clause embedded as Postmodifier in a Nominal Group. Semantically, restricts the scope of reference of the Head (its antecedent).

**delexicalized verb** A verb which has (more or less) lost the semantic force of its 'dictionary meaning'; e.g., *take* in *I'll take a walk* as opposed to *take* in *Take this upstairs*.

**dependent clause** A clause which depends on another in a clause complex, the other being **dominant**. If the dominant clause is labelled α, the dependent is β. Functions as an *expansion* or *projection*.

**determiner** A word class typically realizing Deictic function in the Nominal Group; e.g., *the, a/an*; *this, these, that, those*.

**dummy Subject** Also empty subject/pronoun. A nonreferring pronoun in Subject position; e.g., *it* in *extraposed clause* structures; also *there* in existential clauses: e.g., *There* are three applicants.

**ellipsis** Systematic omission of a lexicogrammatical item; a feature of cohesion.

**embedded clause** A rankshifted clause functioning as a group or part of a group; e.g., as Subject of a clause or as Postmodifier in a group. In practice, equivalent to *rankshifted clause* though the expressions are not synonymous.

**empty Subject** see *dummy Subject*.

**Epithet** An experiential function in the Nominal Group (the others being *Deictic, Numerative, Classifier, Thing* and *Qualifier*). Usually conflates with Modifier but may be Head when Thing is absent. Typically realized by adjective or verb participle. Example (in italics): a *beautiful, old* country house.

**expansion** One of a pair of alternative functions of a continuing clause or dependent clause in a clause complex, the other being *projection*. A clause is linked or bound to another clause in order to develop it, by explanation, addition, description, etc. May also be realized as an embedding.

**extraposed clause** Also postposed clause. A rankshifted clause separated from the Head which it modifies and expressed later in the superordinate clause; e.g., the continuation of a discontinuous Subject with dummy *it* in Subject position, as in: It is obvious *that this will happen*.

**Finite (F)** A function at the rank of clause (the others being Subject, Predicator, Complement, Adjunct). Interacts with Subject in the Mood part of the clause. Precedes Predicator in an unmarked declarative clause and may be fused with Predicator in a one-word Verbal Group. When not fused, it is realized by a modal, a finite auxiliary verb, finite of a copular verb (e.g., *is, seemed, became*) or finite of *have*. (*See also* finite.)

**finite** A finite is the auxiliary verb which in principle has tense and agrees in person/number with the Subject; e.g., *has* in *She has been studying in Osaka*; the first item in a Verbal Group of more than one word; the verbal item in a *mood tag*. A finite Verbal Group is one which has tense and in principle agrees in person/number with the Subject. A finite clause is a clause with a finite Verbal Group. (*See also* Finite.)

**gerund** A 'verbal noun': morphologically a verb (*-ing* form) but distributionally a noun, functioning as Head of a Nominal Group or as Classifier.

**Given** A function in information, contrasting with *New*. Given is treated by the speaker as mutual knowledge to be taken for granted though made explicit.

**group** Rank below clause and above word in the rank scale. Logically analysable as Head +/− Modifier(s). Groups are: Nominal Group, Verbal Group, Adverbial Group, Prepositional Group, Conjunction Group.

**group complex** Combination of two or more groups to fulfil a single function.

**Head** The dominant logical function at the rank of group, the other (dependent) being Modifier. In a Nominal Group, the Head is typically (not always) realized by a noun and usually conflates with the experiential function of Thing. In an Adverbial Group the Head is an adverb, and so on.

**hypotaxis** The binding of unequal elements where one is dominant and the other dependent. Symbolized as α, β, etc.

**Ideational function** One of the three metafunctions (the others being *Interpersonal* and *Textual*). It subdivides into (i) **Experiential:** to do with conceptual content, the representation of 'goings-on' in the world (or elsewhere); (ii) **Logical**: to do with the semantic relations between experiential elements, e.g., Head/Modifier.

**imperative** Option in the Mood system, contrasting with *indicative*. Characterized by absence of *Subject*. Stereotypically associated with the speech act *command*, but there is no one-to-one relationship.

**indicative** Option in the Mood system contrasting with *imperative*. (In fuller accounts it also contrasts with subjunctive and exclamative.) More delicately classifiable as *declarative* or *interrogative*.

**inflection** Grammatically motivated morphological variation in a word; for example: choice between zero and */-s/* at the end of a noun to indicate singular/plural.

**Interpersonal function** One of the three metafunctions (the others being *Ideational*, *Textual*). Concerns the interactional aspect of language, the speaker-hearer dimension: typified by *vocatives*, mood options, modality (expressions of degree of certainty, commitment, etc.)

**Interpersonal Theme** Theme realized as an interpersonal element: e.g., vocative (direct address form), Modal Adjunct (e.g., *maybe, perhaps*), Finite in interrogative. Usually combines with *Topical Theme* in a *Multiple Theme*.

**interrogative** Option in the mood system, contrasting with *declarative* , and, less directly, with *imperative*. A **polar interrogative** is an interrogative 'expecting' the answer *yes* or *no*; a *wh-interrogative* is more open-ended. An interrogative clause is typified by the sequence **F, S** (Subject-Finite inversion); exception: wh-interrogative where wh-word is Subject or part of Subject. Stereotypically identified with the speech act functions *question* and *request* but there is no one-to-one relationship.

**lexical verb** A verb with 'dictionary meaning'; that is, with semantic content other than purely grammatical (contrast *auxiliary* and *copular* verbs).

**marked Theme** A Theme which is untypical; e.g., anything other than Subject in a declarative clause. Markedness is graded: Subject (unmarked) – Circumstantial Adjunct (marked) – Complement (more marked) – Predicator (most marked).

**metafunction** One of the three superordinate functional categories which characterize language. These are: *Ideational, Interpersonal* and *Textual*. They co-exist in all texts.

**metalanguage** Language used for discussing language: grammatical terms, etc.

**Modal Adjunct** *See* Adjunct.

**modal verb** One of a closed set of verbs, always finite but invariant in form; e.g., *may, might, can, could, shall, should, will, would, must*. Where present, the first item in the Verbal Group. Their function is to modulate the verb (i.e., say something about degree of certainty, obligation, etc.), a function similar to that of some *Modal Adjuncts*.

**Modifier** The dependent element in the logical function of the Group (the other – dominant – being Head), subclassifiable as **Premodifier** or

**Postmodifier** according to its position in relation to the Head. In a Nominal Group, Premodifier may be realized by several word classes, stereotypically by determiner and adjective, but also frequently by numeral, noun, and verb participles or combinations of any or all of these; Postmodifier conflates with Qualifier and is usually realized by prepositional phrase, rankshifted clause or participle.

**Mood** (i) A system involving the choices *declarative, interrogative, imperative* and relating to the interaction of Subject and Finite in the clause. (ii) The part of the clause that expresses this.

**moodless clause** *See* non-finite clause.

**mood tag** Also *question tag*. A structure consisting of a Finite (positive or negative) and Subject (pronoun), attached to the end of a declarative or imperative clause, producing a kind of interrogative structure. Example (tag in italics): Sit down, *won't you?*

**morpheme** The lowest rank in the rank scale, immediately below *word*. A constituent of a word, e.g., the word *unsurpassable* breaks down into the morphemes: *un + sur + pass + able*.

**morphology** (i) The form of a word. (ii) The study of word formation.

**Multiple Theme** A Theme made up of two or more Themes, i.e., the *Topical Theme* in a clause plus any *Textual* and *Interpersonal Themes* preceding it.

**New** A function in information, contrasting with *Given*. New is the information which is not to be taken for granted.

**network** A set of inter-related *systems*.

**Nominal Group** A group which can function as Subject, Complement and Complement of preposition in a prepositional phrase. Its Head typically realized by noun or pronoun, but can be adjective, numeral, or determiner.

**nondefining relative clause** Also nonrestrictive relative clause. A dependent clause expanding on (but not restricting the scope of reference of) a Nominal Group in the dominant clause or expanding on the entire dominant clause. Usually signalled by commas or 'comma intonation'.

**non-finite clause** Also *moodless clause*. A clause without a Finite (e.g., *Looking to the west*, they saw land).

**nonrestrictive relative clause** See nondefining relative clause.

**Numerative** An experiential function in the Nominal Group. Usually conflates with Modifier but can be Head. Typically realized by a numeral.

**open set** A set of lexicogrammatical items that can readily have new items added (e.g., common nouns).

**paradigmatic relations** The phenomenon of 'choice' or alternation in the linguistic system; e.g., the choice between *he/she/it* or the choice between *has gone* and *had gone*. In Systemic Functional grammar, described in terms of systems. Identified with de Saussure's two organizing principles of language: *paradigmatic* (or associative) and *syntagmatic*.

**parataxis** The linking of equal elements, symbolized by **1, 2**, etc., in order of occurrence.

**Participant** An element in the ideational function of the clause, typically realized by a Nominal Group. Certain Participant types are associated with certain Process types: e.g., Actor and Goal with Material Process; Senser and Phenomenon with Mental Process.

**parts of speech** A traditional term for *word classes:* typically, *noun, verb, adverb, adjective, preposition, conjunction, pronoun, article, interjection* (most accounts omitting one of the last three). Some can be subclassified.

**past participle** A form of verb. Its most distinctive morphological marker is the suffix *-en* (e.g., *broken, written*), but the most common is *-(e)d* (e.g., *scattered, raced*). Combines with auxiliary *have* for present perfect and past perfect tenses and with *be* or *get* for passive voice. Frequently realizes Modifier in a Nominal Group.

**Predicator (P)** A function at the rank of clause (the others being *Subject, Finite, Complement, Adjunct*). The 'verb' element minus Finite. Follows Finite in an unmarked declarative clause and may be fused with Finite in a one-word Verbal Group. Realized by non-finite auxiliaries and/or lexical verbs. Finite and Predicator together are realized by Verbal Group.

**Prepositional Group** A group with preposition as Head. Combines with a Nominal Group to make a *prepositional phrase.*

**prepositional phrase** A phrase consisting of a *Prepositional Group* and a *Nominal Group.* Note: not the same thing as a Prepositional Group and outside the rank scale. Typically functions as *Postmodifier* in group or *Adjunct* in clause.

**present participle** A form of verb. Invariably has the morphological suffix *-ing.* Combines with auxiliary *be* in continuous (progressive) verbs. Frequently realizes Modifier function in Nominal Group.

**Process** (i) The ideational meaning of a clause: the representation of 'goings-on'. (ii) The ideational meaning associated with the Predicator (and sometimes Finite) in a clause. Type of Process determines the Participant roles available.

**projection** One of a pair of functions of the clause complex, the other being *expansion.* A projection expresses a representation of speech or thought rather than a direct representation of experience; the projection is *direct* or *indirect speech* (or *thought*), respectively *paratactic* and *hypotactic.* It may also be realized as an embedded clause.

**Qualifier** Experiential function in the Nominal Group (the others being *Deictic, Numerative, Epithet, Classifier, Thing*). Conflates with Post-modifier, following Thing. Typically realized by embedded clause, prepositional phrase or participle. Example (Qualifier in italics): the latest round of talks *proposed by the government.*

**question tag** *See* mood tag.

**rank scale** A hierarchy of grammatical constituents (sentence, clause, group, word, morpheme) in which each rank is made up of one or more members of the rank below.

**rankshifted clause** A clause functioning at a lower rank, as part of a group; e.g., embedded as postmodifier in a group or as Subject or Complement of a clause. *See* embedded clause.

**recursion** The process whereby one structure is embedded in another of the same kind; for example, a prepositional phrase in a Nominal Group which is part of a prepositional phrase; a relative clause in a Nominal Group in another relative clause.

**reduced relative clause** Non-finite relative clause (i.e., moodless, lacking the function S and F).

**relative pronoun** Wh-pronoun or *that* realizing Theme in a relative clause.

**Residue** The clause minus the Mood. Includes any of P, C, A, but not S and F.

**restrictive relative clause** *See* defining relative clause.

**Rheme** One of a pair of textual functions of the clause, the other being Rheme. Rheme is that part of the clause which is not Theme. Typically carries the New of Given and New, but there are many exceptions.

**Simple Theme** A Theme (no matter how complex) which is unaccompanied by any other Theme; usually Topical Theme. Contrasts with Multiple Theme.

**Subject (S)** Function at the rank of clause (the others being Finite, Predicator, Complement, Adjunct). Interacts with Finite (F) in the Mood part of the clause; determines person and number agreement of finite verb where this is manifest. Co-refers with the pronoun in a mood tag. Typically realized by a Nominal Group.

**superordinate clause** The clause in which a *rankshifted clause* is *embedded*.

**syntagmatic relations** The linguistic phenomenon of 'chaining'. Items are strung together 'horizontally' as in Subject + Finite + Predicator + Complement; or re+enter+ing. In de Saussure's dichotomy, contrasted with *paradigmatic*, the other organizing principle of language.

**system** A set of lexicogrammatical choices, for example: the polarity system: positive or negative; the voice system: active or passive.

**Textual function** One of the three metafunctions (the others being *Ideational*, *Interpersonal*). Concerns the organization of text: *Theme/Rheme, Conjunctive Adjuncts*, etc.

**Textual Theme** A Theme which is realized by a textual element such as continuative (e.g., *yes, no, well*) or *Conjunctive Adjunct*. Combines with Topical Theme to make a Multiple Theme.

**Theme** One of a pair of textual functions of the clause, the other being Rheme. Usually signalled by its position at the beginning of the clause. Themes are *Topical, Interpersonal* or *Textual* (corresponding to the three metafunctions: Ideational, Interpersonal, Textual). Themes may be *simple* or *multiple*; Topical Theme may be *marked* or *unmarked*. In a clause complex, the entire initial clause can be labelled Theme but it will contain its own Theme/Rheme structure.

**Thing** Experiential function at the rank of Group. Main experiential item in a Nominal Group. Typically conflates with Head. Typically realized by a noun.

**Topical Theme** An ideational element as Theme. Usually the first ideational element in the clause. Conflates with S, P, C or A$^{cir}$.

**unmarked Theme** see *marked Theme*.

**Verbal Group** A group with verb as Head. Realizes Finite and/or Predicator functions.

**vocative** A noun in direct address: *Michael*, can you help?

**wh-word** One of the closed set of words beginning with *wh-* (plus *how*) typically occurring thematically in interrogatives and relative clauses.

**word** Rank immediately below *group* and immediately above *morpheme* in the rank scale. Usually indicated in writing by a space on either side.

**word class** Category of lexical item, roughly equivalent to traditional *part of speech*. Central word classes in Functional Grammar are: noun, adjective, numeral, determiner, verb, preposition, adverb, conjunction (though these can be grouped less delicately or subdivided into more delicate classes).

# References

Adams, P., Heaton, B. and Howarth P. (eds) 1991: *Sociocultural issues in English for academic purposes*, Review of English Language Teaching 1.2, 1–13. London: Modern English Publications.

Andersen, R. 1988: *The power and the word*. London: Paladin Grafton Books.

Anderson, R.C. and Davison A. (eds) 1988: *Linguistic complexity and text comprehension*. New Jersey: Lawrence Erlbaum Associates.

Bach, E. and Harms, R.T. 1968: *Universals in linguistic theory*. New York: Holt, Rinehart and Winston.

Berry, M. 1975: *Introduction to systemic linguistics: 1. Structures and systems*. London: Batsford.

——— 1977: *Introduction to systemic linguistics: 2. Levels and links*. London: Batsford.

——— 1989: Thematic options and success in writing. In Butler, C.S., Cardwell, R.A. and Channell, J. (eds), *Language and literature: theory and practice*. Nottingham Linguistic Circular Special Issue, University of Nottingham.

Bloomfield, L. 1934: *Language*. London: George Allen and Unwin.

Bloor, M. and Bloor, T. 1991: Cultural expectations and socio-pragmatic failure in academic writing. In Adams, P., Heaton, B. and Howarth, P. (eds), *Sociocultural issues in English for academic purposes*, Review of English Language Teaching 1.2, 1–13. London: Modern English Publications.

——— 1992: Given and new information in the thematic organization of text: an application to the teaching of academic writing. *Occasional Papers in Systemic Linguistics* 6, 45–59.

——— 1993: How economists modify propositions. In Henderson, W., Dudley-Evans, T. and Backhouse, R. (eds), *Economics and language*. London and New York: Routledge, 153–69.

Bloor, T. and Norrish, J. 1987: *Written language*. London: Centre for Information on Language Teaching and Research and British Association for Applied Linguistics.

Bloor, T. and Nwogu, K. 1991: Thematic progression in professional and popular medical texts. In Ventola, E. (ed.), *Functional and systemic linguistics: approaches and uses*. Trends in Linguistics Studies and Monographs 55. Berlin: Mouton de Gruyter.

Boas, F. 1964 (originally written 1911): Linguistics and ethnology. Reprinted in Hymes, D. (ed.), *Language in culture and society*. New York: Harper and Row.

Borsley, R.D. 1991: *Syntactic theory: a unified approach*. London: Edward Arnold.

Brazil, D., Coulthard, M. and Johns, C. 1980: *Discourse intonation and language teaching*. Harlow: Longman.

Brieger, N. and Sweeney, S. 1994: *The language of business English: grammar and functions*. London: Prentice Hall.

Brown, P. and Levinson, S.C. 1987: *Politeness: some universals in language use*. Cambridge: Cambridge University Press.

Brown, G. and Yule, G. 1983: *Discourse analysis*. Cambridge: Cambridge University Press.

Butler, C.S. 1985: *Systemic linguistics: theory and applications*. London: Batsford Academic and Education.

Butler, C.S., Cardwell, R.A. and Channell, J. (eds) 1989: *Language and literature: theory and practice*. Nottingham Linguistic Circular Special Issue, University of Nottingham.

Carter, R.A. (ed.) 1990a: *Knowledge about language and the curriculum: the LINC reader*. London: Hodder and Stoughton.

———— 1990b: The new grammar teaching. In Carter, R.A. (ed.), *Knowledge about language and the curriculum: the LINC reader*. London: Hodder and Stoughton.

Channell, J. 1994: *Vague language*. Oxford: Oxford University Press.

Clark, R. and Fairclough, N. (eds) 1990: *Language and power*. British Studies in Applied Linguistics 5. London: Centre for Information on Language Teaching and Research for the British Association for Applied Linguistics.

Cmerjrková, S., Daneš, F. and Havlová, E. (eds) 1994: *Writing vs speaking*. Tubingen: Gunter Narr Verlag.

Coulthard, R.M. 1985: *An introduction to discourse analysis*. London: Longman.

———— 1992: *Advances in spoken discourse analysis*. London and New York: Routledge.

Daneš, F. 1970: An instance of Prague school methodology: functional analysis of utterance and text. In Garvin, P.L. (ed.), *Method and theory in linguistics*, The Hague: Mouton.

———— (ed.) 1974: *Papers on functional sentence perspective*. The Hague: Mouton; Prague: Academia.

Davies, M. 1994: Intonation is visible in written English. In Cmerjrková, S. and Daneš, F. (eds), *Writing vs speaking*, Tubingen: Gunter Narr Verlag.

Dennett, D.C. 1991: *Consciousness explained*. Harmondsworth: Penguin.

Department of Education, Queensland, Australia, 1992: *Literacy for further studies: project report*.

Dik, S. 1978: *Functional grammar*. London: Academic Press.

Downes, W. 1984: *Language and society*. Fontana Linguistics. London: Fontana.

Downing, A. and Locke, P. 1992: *A university course in English grammar*. London: Prentice Hall International.

Drury, H. 1991: The use of systemic linguistics to describe student summaries at university level. In Ventola, E. (ed.), *Functional and systemic linguistics: approaches and uses*. Trends in Linguistics Studies and Monographs 55. Berlin: Mounton de Gruyter, 431–56.

Drury, H. and Webb, C. 1994: Teaching academic writing at the tertiary level. *Prospect* 7, 2–17.

Dudley-Evans, T. 1993: The debate over Milton Friedman's theoretical framework: An applied linguist's view. In Henderson, W., Dudley-Evans, T. and R. Backhouse (eds), 1993: *Economics and language*. London and New York: Routledge.

Fairclough, N. 1989: *Language and power*. London and New York: Longman.

Fawcett, R.P. 1974: Some proposals for systemic syntax. MALS Journal No.1.

——— 1984: System networks, codes and knowledge of the universe. In Fawcett, R.P., Halliday, M.A.K., Lamb, S.M. and Makkai, A. (eds) 1984: *The semiotics of culture and language*. London: Francis Pinter.

——— 1987: The semantics of clause and verb for relational processes in English. In Halliday, M.A.K. and Fawcett, R.P. (eds) 1987: *New development in systemic linguistics: Volume I: Theory and Description*. London: Pinter.

Fawcett, R., Halliday, M.A.K., Lamb, S.M. and Makkai, A. (eds) 1984: *The semiotics of culture and language*. London: Francis Pinter.

Fillmore, C. 1968: The case for case. In Bach, E. and Harms, R.T. (eds), *Universals in linguistic theory*. New York: Holt, Rinehart and Winston.

Firbas, J. 1972: On the interplay of prosodic and non-prosodic means of functional sentences perspective. In Fried, V. (ed.), *The Prague school of linguistics and language teaching*. Oxford: Oxford University Press.

Firth, J.R. 1957: *Papers in linguistics 1934–1951*. London: Oxford University Press.

——— 1964: *The tongues of men and speech*. Oxford: Oxford University Press.

Francis, G. 1986: *Anaphoric nouns*. Discourse Analysis Monograph 11. English Language Research. University of Birmingham.

——— 1990: Theme Workshop. *Network* 13/14, 8–9.

Francis, G. and Kramer-Dahl, A. 1991: From clinical report to clinical story: Two ways of writing about a medical case. In Ventola, E. (ed.), *Functional and systemic linguistics: approaches and uses*. Trends in Linguistics, Studies and Monographs 55. Berlin: Mouton de Gruyter, 339-368.

Fried, V. 1972: *The Prague school of linguistics and language teaching*. Oxford: Oxford University Press.

Fries, C.C. 1952: *The structure of English*. London: Longman.

Fries, P.H. and Francis, G. 1992: Exploring Theme: Problems for research. *Occasional Papers in Systemic Linguistics* 6, 45–59.

Garvin, P.L. (ed.) 1970: *Method and theory in linguistics*. The Hague: Mouton.

Halliday, M.A.K. 1967, 1968: Notes on transitivity and theme in English, 1–3. *Journal of Linguistics*, 3, 37–87 and 199–244; 4, 179–215.

——— 1972: Options and functions in the English clause. In Householder, F.W. (ed.), *Syntactic theory I: structuralist*, Harmondsworth: Penguin.

——— 1973: *Explorations in the functions of language*. London: Edward Arnold.

——— 1974: The place of functional sentence perspective in the system of linguistic description. In Danes (ed.), *Papers on functional sentence perspective*. The Hague: Mouton; Prague: Academia.

——— 1975: *Learning how to mean*. London: Edward Arnold.

——— 1978: *Language as social semiotic*. London: Edward Arnold.

——— 1989: *Spoken and written language*. Oxford: Oxford University Press.

——— 1990: *New ways of meaning: a challenge to applied linguistics*. Paper presented to the Ninth World Congress of Applied Linguistics, Thessaloniki-Halkidiki, Greece.

——— 1993: *Language in a changing world*. Applied Linguistics Association of Australia Occasional Paper 13.

——— 1994 (first edition 1985): *Introduction to functional grammar*. London: Edward Arnold.

Halliday, M.A.K. and Fawcett, R.P. (eds) 1987: *New developments in systemic linguistics: Volume I: Theory and Description*. London: Pinter.

Halliday, M.A.K. and Hasan, R. 1976: *Cohesion in English*. London: Longman.

――― 1989: *Language, context and text: aspects of language in a social-semiotic perspective*. Oxford: Oxford University Press.

Halliday, M.A.K. and James, Z.L. 1993: A quantitative study of polarity and primary tense in the English finite clause. In Sinclair, J. et al. (eds) *Techniques of description*. London: Routledge.

Halliday, M.A.K. and Martin, J.R. 1993: *Writing science: literacy and discursive power*. London: The Falmer Press.

Halliday, M.A.K., McIntosh, A. and Strevens, P. 1964: *The linguistic sciences and language teaching*. London: Longman.

Harris, J. 1824: *The infant's grammar or a picnic party of the parts of speech*. London: Harris and Son. Republished 1977 by The Scolar Press Ltd., London.

Harris, R. (ed.) 1988: *Linguistic thought in England 1914–1945*. New York: Routledge.

Henderson, W., Dudley-Evans, T. and Backhouse, R. (eds) 1993: *Economics and language*. London and New York: Routledge.

Hoey, M. 1983: *On the surface of discourse*. London: George Allen and Unwin.

――― 1991: *Patterns of lexis in text*. Oxford: Oxford University Press.

Hopkins, A. and Dudley-Evans, T. 1988: A genre-based investigation of the discussion sections in articles and dissertations. *English for Specific Purposes* 7, 113–21.

Householder, F.W. (ed.) 1972: *Syntactic theory I: structuralist*. Harmondsworth: Penguin.

Huddleston, R. 1984: *Introduction to the grammar of English*. Cambridge: Cambridge University Press.

Hudson, R. 1984: *Word grammar*. Oxford: Basil Blackwell.

――― 1990: *English word grammar*. Oxford: Basil Blackwell.

――― 1992a: *Teaching grammar: a guide for the National Curriculum*. Oxford: Basil Blackwell.

――― 1992b: A spectator's guide to syntactic theories. *Links and Letters* 1, 25–50. Universitat Autonoma de Barcelona.

Hurford, J. and Heasley, B. 1983: *Semantics: a coursebook*. Cambridge: Cambridge University Press.

Hyland, K. 1994: Hedging in academic writing and EAP textbooks. *English for Specific Purposes* 13, 239–56.

Hymes, D. 1972: On communicative competence. In Pride, J.B. and Holmes, J. *Sociolinguistics*, Harmondsworth: Penguin.

Innis, R.E. 1987: Entry for 'Buhler, Karl' in R. Turner (ed.) *Thinkers of the twentieth century*, London: St James Press.

Jespersen, O. 1909–49: *A modern English grammar on historical principles*. London: Allen and Unwin.

Kress, G.R. (ed.) 1976: *Halliday: system and function in language*. London: Oxford University Press.

――― 1989: *Linguistic processes in sociocultural practice*. Oxford: Oxford University Press.

Kress, G.R. and Hodge, R.I.V. 1979: *Language as ideology*. London: Routledge and Kegan Paul.

Lakoff, G. 1987: *Women, fire and dangerous things: what categories reveal about the mind*. Chicago: University of Chicago Press.

Lakoff, G. and Johnson, M. 1980: *Metaphors we live by.* Chicago: Chicago University Press.

Leech, G.N. 1983: *Principles of pragmatics.* London: Longman.

Lepschy, G.C. 1982: *A survey of structural linguistics* (new edition). London: Andre Deutsch.

Lyons, J. 1977: *Semantics 1.* Cambridge: Cambridge University Press.

—— 1991: *Chomsky* (Third Edition). London: Fontana Press.

Mann, W.C. and Thompson, S.A. (eds) 1992: *Discourse description: diverse linguistic analyses of a fund-raising text.* Amsterdam: John Benjamins Publishing Company.

McCarthy, M. 1991: *Discourse analysis for language teachers.* Cambridge: Cambridge University Press.

McCarthy, M. and Carter, R. 1994: *Language as discourse: perspectives for language teaching.* London: Longman.

Martin, J.R. 1989: *Factual writing: exploring and challenging social reality.* Oxford: Oxford University Press.

—— 1990: Literacy in science: Learning to handle text as technology. In Halliday, M.A.K. and Martin J. (eds), *Writing science: literacy and discursive power.* London: The Falmer Press.

Mey, J.L. 1993: *Pragmatics.* Oxford: Blackwell.

Moore, J. 1979: *Reading and thinking in English.* Oxford: Oxford University Press.

Moore, T. and Carling, C. 1982: *Understanding language.* London: Macmillan.

Munby, J. 1978: *Communicative syllabus design.* Cambridge: Cambridge University Press.

Myers, G. 1989: The pragmatics of politeness in scientific articles. *Applied linguistics* 10, 1–35.

—— 1990: *Writing biology: texts in the social construction of scientific knowledge.* Wisconsin: University of Wisconsin.

Nuttall, C. 1985: *Teaching reading skills in a foreign language.* London: Heinemann Educational Books.

Nwogu, K. and Bloor, T. 1991: Thematic Progression in professional and popular medical texts. In Ventola E. (ed.), *Functional and systemic linguistics: approaches and uses.* Trends in Linguistics Studies and Monographs 55, 369–84. Berlin: Mouton de Gruyter.

Ouhalla, J. 1994: *Introducing transformational grammar.* London: Edward Arnold.

Palmer, F.R. 1974: *The English verb.* Harlow: Longman.

—— 1979: *Modality and the English modals.* London: Longman.

—— 1986: *Mood and modality.* Cambridge: Cambridge University Press.

Pindi, M. and Bloor, T. 1987: Playing safe with predictions: hedging, attribution and conditions in economics forecasting. In Bloor, T. and Norrish, J. (eds), *Written language.* London: Centre for Information on Language Teaching Research for the British Association for Applied Linguistics.

Quirk, R., Greenbaum, S., Leech, G., and Svartvik, J. 1972: *A grammar of contemporary English.* London: Longman.

—— 1985: *A comprehensive grammar of the English language.* London: Longman.

Radford, A. 1988: *Transformational grammar: a first course.* Cambridge: Cambridge University Press.

Reynolds, M. 1990: Classroom power: some dynamics of classroom talk. In Clark R.

and Fairclough, N. (eds), *Language and power*. British Studies in Applied Linguistics 5. London: Centre for Information on Language Teaching Research for the British Association for Applied Linguistics.

Robins, R.H. 1967: *A short history of linguistics*. London: Longman.

Sampson, G. 1980: *Schools of linguistics: competition and evolution*. London: Hutchinson.

Sapir, E. 1921: *Language: an introduction to the study of speech*. New York: Harcourt, Brace and World.

de Saussure, F. 1916: *Cours de linguistique générale*. Paris: Payot.

———— (translated W. Baskin) 1959: *Course in general linguistics*. London: Peter Owen.

Scott, F., Bowley, C., Brockett, C., Brown, J. 1968: *English grammar*. London: Heinemann Educational.

Short, M. (ed.) 1988: *Reading, analysing and teaching literature*. London and New York: Longman.

Siewierska, A. 1991: *Functional grammar*. London: Routledge.

Sinclair, J. 1972: *A course in spoken English: grammar*. London: Oxford University Press.

———— 1991: *Corpus, concordance, collocation*. Oxford: Oxford University Press.

Sinclair, J. and Coulthard, R.M. 1975: *Towards an analysis of discourse: the English used by teachers and pupils*. Oxford: Oxford University Press.

Sinclair, J., Fox, G. and Hoey, M. (eds) 1993: *Techniques of description*. London: Routledge.

Stubbs, M. 1986: A matter of prolonged fieldwork: notes towards a modal grammar of English. *Applied Linguistics* 7, 1–25.

Swales, J.M. 1984b: Research into the structure of introductions to journal articles and its application to the teaching of academic writing. In Williams, R., Swales, J. and Kirkman (eds), *Common ground: shared interests in EAP and communication studies*. Oxford: Pergamon.

———— 1990: *Genre analysis*. Cambridge: Cambridge University Press.

Tadros, A. 1981: *Prediction in text*. Discourse Analysis Monograph 10. English Language Research. University of Birmingham.

Thomas, S. and Hawes, T.P. 1994: Reporting verbs in medical journal articles. *English for specific purposes* 13, 171–86.

Thompson, G. and Yiyun, Ye 1991: Evaluation in the reporting verbs used in academic papers. *Applied Linguistics* 12, 365–82.

Toolan, M. 1992: *Language, text and context: essays in stylistics*. London and New York: Routledge.

Tyler, A. 1994: The role of syntactic structure in discourse structure: signaling logical and prominence relations. *Applied Linguistics* 15, 243–62.

Ventola, E. 1983: Contrasting schematic structures in service encounters. *Applied Linguistics* 5, 275–86.

———— 1987: *The structure of social interaction: a systemic approach to the structure of service encounters*. London: Francis Pinter.

———— (ed.) 1991: *Functional and systemic linguistics: approaches and uses*. Trends in Linguistics Studies and Monographs 55. Berlin: Mouton de Gruyter.

Ventola, E. and Mauranen, A. 1991: Non-native writing and native revising of scientific articles. In Ventola E. (ed.), *Functional and systemic linguistics: approaches and uses*. Trends in Linguistics Studies and Monographs 55. Berlin: Mouton de Gruyter.

Whorf, B.L. (edited and with an introduction by J.B. Carroll) 1956: *Language, thought and reality: selected writings of Benjamin Lee Whorf.* Cambridge, Massachusetts: MIT Press.

Widdowson, H.G. 1979: *Explorations in applied linguistics.* Oxford: Oxford University Press.

———— 1984: *Explorations in applied linguistics 2.* Oxford: Oxford University Press.

———— 1990: *Aspects of language teaching.* Oxford: Oxford University Press.

Williams, R., Swales, J. and Kirkman, J. (eds) 1984: *Common ground: shared interests in EAP and communication studies.* Oxford: Pergamon.

Willis, D. 1991. *Collins Cobuild student's grammar.* London: Harper Collins.

Young, D.J. 1980: *The structure of English clauses.* London: Hutchinson.

# Index of Authors

# Subject Index

References are to page numbers. Please also see the separate Index of Authors.

Notes.
P.77   dear definition of 'ideational'
P.86   textual function

Q.
P.75
P.82
P.96